THE LAST OF THE LASCARS

DEDICATION

'He dreamed of the ship on the sea,
That would carry his father and he,
To a place they could never be found,
To a place far away from this town,
A Newcastle ship without coals,
They would sail to the island of souls.'

Sting, *The Soul Cages* (1991).

This book is dedicated to the loving memory of my great-grandfather, George Paul Oldacre Parker (1893–1981), who formerly worked as a fireman (stoker) on a Swedish merchant steamer vessel on his passage home to Britain in 1924 from Australia, travelling through Singapore, India, Aden, Suez and the Mediterranean.

THE LAST OF THE LASCARS

YEMENI MUSLIMS IN BRITAIN, 1836–2012

Mohammad Siddique Seddon

KUBE
ACADEMIC

The Last of the Lascars: Yemeni Muslims in Britain, 1836–2012

First published in England by Kube Publishing Ltd.,
Markfield Conference Centre
Ratby Lane, Markfield,
Leicestershire LE67 9SY
United Kingdom
Tel: +44 (0) 1530 249230
Fax: +44 (0) 1530 249656
Website: www.kubepublishing.com
Email: info@kubepublishing.com

CIP data for this book is available from the British Library.

ISBN 978-1-84774-036-6 *casebound*
ISBN 978-1-84774-035-9 *paperback*
ISBN 978-1-84774-068-7 *ebook*

Cover design: Fatima Jamadar
Book design: Naiem Qaddoura
Typesetting: Nasir Cadir

Printed by IMAK, Istanbul, Turkey

CONTENTS

ACKNOWLEDGEMENTS

ALL PRAISE IS DUE to Allah, the Almighty, the Sublime. May his Peace and Blessings be upon his beloved final Prophet and Messenger, Muhammad. I am profoundly grateful to the Yemeni community of Eccles, Greater Manchester, for opening up their homes and their hearts to me during my on-going research into British Yemenis that originally began as a doctoral study in 2001, for which I am also eternally thankful to Professor David Waines for his wise and patient supervision of the original thesis and his useful comments and advice on this subsequent publication. I would like to record my sincere gratitude to the Islamic Foundation, Professor Kurshid Ahmad, Dr Manazir Ahsan and all former colleagues for their financial, spiritual and intellectual support during my years of postgraduate study and research. My particular thanks also goes to Muckbil Ahmad, Gadri Salih, Aziz Bugati, Ali Lehji, Tariq Mahyoub, Ali Mawri and Rabiea Shaker, along with Abdulalim al-Shamiri, Adnan Saif and Imtiaz Ahmad Hussain and his family for all their gracious hospitality and tireless help. I would also like to express my sincere appreciation for the works of K. L. Little, Sydney Collins, Bahr Ud-Din Dahya, Fred Halliday, Richard Lawless and Humayun Ansari for their earlier studies on British Yemenis which have both informed and shaped this monograph. I am deeply indebted to Peter Fryer for granting permission to reproduce his wonderfully insightful photographs in this publication and to Yahya Birt and his colleagues at Kube Publishing for their support in this publication project. My parents and my sisters also need to be publicly acknowledged and personally thanked for both nurturing and tolerating my acute eccentricity and nomadic spirit. Finally, I must record my heartfelt love and eternal gratitude to my wife and children.

Mohammad Siddique Seddon
University of Chester
August 2013

CHRONOLOGY

10th to 2nd Centuries BCE

The kingdoms of Saba', Ma'īn and Qahtān flourished through the development of the spice and incense trade through southern Arabia.

2nd Century BCE to 6th Century CE

The Ḥimyarite dynasty asserts its ascendency over ancient Yemen until it was usurped by a period of Ethiopian rule that was ended by a Persian invasion by the sixth century CE.

7th Century

Islam is established in Yemen. Sunni Muslims of the Shāfi'ī school settle the coastal regions while the Zaydī branch of Shia Islam dominates the highlands.

9th Century

The Rassid dynasty is founded by a Zaydī Imām who establishes rule over most of ancient Yemen.

12th Century

Ṣalāḥ al-Dīn Ayyūbī's elder brother conquers Yemen and founds a dynasty with Ta'izz as its capital.

13th to 15th Centuries

The Rasūlid dynasty establishes its power in Yemen with its influence stretching as far as Makkah and Ḥaḍramawt.

1515
The Egyptian army is employed in Yemen to protect the port of Aden from successive Portuguese offensives.

1517
An Ottoman offensive using Egyptian forces conquers Yemen and remains in occupation on behalf of the Turks.

1529
A Turkish Pasha is installed as Governor of the Yemen by the Ottomans.

1609
John Jourdain, a representative of the British East India Company, becomes the first recorded Englishman to enter Yemen.

1728
The ʿAbdalī sultanate of Laḥīj becomes independent of the Zaydī Imām and captures Aden. Soon afterwards the Imām loses control of the ʿAwlaqī and Yāfiʿ regions of southern Yemen.

1818
Ibrahim Pasha, Ottoman Governor of Egypt expels the Wahhābīs from Yemen and occupies the main ports.

1835
Captain Haines docks at Aden and surveys the port for the British East India Company.

1836–1872
Rebellion and insurgency shifts power between Ottoman Turk and Zaydī Imām ascendency in north Yemen with the Turks finally capturing Sana'a and establishing full occupation of north Yemen.

1839
The British Protectorate is established at Aden after its capture by the British East India Company. A 'Treaty of Friendship' between the British and Sultan of Laḥīj, followed by similar treaties with other local rulers of territories adjacent to Aden.

1853
Aden is declared a 'free port' by the British East India Company, increasing its commercial revenues.

1856
The Reverend Joseph Salter establishes his Asiatic Strangers Home at London's East India Docks, aimed at proselytizing amongst the large numbers of non-Christian lascars.

1857
Captain Luke Thomas becomes the first independent British trader to establish business at Aden. A lascar sailors' home is established in Glasgow.

1869
The opening of the Suez Canal increases Aden's importance as a regional trading port.

1881
A lascar sailors' rest is established in Cardiff to cater for the large numbers of Yemeni sailors present at the port.

c.1900
Shaykh Abdullah Ali al-Hakimi, the charismatic spiritual reformer of British Yemenis, is born in a Dhubḥānī village in north Yemen.

1914–18
A convention with Turkey defines the frontier of the Aden Protectorate with the Ottoman Empire. Thousands of Yemeni lascars volunteer to serve on seconded merchant vessels in defence of Britain at the outbreak of the First World War.

1919
A riot erupts at Mill Dam, South Shield docks, when Yemeni lascars are refused work on British ships and are abused and beaten by indigenous white sailors. In the aftermath, 13 Yemenis are arrested and imprisoned and further riots involving Yemeni and English sailors occur in Liverpool, Cardiff and London docks.

1925
The Special Restriction (Coloured Alien Seamen) Order establishes limiting quotas by the British government for 'Arab and Coloured' sailors on British vessels along with the compulsory registration within seven days of docking, at local police stations.

1932
Aden is taken from the control of the Government of Bombay and formed into a Chief Commissionership under the central Government of India.

1934
Shaykh Abdullah Ali al-Hakimi receives permission (*ijāzah*) from his Algerian Sufi shaykh, Aḥmad ibn Muṣṭafā al-'Alawī, to establish *zawāyā* (Sufi lodges) among the Yemeni communities settled in British ports.

1936
Under the spiritual leadership of Shaykh Abdullah Ali al-Hakimi, the South Shields Yemeni community purchases *The Hilda Arms*, a former public house, and establishes the 'Zaoia Allaoia Islamia Mosque'.

1937
Aden becomes a Crown Colony and is finally ruled independently of India.

1941
Nur al-Islam Mosque, Cardiff, is bombed by a German aeroplane during the war. Miraculously, the praying congregation are all unharmed, but the mosque is destroyed.

1943
The official reopening of the Nur al-Islam Mosque after it was reconstructed with a government grant of £7000 courtesy of the India Office.

1945
'Second wave' migration of Yemenis to Britain occurs into the industrial cities of Birmingham, Manchester and Sheffield, as a result of post-World War Two single-male, Commonwealth and colonial economic migration to the UK.

1948

The Zaydī Imām, Hamid al-Din, is assassinated by revolutionary anti-Imāmate forces in north Yemen. Shaykh al-Hakimi launches the publication of *Al-Salam*, his anti-Zaydī Imām newsletter, which is Britain's first Arabic language periodical.

1953

Shaykh al-Hakimi leaves Britain permanently for Aden after he is ousted by his former deputy, Shaykh Hassan Ismail and the pro-Zaydī Imām Shamīrī tribesmen from amongst the British Yemeni community.

1956

After almost 30 years of faithful service to the Yemeni community, Shaykh Hassan Ismail returns home to Yemen after his *ḥajj* to Makkah. His adopted British Yemeni son, Shaykh Said Ismail, becomes replacement *imām*, aged just 25.

1962

The Zaydī Imām, Ahmad, dies and is succeeded by his son, Muhammad al-Badr, who flees Yemen after just one week of ruling when an assassination attempt fails during a successful *coup d'état* by revolutionary forces. In Britain, the Commonwealth Immigration Act 1962 becomes law, which requires migrant Commonwealth and colonial workers to acquire either a visa or work permit before entering the UK. As a result, large numbers of family dependants join them in Britain.

1970–80

Yemeni wives and children begin to join their 'second wave' migrant husbands in the industrial cities of Birmingham, Manchester and Sheffield.

1980

Large numbers of Yemenis migrate from Britain as a result of economic depression and mass unemployment to work in the prosperous Arabian Gulf.

1991

North and South Yemen are reunified under the initiative of the North Yemen President, Ali Abdullah Salih.

1991–92

The First Gulf War. President Saddam Hussein of Iraq orders the invasion of Kuwait and the newly-reunified Yemen abstains in a UN Security Council vote to condemn Iraq's aggression. As a result, Saudi Arabia and other Gulf Arab states evict around one million Yemeni workers with immediate effect.

1995–2002

'Prince' Naseem Hamid, Sheffield-born British Yemeni boxer, becomes the featherweight boxing champion and defends a series of world champion titles until he retires, undefeated, in 2002. In the process, he puts Yemen 'on the map' and imbues young British Yemenis with a sense of pride and belonging.

2001

The 9/11 terror attacks using hijacked planes to fly into the Twin Towers, New York, and the Pentagon, Washington, kill thousands and precipitate the War on Terror. Osama Bin Laden's al-Qaeda Muslim terror group claim responsibility with a number of Yemeni-origin Arabs connected with both to the attacks and the organization.

2005

The 7/7 terror attacks on the London transport system kills over 50 people. The British government increases its security and surveillance of the British Muslim community with a particular focus on British Arab (including Yemeni) communities.

2010

The pro-democracy movement inspires the so-called 'Arab Spring' across the Arab-Islamic region.

2011

The revolutionary pro-democracy movement in Yemen eventually forces President Ali Abdullah Salih from office after hundreds of civilians are killed by his forces and he survives an assassination attempt. In Britain, Shaykh Said Ismail Hassan passes away after a long illness, ending his 55 years of service as *imām* to the Cardiff Yemeni community at the South Wales Islamic Centre.

2012

The Yemeni community in Cardiff revives street parades originally organized by Shaykh al-Hakimi and continued by Shaykh Hassan Ismail and Shaykh Said Hassan. Their reinstitution by the ʿAlawī *ṭarīqah* is done in honour of the recent passing of Shaykh Said Hassan Ismail.

LIST OF ILLUSTRATIONS

TRANSLITERATION TABLE

Arabic Consonants:

Initial, unexpressed medial and final:

ء	ʾ	د	d	ض	ḍ	ك	k
ب	b	ذ	dh	ط	ṭ	ل	l
ت	t	ر	r	ظ	ẓ	م	m
ث	th	ز	z	ع	ʿ	ن	n
ج	j	س	s	غ	gh	هـ	h
ح	ḥ	ش	sh	ف	f	و	w
خ	kh	ص	ṣ	ق	q	ي	y

Vowels, diphthongs, etc.

Short:	ـَ	a	ـِ	i	ـُ	u
Long:	ـَا	ā	ـُو	ū	ـِي	ī
Diphthongs:			ـَوْ	aw		
			ـَيْ	ay		

FOREWORD

'To be rooted is perhaps the most important and least recognised need of the human soul', wrote the philosopher Simone Weil. The popular perception is that Muslims lack roots in British soil: they have arrived only recently, and, as a consequence, they do not possess deep historical and organic links with the customs, traditions and values of British society. This perception has been damaging for communal harmony since it has been deployed to set boundaries that, arguably, categorize, alienate and exclude Muslims, by calling into question their emotional ties, loyalties and claims of belonging to this country; namely, a version of 'this is our country and by implication not yours', through which claims to greater entitlement are frequently, if not always explicitly, asserted. In this discourse, British Muslims are viewed as a huge problem in need of a solution, and much media, political and academic energy is focused upon attempts to understand them.

The difficulty in achieving this understanding, however, is that British Muslims have come to be portrayed inaccurately as undifferentiated, isolationist, opposed to modern, secular norms and values, and as immune to processes of change. Generalizations abound, and the diversity of Muslim life is cast aside, creating a homogeneous and monolithic image instead that throws up negative stereotypes that militate against constructive interaction. Instead of mutual goodwill, division, distrust and Islamophobia have resulted. But such perceptions ignore visible evidence of the on-going fusion that is taking place between Muslims and British society, each drawing inspiration from the other to enhance the future cultural development of us all. They also belie historical scrutiny and deny Muslim legitimacy, ownership and a stake in Britain.

By looking at the historical evolution of one of Britain's oldest Muslim communities – Yemeni lascars or sailors – this rigorously researched book demonstrates their rootedness, and, by arguing that they have as much claim on this land as anybody else, represents a very welcome contribution to this discourse. Against the backdrop of racially-charged debates about immigration and questions of identity, especially since 9/11, Mohammad Seddon offers a timely exploration of how one particular set of Muslims have sought to establish themselves as an integral part of the British community over a period of 200 years. By focusing specifically on the history of these Yemeni Muslim sailors, he examines the long legacy of connections and interactions that have progressively bound their community to this country, and so locates broader present-day debates about the construction of British Muslim identities, religious belief and citizenship within a more textured historical frame. What we are provided with is a fascinating account of the economic, political, social and cultural dynamics of their lives, which is woven into the wider context of a rapidly changing imperial and post-colonial British society, where race, religion, gender and class intersect.

By investigating official and popular attitudes to their presence, and the differing responses of these Yemenis, this study challenges accepted wider notions of migration and settlement patterns, deepening our understanding of their contributions to British society as well as their role in the two world wars. It offers unique insights into their everyday lives, their internal organization and dynamics, into the links with their country of origin, and relations with their 'host' communities. In the process, it sheds fresh light on the nature of religious authority, representation and civic engagement, and successfully uncovers aspects of British history that have thus far remained in large part neglected. What emerges from this fascinating narrative is a deeply informed understanding not only of the resilience of British Yemeni Muslims' daily lives but also the dynamic of their institutions such as families, mosques, and religious leadership, and their social and political significance in today's Britain.

This is a study written in the tradition of 'history from below'; by making them, the 'subaltern', the subject of history, it represents an attempt to democratize history. It is also an attempt to understand a group of people considered to be incidental to the making of history and hence of little historical interest.

By seeking to get inside their minds to discover how and why they behaved in the ways that they did, what they achieved and how far their aims were realized, it is clear that the politics of Yemeni Muslim lascars were not marked simply by acquiescence, accommodation, compromise and negotiation but also by resistance. But the adoption of this historiographical approach does inevitably present challenges. How does someone write an historical narrative drawing largely upon fragmentary and scattered sources, such as scarce personal life stories and memories? Seddon grapples with these challenges with considerable success, enabling a more inclusive and arguably less biased account to emerge than would be possible through the 'mainstream' writing of history. Of course, while many questions are answered, new ones are inevitably raised, and much still remains to be researched on the experiences of Britain's Muslim communities. In this respect, Seddon's study has done its job – stimulating further interest in an important aspect of British history, namely the reconfiguration of Yemeni Muslim identities, constructed through different antagonisms and processes of enculturation, and the effect that this has had in locating them socially in multiple positions of marginality and subordination.

Humayun Ansari
Royal Holloway, University of London
November 2012

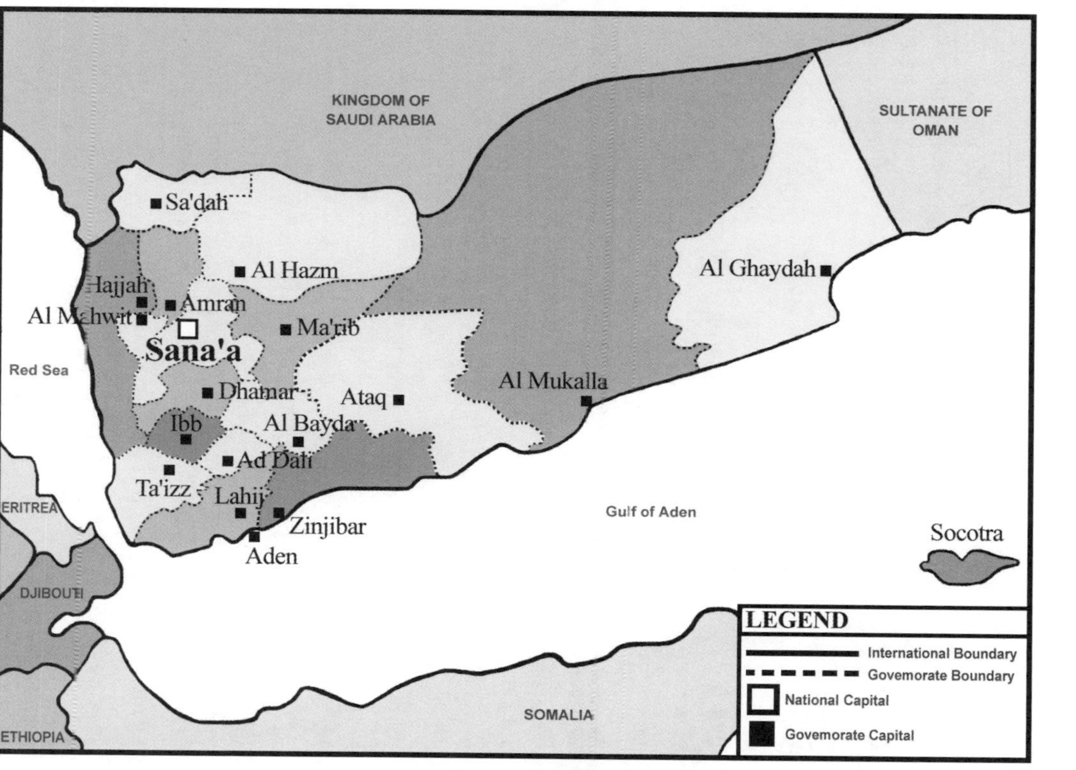

A map of modern Yemen

PROLOGUE

MUCH OF OUR KNOWLEDGE and understanding of Muslims in the UK is informed by the post-Second World War economic migration of post-colonial and Commonwealth single-male, South Asian workers and labourers to the factories and industries of late twentieth-century Britain. This is because this particular migration phenomenon has had the most significant impact on modern Britain, indelibly changing and reshaping our society across its social and political spectrums. The contemporary British 'migration experience' has also produced a plethora of academic writings engaged with a multitude of disciplines, producing many sociological theories all attempting to explain and quantify the effects of large-scale Muslim settlement on wider society. But where the end of the twentieth century witnessed a proliferated interest of Islam and Muslims in Britain and the West, not just through academic studies, but also through media representations, social debates and political legislation, the beginning of the previous century was instead marked by indifference and a degree of colonial cajolery towards the subjugated Muslim 'other' in imperial Britain.

Yemeni migration and settlement to Britain not only spans the breadth of these two historical events and particular migration experiences, it precedes both events by more than half a century. As a result of the early migrations to Britain, Yemeni communities in Cardiff and South Shields represent the oldest continuous Muslim presence in the UK. Yet, their story has remained largely unknown and virtually untold. In exploring the unique history of Yemeni Muslims in Britain, this study asserts that the generally-accepted beginnings of Yemeni community settlement in Britain, thought to be around the 1880s, needs to be revised to a point some 50 years earlier. As this book suggests, there is some evidence to challenge current received opinion.

Although the British Protectorate at Aden was not established until 1839, after its capture by the British East India Company (EIC), the company's vessels had been visiting the port from as early as 1609 when it was then under Portuguese control. By 1829, the EIC considered making Aden a coaling station for its various steam vessels travelling from the Far East, India, Africa and Europe, transporting raw materials from the colonies and then shipping out finished manufactured goods from Britain to the world. In 1835, Captain Haines, an employee of the British East India Company, docked at Aden and prospected the port on behalf of the Company as a possible major strategic coaling station and entrepôt for British vessels and goods sailing to and from India and the Far East. Almost immediately, Company ships began docking at the port. In much the same way that Indian lascars[1] found their way to British ports on EIC vessels from the ports of Calcutta and Bombay as early as the seventeenth century, it is reasonable to assume that Yemeni *baḥriyyah* (sing., *baḥrī*, meaning literally 'of the sea', but understood as 'sailor'), extremely competent at negotiating the sea trade winds to India and China from the Arabian Peninsula for more than two millennia, also signed up on British ships either sailing from Aden, East Africa or India. What is certain is that, by the 1830s, Yemenis from the southern Yemen tribes, allied through treaties with Britain, would have joined British merchant vessels. This fact is also evidenced by the rapid population increase of Aden after the British occupation. Further, the Aden Protectorate was ruled by the British through the India Office from 1839 until 1937, when it finally received 'Colony' status and was then ruled as a separate entity from India. Before 1937, 'Adenese' subjects would have been administered and, therefore, considered as colonial Indian subjects, thus adding to the 'invisibility' of Yemeni sailors among the lascars residing in British ports. It is for the above stated reasons that the timeline for Yemeni migration and settlement in Britian needs to be located around 1836 rather than the 1880s.

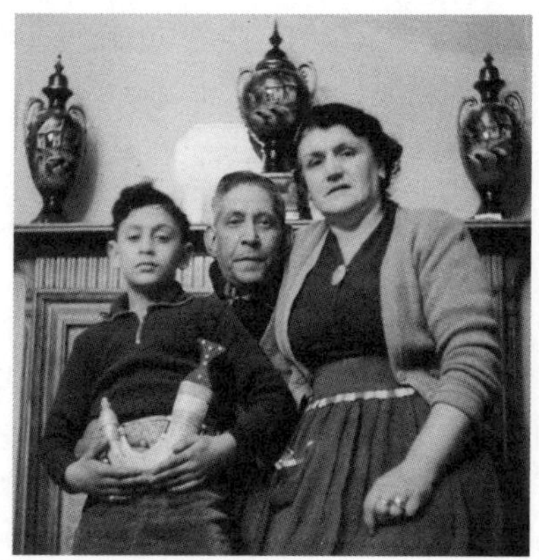

0.1 – Saeed Hassan (al-Hubabi), his wife Josephine and their son, Saeed Kasseum in the living room of their family home in Liverpool, circa 1950.

But who are the Yemenis, from where do they originate and why did they settle in Britain? The publication before you is presented as a historical narrative that not only addresses the above important questions, but also captures the British Yemeni story by constructing a detailed and integrated account extracted from contemporaneous writings, newspaper reports, magazine articles, personal accounts, achieves and recollections collected through ethnographic research and both general and academic publications. The book is also largely informed by my own research on British Yemenis that was originally undertaken as a doctoral thesis.[2] The eclectic source material used in this publication has been woven together to produce a comprehensive social history of Yemeni Muslim migration and settlement in Britain from the earliest time to the present. The personal narratives, recollections and family histories of British Yemenis are an extremely important and unique source of material that both inform and shape the details of this book's chronological narrative. An example of how rich a single family history can be in terms of individual members, their lived experiences and the specific events that mirror the wider context of British Yemeni history in which they unfold, are explored in this publication and briefly exampled below.

Gadri Salih is a British Yemeni who was born in Eccles, Greater Manchester, in 1975. He is the fourth generation of his family to be born in Britain and also to have migrated to Britain over the last 120 years or so. Gadri's incredible family story offers an amazing 'snap-shot' of a unique British Muslim history that is practically unknown to most. Gadri's maternal great-grandfather, Said Hassan, a lascar sailor from Radā', a provincial town in the northern highlands of Yemen, came to Britain in the late nineteenth century, most probably around 1890. Known locally in South Shields and Liverpool as 'Al-Hubabi', Hassan soon established himself as a boarding house owner in the Holborn area of South Shields, where a growing number of Arab-only lodgings were founded for the numerous lascar sailors. The term 'lascar', is an anglicized version of the Arabic term *al-'askar* meaning, 'one employed in military service', and it was used by the colonial British to mean an 'oriental merchant sailor' originally connected to the British East India Company, established in 1600. The term is actually unfamiliar to most Yemeni sailors who instead used the Arabic term, *baḥrī*, to describe their merchant sailing profession. The former lascar, Hassan, became extremely wealthy as a result of his entrepreneurial skills, eventually owning several boarding houses, an import-export business between Aden and the UK, a small shipping company with a flagship called *Sheba* on which Gadri's grandmother and her siblings travelled to the Yemen from South Shields in the early 1930s. Further, on 5 June 1929, Said Hassan applied to South Shield's Town Council for a licence from the Watch Committee to operate a private bus service from South Shields to London. While Alderman Lawson could see no genuine reason why Councillor Cheeseman disagreed to the granting of the licence, on the racist grounds that South Shields had, he said, become a 'dumping ground for other places as far as the Arabs were concerned', additionally, Councillor Scott took further exception to the fact that Said Hassan, as an Arab boarding-house keeper, could afford to spend £2000 on a bus when, he said, 'some English lodging-house keepers could not even pay their rent.' However, despite the unusual and rather discriminatory objections, the council agreed to grant the licence.[3] Hassan also met Prince Hussein, son of the ruling Zaydī Imām of what was then North Yemen, during the Prince's visit to South Shields between 21st and 22nd May 1937. Richards Lawless' book, *From Ta'izz to Tyneside* (1995), contains a photograph of Said Hassan accompanied by his wife, Josephine Hassan (neé Irwin) meeting the Prince in his boarding house during the visit, in which Hassan was presented with a ceremonial *jambiyyah* (Yemeni dagger) by the Prince.[4]

Although a shrewd and accomplished businessman, Hassan's many boarding house properties were actually legally registered in other people's names and when economic depression led to mass unemployment among the Yemeni sailors in South Shields, Cardiff and Liverpool, many boarding-house keepers were bankrupted simply because their lodgers could not pay their keep. In October 1930, six Arab boarding-house keepers from South Sheilds wrote to the Under Secretary for India, requesting financial help for the stranded sailors and listing a number of boarding-house keepers who were owed considerable debts by their borders. Among those listed was, 'Mrs Said [Josephine] Hassan of 10 Chapter Row, £672', a huge amount of money at that time. It is possible that financial difficulties forced Said Hassan and his family to eventually relocate to Liverpool by the end of the 1930s where he purchased a large, detached, Victorian mansion house, 'The Hollies', former family home of Frank Hornby, MP, (1863–1936), the founder of the Hornby toy manufacturing company, creator of Meccano and Hornby Trains, and later an MP, on Station Road, in Maghull, Liverpool, complete with its own grounds. Gadri's mother remembers visiting the house during her early childhood in the 1950s and sitting at a huge dining table where all the family would eat together, with grandfather al-Hubabi sitting at the head of the table.

0.2 – Muhammad al-Hubabi, in front of his father's luxury car, taken in Liverpool, circa 1950.

Once re-established in Liverpool, Hassan acquired a number of properties, possibly boarding houses to service the Yemeni sailors visiting and lodging in the port city. One Yemeni migrant worker, Muhammad Kasseum, originally from Ta'izz in North Yemen, arrived in Liverpool in the late 1930s after living in Marseilles, the southern French port, for seven years. Kasseum eventually married Said and Josephine Hassan's daughter, Attegar, and the couple first lived in Liverpool before moving to Eccles, Greater Manchester, in the late 1950s. Gadri's family were one of the first Yemeni families to settle in Eccles and his maternal aunt, Farida Qarina Salih Ali Qaadiri, born in 1952 in Liverpool, is the first Muslim to be buried in the Eccles and Patricroft Muslim Cemetery, after she sadly passed away on 9th September 1972, aged just 20. Kasseum and his wife had a number of children, some born in Liverpool and others in Eccles and he soon established two Arab cafés in the town. The first was located in nearby Monton, but, by 1969, Kasseum had established a new café on Liverpool Road, facing Eccles Town Hall. Kasseum was also a local Yemeni community organizer and, in 1961, on his initiative he organized Arab film shows at the local cinema. Eccles Justices gave Mr Swindlehurst, the proprietor of the Regent Cinema, permission to open on Sunday afternoons to cater for the town's growing Yemeni population. In June of the same year, the film *Samson and Delilah* in Arabic, was screened and shortly after there were regular showings of Arabic films and musicals.[5] By the early 1960s, a sizeable number of Yemenis had migrated to the industrial cities of the UK to work in the heavy industries of booming post-war Britain. This particular Yemeni migration to Britain is known as 'second wave migration'. Gadri's father, Salih Ali Audhali, originally came to Sheffield in the 1950s from Radā', North Yemen, and he moved to Eccles in the early 1960s. 'Audhali' was not Salih's real name but, rather, the name of a regional southern Yemeni tribe that was allied to the British Protectorate at Aden.

Once established in Eccles, Salih married Muhammad Kasseum's daughter, a third-generation, British-born Yemeni. Gadri describes the transnational tribal marriage connections in his family as being comparable to a chess game in which, 'the pieces are moving from the black squares to the white and from the left to the right until you get to the end [of the board]'.[6] By the late 1970s, economic recession had gripped Britain's manufacturing industries and large numbers of migrant Yemeni workers with very few transferrable skills were facing unemployment. As a result, a significant number took up employment opportunities in the Arabian Gulf, along with Gadri's father, who initially moved to Saudi Arabia to work in the oil industry. In 1981, once established in Saudi Arabia, Salih sent for his family to join him from Britain. Gadri and his family soon settled into their new life in the Middle East, attending school and growing up in a culturally traditional and religiously conservative Saudi society relatively happily for ten years until the outbreak of the first Gulf war in 1991.

When the former president of Iraq, Saddam Hussein, invaded Kuwait, Yemen, then one of 15 countries serving on the UN Security Council, abstained from the UN vote condemning Iraq's actions. As a result, all Yemeni migrants in Saudi Arabia were expelled from the country. In effect this meant that almost one million Yemenis were forced to return to the Yemen virtually overnight. Salih was forced to leave his business and home with his family taking almost nothing with them but the clothes on their backs. Shortly after returning to the Yemen, Salih sadly passed away, forcing Gadri's mother and younger siblings, as British subjects, to return to the UK in 1997 where they had extended family. As a then newly-married man, Gadri remained in the Yemen along with a couple of older married sisters but in 1998 he decided to pay a surprise visit to his mother and family in the UK. After his KLM flight stopped at Jeddah, Saudi Arabia, to take on more passengers to fly to Manchester via Amsterdam, his plane then suffered an engine fire immediately after take-off, forcing a return landing to Jeddah where it was discovered that both engines had actually failed! Nine hours later Gadri boarded a British Airways flight this time flying to London, Heathrow. Once in London, Gadri was obliged to make his own way to Manchester. However, disorientated by his difficult and redirected flight and unaware as to how he might find his way to Manchester, he approached 'a very tall police officer' saying:

> I'm lost. He [the policemen] said, 'What's the story?' I said I was on the KLM [flight], I was supposed to go to Amsterdam, then Manchester, this is what happened. ... What am I supposed to do? I'm in London, I've never been here in my life. And he said, 'You've got a Manchester accent!' ... He said, '[You've been away] eighteen years you say? You've still got that Manchester accent!' But he helped me, and he took me [to the ticket office] to buy a ticket for the train. ... He got me on the train.[7]

Gadri was then aided at Paddington Station by two Algerians who eventually helped him board a train for Manchester and contacted his family to arrange for them to meet him at the station in Manchester, after recognizing Gadri was an Arab, who was ironically lost in his own country! Gadri Salih's family narrative crystallizes some of the key historical and sociological themes pertinent to British Yemenis explored in this monograph; migration, diaspora, discrimination, community settlement and formation, religion, culture, politics, being and belonging. This book traces the transformation of a nascent group of colonial, oriental merchant sailors into a thriving community as Britain's oldest established Muslims, but who are practically invisible.

0.3 – Gadri Salih, great-grandson of al-Hubabi, and his fifth-generation, British Yemeni children at their home in Eccles, Greater Manchester.

The first chapter of this book provides a brief history of Yemen from ancient times as a centre of the production of frankincense and myrrh that was much sought after in the ancient world. The incense and spice trade turned Yemen into a place of legend and myth, as well as a very wealthy region both through international trade and agricultural production in its southern highlands. The production of incense and export agriculture meant that ancient Yemen needed its established camel caravan routes to carry goods to Babylonia and Byzantium and its developed entrepôts, which included Aden, to ship merchandise to Upper Egypt, the Mediterranean and across to Abyssinia via the Red Sea and through the Gulf of Aden to the Indian Ocean to India, the Far East and China. The ruling Sabean and Ḥimyarite kingdoms shaped the changing fortunes of the Yemeni people as a combination of economic shifts and natural disasters afflicted the prosperous region and it fell into rapid decline. *Arabia Felix* or 'Felicitous Arabia', as the Romans had called it, soon went from being the 'land of plenty' to the 'land of empty'. The northern highlands of Yemen had been influenced by Byzantine Christianity for many years both from the Hellenistic world and from across the Red Sea in Africa. But when the Ḥimyarite king, Dhū Nawwās converted to Judaism and began persecuting his Christian subjects in Najrān, the powerful Abyssinian kingdom invaded in the early sixth century CE (Common Era) to remove the king and re-establish Christianity as the dominant religion of the Yemen until the introduction of Islam in the early period of Muhammad's mission.

Dominated for a millennia by the minority ruling Zaydī Imāms, a branch of Shii Islam, the harsh topography and differing terrains of the Yemen have meant that imposing total rule over the whole country has never been completely achieved and the ancient tribal hostilities between the dominant Kathīrī and Quʿaytī tribes of the southern desert region of Ḥaḍramawt were eventually exploited by the British in the mid-nineteenth century who desperately sought to control the port of Aden to protect its imperial, global entrepreneurialism. It is at this juncture that the historical narrative of this monograph begins as thousands of Yemenis sought employment on ships sailing from Aden, with many sailing to Britain from as early as the 1830s. The establishment of the British Protectorate at Aden in 1839 effectively precipitated the creation of two Yemens; the former northern socialist, Yemen Arab Republic (YAR) and the former southern Marxist, Peoples Democratic Republic of Yemen (PDRY). Britain's colony at Aden lasted until 1967 when they were eventually ousted after a fierce independence war. Throughout the changing fortunes of Yemen's long history, migration and diaspora have been common themes, as Yemenis sought a better life elsewhere through trade or work.

The second chapter explores the earliest arrival and settlement of Yemenis sailors to the British port cities of Cardiff, South Shields, London, Liverpool and, later, Manchester, as recounted through the personal narratives and tales of lascars present in imperial Britain. The writings of the Reverend Joseph Salter, who worked as a Christian missionary amongst South Asian, Arab and Far Eastern Oriental sailors for many years produced two published accounts of his philanthropic missionary work amongst the abandoned and desperate lascars scattered across the port cities of Britain in the nineteenth century. They provide harrowing accounts of the deprivation and discrimination suffered by many of the early lascars. As the British Empire rapidly expanded, the terminologies and typologies relating to its colonial subjects became devoid of the details and nuances of specific ethnic subgroupings and instead the ubiquitous term 'lascar' was applied to any oriental sailor whether he came from Malacca, Bombay or Aden. In the use of this overarching term, ethnic subgroups; like the Malays, Indians and Yemenis, became subsumed as they were woven into the collective term, 'lascar'. It is therefore more than likely that the 'Arabs' referred to by the Reverend Joseph Salter, during his nineteenth century missionary work among the Oriental sailors stranded in British ports, were in fact Yemenis. As my research confirms, Yemeni settlers were recorded in the port of Cardiff as early as the 1860s. This particular form of early migration was largely facilitated through the custom of the *muqaddam* ('representative') and the *muwassiṭ* ('middleman'), who acted as subcontractors to the shipping agents and port authorities in providing ships' crews, usually made up of around 12 Yemeni lascars from the same tribe. In the process, the *muqaddam* or *muwassiṭ* would invariably profit from a small fee and commission from both the shipping agent or port authority and the employed Yemeni lascar.

As the lascar presence increased across British docklands, a series of discriminatory legislation aimed at limiting the numbers of lascars in the ports and shipping industry was put into place from the mid-nineteenth to the mid-twentieth centuries. The lascars faced an unbelievable degree of racism and discrimination and the contemporaneous accounts of their difficult and often squalid living conditions also document a number of unique examples of early Muslim ritual practices and religious rites within the then burgeoning British Muslim community. Amongst the new measures aimed at curtailing lascar settlement in Britain were 'coloured only' sailors' rests and lodging houses. In the process, there was a pairing-off of lascars who wished to lodge with people of the same language and culture as themselves and, as a result, 'Arab only' boarding houses began to appear in South Shields, Cardiff and Liverpool. However, despite the exclusionary measures, Yemeni sailors not only continued to inhabit the port cities but many began to marry local women and raise families, forming tight-knit communities identified by their racial and religious otherness and contrasted with the wider society of the various cities in which they settled. The multi-racial, multicultural docklands communities largely settled by Yemeni lascars became exoticized by the locals and Cardiff's Butetown docklands area became known as 'Tiger Bay', South Shields' Holborn and Laygate areas were named locally as 'Little Arabia' and the Trafford Park area of Manchester Docks, was known as the 'Barbary Coast'.

Chapter 3 explores the nascent formation of early Yemeni communities across the British port cities and the emergence of the Arab boarding houses and cafés that facilitated the cultural and religious needs of the settling lascars. The chapter illustrates that despite the development of small, 'incapsulated'[8] communities, many lascars faced extremely high levels of discrimination as their white maritime peers raised continued objections to the 'black and coloured' seamen commissioned at cheaper rates by the shipping companies. Ironically, the establishment of national labour unions in the British shipping industry were mobilized in an effort to reduce the numbers of non-white sailors employed on ships. By the turn of the twentieth century, it was estimated that the number of 'coloured' seamen working on British vessels was around a staggering 40,000. However, union pressure resulted in a huge reduction of almost a third by 1912. In a desperate bid for work, Yemeni sailors were forced to travel between the docks of Cardiff, South Shields, London, Hull, Liverpool and Manchester, a phenomenon known as the 'Tramp trade'.

By the outbreak of the First World War in 1914, the situation of Yemeni lascars took a dramatic turn when the British government was forced to rely on its colonial subjects to aid the war effort. Thousands of Yemenis based in British ports volunteered to serve on seconded merchant vessels used to ship vital supplies to the troops deployed in Europe, North Africa and the Middle East. Additionally, the increase in demand for colonial sailors to replace the British men in military service provided further employment opportunities for Yemeni lascars while others found jobs in the munitions factories of Manchester or the shipbuilding and auxiliary industries such as the timber yards. By 1919, serious economic recession and major changes in the shipping industry meant that many Yemeni lascars became redundant. In the increasing racial tensions that flared up in the interwar period during the desperate search for work within the shipping industry, a number of so-called 'Arab riots' broke out across the British ports. Newspaper articles inflamed the situation by making a series of unfounded claims against the minority lascars. As the race riots continued, on and off until the 1930s, the army was often employed to quell the disturbances. The developing Yemeni community faced a litany of discriminatory abuse that was aimed not just at the settler migrants, but at their indigenous wives, who were accused of being sexually deviant because of their liaisons and marriages to the Arabs, and their 'mixed race' children, who were portrayed as the 'half-bred' by-products of what were considered to be most unsavoury matrimonies. The social exclusion faced by the Yemeni communities directly after the First World War resulted in their effective marginalization across all realms of British public and social life, despite the huge sacrifices the community had made in defence of Britain during the war.

If invisibility is a recurring theme in the history of Yemeni settlement in Britain, Chapter 4 explores their growing visibility as a direct result of the later employment struggles that directly follow the First World War and the interwar economic depression of the 1920s and 1930s. Yemenis initially lost their visibility and became submerged into broader racist and discriminatory terms such as 'blacks' and 'Arabs' during this period. It was during the interwar years that three significant events occurred relating to British Yemenis. The first was the forced and voluntary repatriation from Britain of large numbers of unemployed Yemenis during the great depression of the early twentieth century. In addition to the imposed deportations, thousands of Yemenis returned voluntarily or sought better employment opportunities in the developing Arab Gulf countries. The second event was the introduction of a spiritually dynamic and well-organized religious movement that took root across the British Yemeni communities from the 1930s to the mid-1950s. This movement, the ʻAlawī Sufi *ṭarīqah*, introduced by the charismatic Yemeni religious scholar, Shaykh Abdullah Ali al-Hakimi, who transformed the lives of the Yemeni sailors, their British Muslim convert wives and their 'mixed race' (or *muwalladūn*) children.

Once again, the Yemeni community moved from being unassuming and unseen to becoming religiously and culturally distinctive and highly visible. The experience of the ʻAlawī Sufi *ṭarīqah* within the British Yemeni community is a unique and fascinating chapter of British Muslim history that completely transformed the British Yemeni communities. Al-Hakimi, almost single-handed, established a number of religious centres across the towns and cities where Yemenis were located. He also educated the many indigenous wives of the sailors, founding Islamic classes along with Qur'ān classes for their children. During significant religious festivals, street parades were organized across the port cities in which Yemenis were settled. The third event was the dramatic change in the shipping industry as vessels moved from steam power, provided by coal shovelled into the engine boilers by Yemeni lascar, 'stokers' or 'donkeymen' to oil-fuelled ships. This development forced an 'inward migration' of Yemeni communities into the industrial centres of urban Britain, away from their traditional maritime employment and isolated multicultural docklands communities. In the process, this migration created new communities of urbanized and industrialized British Yemenis shaped by the factories and steelworks in the manufacturing cities of Birmingham, Sheffield and Manchester.

The employment struggles of Yemeni settlers to Britain by the mid-twentieth century were compounded by the wider economic depression that plagued Western Europe for decades after the First World War. Added to this was the blatant discrimination Yemenis, their British wives and 'mixed race' children constantly confront. In the face of increasing hostility and exclusion, Yemeni sailors and industrial labourers began to mobilize through the trade union movement. Further, as the politics of the Yemen shifted by the late twentieth century, so too did the leadership of the British Yemeni community which had been led and motivated so charismatically by its spiritual guide, Shaykh Abdullah Ali al-Hakimi, for almost two decades. Al-Hakimi was originally welcomed by the British government and his spiritual reforms within the community were seen as a much needed antidote to the rising politicization of the British Yemeni communities and their increasing militant trade unionism. His inspiring spiritual leadership instilled the community with a sense of pride and belonging, both religiously and culturally. However, al-Hakimi's efforts were thwarted by his political ambitions aimed at a free and united Yemen, rid of its archaic and outmoded, medieval, theocratic ruler in the shape of the Zaydī Imām in the North and the colonial occupation of British imperialists at the port of Aden. These ambitions were to prove extremely costly to al-Hakimi both upon him personally and upon the community and spiritual order he worked so tirelessly to establish. As al-Hakimi's reformist aspirations increasingly began to focus on removing the autocratic Zaydī Imām, the British government began to distance themselves from him, fearing his revolutionary politics would not only disrupt their cordial diplomatic relations with the Imām in North Yemen, but would also lead to a revolt to their control of south Yemen. But when the dominant Shamīrī tribe, originating from the province of Ta'izz, took exception to his anti-Imāmate stand and what they saw as his 'meddling' in the politics of Yemen, the rift between the Shaykh and his *ṭarīqah* adherents became irreconcilable and al-Hakimi was forced to leave Britain for the Aden Protectorate in 1953. This move saw the former assistant to Shaykh al-Hakimi, Shaykh Hassan Ismail, becoming the *murshid* (spiritual guide) of the 'Alawī *ṭarīqah* in the UK. The chapter explores al-Hakimi's far-reaching influence and indelible impact on the Yemeni community in mid-twentieth century Britain.

Chapter 6 follows the development of the 'Alawī *ṭarīqah* when Shaykh Hassan Ismail, al-Hakimi's former deputy and subsequent replacement, permanently returned to Yemen in 1956 after electing his adopted UK-born British Yemeni son, Shaykh Said Hassan Ismail, as the new *murshid* of the 'Alawī *ṭarīqah*. The legacy of Shaykh Said's consistent and loyal service to the Yemeni community in

Cardiff spanned over 50 years and was rooted in a distinctly British Muslim context, largely reflected in the Shaykh's own idiomatic British Yemeni identity. However, while claims to wider notions of Britishness became a developing feature of British Yemeni identity experiences in the latter part of the twentieth century, post-Second World War economic migrants coming directly from the Yemen into the industrial metropolises of Britain through a 'second wave' migration were experiencing varied degrees of cultural adjustment. The settlement of these new migrants was facilitated through the same tribal networks and *muwassiṭūn* ('middleman') systems employed by the Yemeni lascars to British port cities over a hundred years earlier. Although new Yemeni settlers still faced degrees of racism and discrimination in their places of work and settlement, social and political changes in Britain and Yemen meant that the migrant labourers were both better politically educated and actively organized as a result of both Marxist and socialist governments in North and South Yemen, respectively. In the UK this developed political awareness saw the establishment of the Yemeni Workers Union and the affiliation of many Yemeni workers with other established British Trade Unions.

At the local British Yemeni community levels, the politicization of Yemenis sparked the establishment of many cultural institutions and community organizations that galvanized the emerging innercity Yemeni communities locally, nationally and internationally, through which diaspora Yemenis were able to mobilize and work towards seriously developing their communities in the UK and Yemen. By the 1970s, economic recession hit the UK's manufacturing industries hard and the resultant mass-unemployment impacted directly on the 'second wave' Yemeni communities across the northern industrial cities. Britain's Black and Asian communities, largely established through postwar economic migration, were 'scapegoated' and transmogrified by the media and ruthless politicians from loyal and hard-working employees into lazy and unemployed 'scroungers' almost overnight. The Yemeni response was a degree of 'mass migration' to the more prosperous and opportune climes of the developed Arabian Gulf, thus creating another transnational Yemeni link and migration narrative as witnessed by Gadri Salih's opening story. For those who stayed, their fate was to be once again subsumed by invisibility into the wider debates of immigration, integration, loyalty and belonging and a perceived failed multiculturalism. In the ensuing and highly controversial debates, demonstrations and ultimate riots a distinct sense of British Yemeni identity emerged in the presence of a much-needed role model and hero; the Sheffield-born boxing phenomenon, 'Prince' Naseem Hamid. As one young British Yemeni put it; '[When] "Prince" Naseem came on the scene...it was, "I'm from the Yemen, you know 'Prince' Naseem?" And, that made it like alright and cool.' Hamid's singular contribution to British Yemeni identity represented a tangible manifestation of the resultant hybrid and hyphenated multiple identities as British Arabs, British Yemenis and British Muslims that was increasingly experienced by succeeding generations.

The final chapter explores the contemporary setting, present conditions and current developments of the Yemeni communities across Britain through a number of leading research studies and publications by academics, journalists and writers. Some key observations offered by various studies conducted on British Yemeni communities assert a multitude of often conflicting interpretations from 'invisibility' and 'incapsulation' to the description of Britain's oldest Muslim community as representing both a genuine expression of 'British Islam' and 'English Muslims'. The phenomenon of 'second wave' migration of single-male Yemenis to the industrial metropolises of post-World War Two Britain is contrasted with the earlier port settlements of the nineteenth-century lascars. A number of commentators viewed the Yemeni communities, particularly the South Shields community, as fully integrated members of the wider societies into which they settled. This reality, they assert, has been largely established as a result of the intermarriages and subsequent generations of settlement in their various locales.

The chapter also explores the custom, merits and dangers of chewing *qāt*, a plant indigenous to the Yemen, whose leaves are chewed in communal gatherings of males on a daily basis in Yemen but less frequently here in Britain. Media scrutiny regarding the easy availability of *qāt* in the UK has periodically presented its consumption with the same panic and fear as that of 'hard' drug use, demanding an outright ban of *qāt* that is simply reactionary. This chapter instead offers critical assessment of the consumption and use of *qāt* amongst British Yemenis based upon an examination of its physical and medical affects as well as its cultural significance.

The chapter also investigates the various degrees of community development and capacity building across the British Yemeni communities by comparing the largest, settled in Birmingham, to the smallest, living in Eccles, Greater Manchester, and examining how population size affects the 'visibility' and, consequently, the amount of investment and support from the local authorities these communities might receive. The comparison details the successful development of Birmingham's Bordesley Centre, managed by the largely Yemeni-run Al-Muath Trust. The Centre is an institute that serves, not only the large settled Yemeni community, but also the majority of ethnic minority communities within the locale. The current growing confidence and community development sprouting across the British Yemeni communities is predominantly absent from the studies examined in this chapter despite some writers speaking about British Yemenis as 'successfully integrated', even describing them as 'English Muslims'. Conversely, the research monographs of Richard Lawless and Fred Halliday express the experiences of Yemenis in Britain as the 'end of an era' of a community that lives in the 'remotest village', whose lives are both separated and 'invisible' to the wider society in which they live, as 'incapsulated' communities.

The Epilogue to this social history discusses the British Yemeni community in the wider contexts of Arab communities in Britain and the related issues of visibility and recognition by local and national governments in terms of their specific needs and concerns. It is evident from the studies referenced and cited that there is a large degree of marginalization when it comes to addressing both the misrepresentations of the many diverse Arab communities in the UK, as either pathologized 'Islamic terrorists' operating as al-Qaeda 'sleeper cells' or 'rich petroldollar Shaykhs' who inhabit the nightclubs and casinos of London. Coupled with the subject of representation beyond misleading stereotypes has been the previous problem of establishing an accurate population statistic for the number of Arabs in Britain before the new inclusions in the 2011 census statistics.

The works of Madawi al-Rasheed and Camilla Fawzi El-Solh provide startling and powerful arguments for more nuanced representations and greater academic research into Arabs in Britain. The emergence of Arab community mobilization as a direct result of 9/11 and the subsequent US-led 'War on Terror' initiatives; the invasion of Afghanistan and, then later, Iraq, the intensive securitization of Arab communities in US, Britain and Europe, and the high numbers of 'extraordinary renditions' – the cruel euphemism for the numerous unexplained disappearances of Arab Muslims from across the globe into US-facilitated incarcerations, devoid of any human rights – have all witnessed a high degree of organized British Arab responses. For example, the 'Stop the War' campaign supported by the Muslim Association of Britain (MAB) attracted large numbers of young British Yemenis into its ranks. Further, the current pro-democracy movement sweeping across the Arab-Islamic Middle East has seen rallied support from the Arab communities in Britain, manifest through many demonstrations, fund-raising events and representations of the various revolutionary movements in the British media. This is particularly true in the case of the British Yemeni community towards the final days of Ali Abdullah Salih's presidency.

Another issue is the question of Fred Halliday's asserted 'invisibility' of the British Yemeni community which is addressed in the Epilogue through a specific case study of the population statistics according to the 1991 and 2001 Census for the Yemeni community of Eccles, Greater Manchester, and the subsequent local authority's responses to the prevailing socio-economic conditions of that community. The case study records the dramatic shift in local authority funding and resources once a serious discrepancy between the 'official' population figure and a much higher figure, based on quantitative ethnographic research, had been established for the Yemeni population. Thus, almost immediately transforming that particular community from being 'invisible' and underdeveloped into one that is both visible and organized.

The politicization of Muslim identity appears to be an increasing inevitability for Muslim minorities in the post-9/11 political climate of western societies. Yet how much is this phenomenon actually internal to the experiences and realities faced by young British Yemenis is an interesting question. Current research into 'British Muslim Arab' identity has been undertaken by Carol Nagel and Lynn Staeheli, which included a significant proportion of young British Yemeni respondents. Their research findings have been examined as a means of exploring the idea of 'Muslim', as both a public and political identity, based on the qualitative research interviews in their study. Surprisingly, they noted that while levels of personal religiosity varied, most respondents appeared to reject the idea of a 'British Muslim' identity because it was both inherently politicized and largely unrepresentative of their personal experiences of religion and politics. What is clear from the detailed study is that the majority of the views of the young British Arabs questioned are in counterdistinction to the perpetuated association between Islam and political extremism, whilst acknowledging the place of religion and religious identity in the public realm.

Finally, this study concludes with a concise discussion on the notion of traditional tribal belonging in the particular context of transnational and diaspora Yemeni networks. Translocal tribal politics often forms part of the intra-community dynamics of the British Yemeni communities. However, the tensions and disputes between various tribal allegiances only occasionally surface and may even remain invisible to the outsider. Moreover, the need to conform to the collective conventions of tribal traditions and mores is essentially self-imposed, particularly in the diaspora. Global dimensions of Yemeni identity, both religious and cultural, have become unique features of 'Yemeniness' and aspects of 'translocal tribalism' are important facets of identity for young British Yemeni males. The cumulative affects of the modern manifestations of what it means to be both British and Yemeni have produced an amazing and resilient community of Arab Muslims in the UK who have established themselves for almost 200 years as the country's oldest settled Muslim community, complete with its own unique and fascinating historical narrative.

As Arabic is the literary language of Yemenis and Islam, Arabic terms have been used and explained throughout the book, and a glossary of the major words appears at the end. Spellings considered to be correct by the wider Muslim academic community have been adopted: for example 'Shaykh' and 'Muslim' rather than 'Sheikh' and 'Moslem'. Diacritical marks have been used for unfamiliar Arabic terms except where standard names, placenames and terms are commonly used. In quotations, the terms and spellings used by the original authors have been reproduced so that variant spellings such as 'Mohammed', 'Moslem', 'tariqa' and 'sheikh' are found. The italicization, punctuation and spelling in the quotations all appear as they do in their original texts. It is customary for peace and salutations to follow the names both of Islamic Prophets and Muhammad's companions, but these have been omitted in this book.

YEMEN: A BRIEF HISTORY OF *ARABIA FELIX*

The port of Aden at the tip of southern Yemen has been historically described as the 'gateway to China' largely because ancient Arab mariners used the port as a midway point in the maritime trading routes between the eastern coast of Africa, the Mediterranean, via the desert caravan routes, and India, China and Malay.[1] The oceanic 'super highways' created by Yemeni and Omani merchant seamen ensured that Arab colonies were well established in East Africa and India long before the advent of Islam in the seventh century CE. In the Yemeni context, these important trade routes were traditionally dominated by the two ruling tribes of the Kathīrī and Quʿaytī emanating from the fringes of Ḥaḍramawt in *al-Rubaʿ al-Khālī* ('The Empty Quarter') desert of the southern Arab Peninsula. Ancient histories of Middle Eastern civilizations make very little reference to Yemen, focusing instead on the wonders of Babylon and Pharoanic Egypt. The general absence of any narrative of ancient Yemen, however, cannot deny its unique importance in the economic development of the region from around 2000BCE until 700CE. In this period, Yemen was a flourishing area ruled by a number of important kingdoms who advanced the region's prosperity and technological development. The pre-Islamic civilizations of Awsān, Ḥaḍramawt, Ḥimyar, Maʿīn, Qatabān and Saba' were ancient kingdoms whose histories shaped the very nature of what we know today as Yemen.[2] It is only their remoteness in relation to modern population centres that have made the abandoned desert ruins of these previous civilizations the subject of myth and legend.

In more recent times, Yemen's virtual encapsulation, as a result of almost a thousand years of Zaydī Imāmate-rule, cut the region off from the rest of the world, resulting in a further ignorance of the country's rich and epic history. It is only in the last 200 years that Western explorers, often at great personal risk, have been able to penetrate Yemen's unforgiving landscapes of remote and rugged mountains and vast barren deserts to reveal many of its important archaeological sites and lost ancient settlements. Modern excavations of these now isolated sites have revealed not only their former glory as centres of advanced civilization, but also their key role in the extremely lucrative trade in rare spices and expensive incenses. The abandoned ancient trading entrepôts were vital to the commodities and rites of the ancient world. In Pharoanic Egypt and ancient Babylon, the use of frankincense and myrrh in the religious rituals of mummification and the employment of aromatic gums as precious commodities used in medicines, cosmetics and foods was acknowledged across the ancient world. Egyptian demand for these rare goods established permanent trade routes to the incense-producing areas of Ḥaḍramawt and Ẓufār in Southern Arabia. This lucrative trade was then further extended to later Greek and Roman civilizations to the north of Arabia via the vast camel caravans of the incense routes. This international trade enabled the regional kingdoms and their capitals to flourish that saw the establishment of a number of important seaports including Qānā in the south of Arabia and Gaza in the north.[3] Economic cooperation was vital to all the kingdoms of the region and, despite often on-going hostilities between various regional sovereignties, protection for trade caravans was ensured through a system of 'commissions' or taxes from the merchants in return for safe passage through tribal territories across the deserts and highlands. However, protected travel could only be assured where traders adhered strictly to a prescribed and widely recognized route and any breaches could often result in the penalty of death.

1.1 – A British stamp from the Aden Protectorate published in the 1960s displaying an early etching of the port.

Whilst relatively little is known regarding the administration and organization of the various ancient kingdoms of the region, archaeological evidence and research suggests that the majority were polytheist, with a number of ancient temples and places of worship dedicated to astrological deities such as the sun, the moon and other celestial entities.[4] Further, the excavation of burial sites also indicates a belief in an afterlife by the presence of a number of personal possessions included in many graves. Archaeologists also interpret the gradual development of simple stylized sculptural forms into intricate three-dimensional figures, complete with individual features, as suggestive of the wealth and influence generated through the highly profitable incense trade that exposed these relatively isolated societies to more advanced civilizations. The distinctive and fairly rapid shift from simple geometric designs to greater developed floral shapes and patterns indicate clear Hellenistic influences. Architecturally, the design of the original temples, constructed of rectangular buildings flanked with square shaped columns, is contrasted with the later buildings which appear to replicate the hallmarks of Greek and Roman architectural motifs.

Ancient Rulers and Kingdoms

Although historians generally refer to the overarching ancient civilization of the region as Sabean, the kingdoms of southern Arabia were largely contemporaneous and did not succeed each other. Rather, different kingdoms reached their civilizational peak at different times. For example, by the third century CE, the Ḥimyarite kingdom exercised its hegemony over the neighbouring kingdoms of Saba', Dhū Raydān, Ḥaḍramawt and Yamnat and, a century later, Ḥimyarite ascendancy included rule over the Bedouins of the highlands and lowlands, forming the first political unification of southern Arabia under a single ruler. Before Ḥimyarite ascendancy, the Sabeans had dominated the region for well over a thousand years, creating a kingdom whose influence reached far beyond tribal tributaries. Equally, the people of the Ma'īn kingdom in the north of the region were economic stalwarts whose commercial exploits and interests reached as far as the Nabatean city of Petra in central Arabia and several countries around the Mediterranean. However, it was only the kingdom of Ḥaḍramawt that produced the much-needed luxury commodity of frankincense, from the Dhofar region, which was shipped through the ancient port of Qānā, today known as Bi'r 'Alī, thereafter transported overland through Shabwah.[5]

In the ancient world, the consumers of the expensive incenses were never informed of their precise origins, hence the legends and myths that surround the early medieval spice and incense trade. For example, Heredotus wrote that incense growers lived in isolated groves and were forbidden marital relations with women or to attend funerals. He also claimed that the mythical groves which produced the precious incense were guarded by winged serpents. But such fables were probably largely the result of overzealous Yemeni incense merchants who wished not only to preserve the high prices sought for their wares, but also to protect the sea routes they had mastered to India and China by learning to negotiate the monsoon winds.[6] The ancient sea routes brought in further expensive luxuries such as spices and silks which all passed through Yemeni ports on to camel caravan routes through Arabia into Greek and then later Roman domains. So fruitful were Yemeni merchants in the trade of precious commodities, that the Romans believed that the Arabian Peninsula was the producer of all such expensive items, prompting them to describe the Yemen as *Arabia Felix* ('Fortuitous Arabia'). But the exotic and mysterious image of Arabia, cultivated by the Romans, overlooked the harsh realities of life in the region in which the majority of the population were held in virtual serfdom, working the irrigated foothills of the highlands in the production of much-needed agricultural produce. Evidence of this early sophisticated agricultural society is best seen in the ancient remains of the huge rock monoliths of the former Ma'rib Dam. These now strange free-standing structures are all that remain of the colossal *wādī* (valley) sluices that trapped the rainfall running down the valleys, forming a complex irrigation system constructed by the ancient Sabean civilization that is believed to have irrigated more than 16,000 hectares, producing food for an estimated 300,000 people.[7]

The Ma'rib Dam is a legend that even finds references in the Qur'ān (Sūrah 27, *Al-Naml* and Sūrah 34, *Saba'*) and is linked historically to the Old Testament Queen of Sheba (or, Bilqīs), who was said to have visited King Solomon's (Sulāymān) court in ancient Palestine (10 Kings: 1–3, Chronicles: 1–2). Scripture offers only sketchy descriptions of the events and no absolute narrative exists as to the exact detail of the ancient queen, her epic journey to Solomon's seat and the details of her kingdom. Archaeological excavations of these ancient Sabean sites are slowly beginning to offer further evidence of this once great civilization. The collapse of the Ma'rib Dam in the fifth century CE, and its ill-fated restoration that resulted in its ultimate collapse 100 years later, is seen as the catalyst for the demise of the Sabean civilization. Although historians suggest that the collapse of the Ma'rib Dam was actually only a contributory factor to the wider downturn in the incense trade from the fourth century CE onwards when the Romans discovered their own sea routes to India in search of the origins of the spices and incense they sought. Further, the political shifts within the Roman Empire as the Eastern Empire quickly acceded saw the capital transferred from Rome to Constantinople in 395CE, which meant that a new overland route to India and China opened up through ancient Persia and Afghanistan. Added to this was the spread of Christianity across Byzantium in the fourth and fifth centuries CE, which hailed a major change from the previous pagan rituals that had relied on incense for its religious rites.

As develoments in the Western and Eastern Roman Empires took their toll on the international incense trade in the Yemen, internal transformations within the region also began to have their impact. The relatively sophisticated kingdoms and civilizations that had developed as a direct result of the boom in the incense and spice trades slowly began to deteriorate as the previous wealth that flooded into the region gradually dried up. This serious economic decline in the region brought about a re-nomadification of Southern Arabia as the former prosperous centres suffered from economic deprivation.[8] Consequently, the highly-developed irrigated agricultural societies that sprouted out of the practical need to feed the booming economic centres also fell into rapid decline. The resultant effect was a complete cessation of market economies based on the luxury commodities of spice, silk and incense. As a consequence, what had previously been hailed by the other great civilizations as the 'land of plenty' quickly became the 'land of empty'.

The northern highlands of the region had for many years been influenced by Byzantine Christianity, both from the Hellenistic world and the Abyssinian Empire. Yet, whilst Christianity had influenced the beliefs and culture of the northern Ḥimyarite kingdom, when the last Ḥimyarite sovereigns converted to Judaism, the situation for the majority Christians in the region of Najrān became that of religious persecution at the hands of the zealot Jewish king, Dhū Nuwwās, prompting an invasion by the Abyssinians around 518CE. Towards the south, the ancient prosperous kingdoms of Saba', Ma'īn, Qatabān, Awsān and Ḥaḍramawt, all evaporated as their various populations either reverted to a Bedouin existence, trekking the ancient oasis routes of the Empty Quarter desert or settled the highland slopes to carve out small agricultural communities. The residue of these ancient Yemeni civilizations remains deep-rooted in the collective conscience of their descendants and is often manifest in the modern-day constructions of Yemeni homes, whether they are mountain village dwellings that hang precariously off the rocky ridges, the urban settlements of regional and provincial cities, or the Manhattan-like multi-storey tower blocks of Shibām in Wādī Ḥaḍramawt. Beyond the unique architecture of the Yemen, which pays homage to past civilizational glory, are the ancient tribal customs (*'urf*) that encapsulate moral and ethical codes of mutual coexistence and run parallel to the religious codes of the Islamic *sharī'ah* and the modern secular legislation of a burgeoning democratic nation-state. Never too far behind the modern tropes and trappings of contemporary Yemen are the ancient reminders of a civilization with a unique and ancient past.

In the pre-Islamic period the Yemeni people are considered to be the 'original' Arabs, *al-'arab al-'āribah*, or what Ismail Raji al-Faruqi translates as 'the Arabizing Arabs', in contrast to *al-'arab al-musta'ribah*, or, the 'Arabized Arabs'.[9] Paul Dresch refers to an Islamic Prophetic tradition, which declares the Yemenis to be the original Arabs, is often used to substantiate this genealogical and civilizational claim.[10] The topography of the Yemen has largely contributed to the social, cultural and political development of the country and there are three principle geopolitical regions that have had a determining effect on the different socio-political groupings and historical worldviews of the peoples of Yemen.[11] The western and northern mountain highlands have always been virtually impervious to invasion or outside domination, rendering it autonomous of any imposed and centralized form of national government. The southern uplands have provided a relatively stable and suitable environment for the establishment of more urban and organized societies conducive to structured forms of government or state building. Tihāmah occupies the precarious location between the mountains and the sea, leaving its people open to historic invasions from both directions. This geographical vulnerability has hindered the establishment of any local rule and Tihāmah has historically been the political battleground of foreign and Yemeni ruling powers.[12] Tribal bonds and allegiances have also often stunted the development of any central authority or unifying government. Most Yemenis belong to a tribe, clan or lineage and tribes inhabit defined regions and territories each ruled by a tribal elder, or shaykh. These regions are governed by a combination of their own *'urf* (local tribal customs) and *sharīʿah* (Islamic law) according to its specific theological tradition.[13] Furthermore, each tribe and region preserves inherited genealogies and distinct historical narratives. Yet despite the apparent hindrance of tribalism, there have been several forms of government in the 5000 year-old history of the Yemen. However, few rulers managed to exercise total rule over all regions of the Yemen and even fewer could claim absolute allegiance to their rule.[14]

Islam and the Zaydī Imāms

The modern country of Yemen geographically occupies the southwestern tip of the Arabian Peninsula, *Jazīrat al-ʿArab*, bordered on the west by the Red Sea and to the north and the east by Saudi Arabia and Oman respectively. The land mass covers an area of 74,000 square miles with a coastal mountain range and a central plateau that rises to over 12,000 feet above sea level.[15] The land between the mountain highlands and the Red Sea is extremely fertile and is often described as the 'Garden of Arabia'. It is also the most densely populated region and the place where the capital city, Sana'a, is located. Sana'a is surrounded by many remote highland settlements and mountain villages with isolated rural communities living in harsh and rugged terrain.[16] The average settlement size is less than 90 people. The three main geographical regions of the Yemen are Bāb al-Mandab, Tihāmah and Ḥaḍramawt. Bāb al-Mandab is the strait running from the southern tip along the Red Sea to Saudi Arabia. Tihāmah, is a largely barren, desert plain south of the central plateau and, apart from the developing city of Hodeidah and a few traditional trading ports like Zabīd and Bayt al-Faqīh, it is relatively uninhabited. Tihāmah's expanse leads to the eastern craggy peaks of the central Yemen. Towards the central mountain area lies the city of Taʿizz and further north other historical and religious centres include, Kawkabān, Ḥajjah, Ṣaʿdah and Shahārah. In the south lie Dhamar, Ibb, Jiblā and Radāʾ. The eastern escarpment peters away into the great vacuous expanse of Ḥaḍramawt and the Empty Quarter, a vast desert and ancient home to the people of Saba' and Maʿīn. Many towns in the far eastern part of the Yemen are reminders of a great civilization long pre-dating Islam – Barāqish, Ma'rib[17] and Ẓafar, a region now only inhabited by Bedouins. The current population of the Yemen is estimated to be around 18 million, four times what is was in 1900. With a growth rate of approximately 3.7% annually, it would appear that the population has almost doubled every 20 years.[18] The region is home to a civilization with both an ancient biblical past and a turbulent modern history.

Yemenis have traditionally been travellers and, long before the Islamization of the Yemen, early migrations to central Arabia and Mesopotamia are traced through ancient tribal histories and genealogies.[19] A Qur'ānic reference to the collapse of the Ma'rib Dam, that had provided essential water irrigation for the ancient Yemenis, is cited as a major catastrophe, which resulted in a massive population displacement through the migration of the ancient inhabitants.[20] The tradition of migration continued after the Yemenis accepted Islam and Dresch notes wryly, 'Yemen, like Scotland or Ireland, has often exported population, and in Islam's first centuries Yemeni names spread through most of the known world.'[21] In the first Islamic citadel of Madīnat al-Nabawiyyah,[22] formerly known as Yathrib, the two leading tribes of ʿAws and Khazraj had originally migrated from the Yemen.[23] Both tribes were instrumental in accommodating the migration and asylum of the Prophet Muhammad and his early followers from persecution in Makkah into a city, Madīnah, that soon became the political and cultural centre of Islam. Later, as part of the regional diplomatic missions to the city, a delegation of Byzantine-ruled Christians from the Najrān region of the historical Yemen visited the Prophet. Their discussions lead to a ratification and formalization of a previously-agreed allegiance and tribute, with the Christians retaining their religion and a Muslim emissary, Abū ʿUbaydah ʿĀmir ibn al-Jarrāḥ, appointed as a judicial authority over their affairs.[24] Most of the Yemen came under the fold of Islam within the Prophet's lifetime and he is reported to have said of them, 'Here come the people of the Yemen, tender of heart and good intention. *Īmān* (faith) is Yemeni and *ḥikmah* (wisdom) is Yemeni.'[25] Furthermore, when the Yemeni tribe of Daws converted *en masse* to Islam with al-Ṭufayl, they also made a mass migration from their homeland to the Prophet's city.[26]

1.2 – A postcard of the picturesque Bāb al-Yaman, the entrance to Sana'a al-Qadīmah or 'old Sana'a', circa 1970s.

In the Malaysian Archipelago, Yemeni traders and merchants, like the Omanis, contributed to the introduction of Islam in China, Malaysia and Indonesia long before other Muslim settlers from India and Persia. Arabs had long established an ancient sea trade route to China but, as more accurate forms of navigation were developed in the early medieval period by Muslim sailors, trade and travel to the Far East from the Arabian Peninsula intensified. As a result, N. A. Balouch has commented: 'within the first two centuries of the Hijrah this old sea route developed into an Ocean Highway for international trade and commerce.'[27] Yemenis, particularly the

Sayyids, the bloodline decendents of the Prophet Muhammad, presented themselves as formidable economic opponents to frustrated Dutch merchants in eighteenth-century Malaysia.[28] It would appear that the historical trading links between the Yemen and the Malaysian Archipelago, which pre-dated Islam, were used to extend trade and to proselytize Islam peacefully and mutually rather than by force or conquest.[29] South Asia was well known in pre-Islamic Arabia as Hind and the Yemenis had historically traded in spices from the Subcontinent.[30] The name 'Hind' was a popular female name amongst pagan Arabs and in his eight-volume work titled, *Kitāb al-Tabaqāt al-Kabīr*, Abū 'Abdullāh Muhammad ibn Sa'd gives references of at least 14 women of Makkan and Madīnan origin bearing the name 'Hind'.[31] Further, Hind bint al-Khāṣṣ, a pre-Islamic legendary figure in popular Arab folklore was renowned for her eloquence, quick-wittedness and repartee. Her name 'al-Khāṣṣ' ('the special') implies that she was the offspring of a marriage between a human father and a *jinn* ('genie') mother. The legend is fuelled by the fact that pagan Arabs believed that any human possessing exceptional qualities, brilliance of mind or endowed with any natural gift was probably due to the intervention of the *jinn*.[32] Martin Lings also refers to two prominent women of Makkah, Hind bint 'Utbah Umm Mu'āwiyah, the wife of Abū Sufyān, a tribal leader of the Quraysh, and Umm Salamah or Hind bint Abī Umayyah. Hind bint 'Utbah's son Mu'āwiyah was later to become the Muslim governor of Syria and Umm Salamah became a wife of the Prophet after her husband, Abū Salamah, died from the injuries he received in the battle of Badr.[33] Whilst the region of Hind appears to have captured the imagination of pre-Islamic Arabs, in the early spread of Islam in India, perhaps the only Yemeni contribution was the migration of Ismā'īlī *dā'īs*, or proselytizers, into the region of Gujrat.[34] One cannot overlook, however, the later influence of eighteenth-century reformist Yemeni scholar, Muhammad al-Shawkānī (1760–1834CE), on the newly developing approaches to *sunnah*, *taqlīd* and *ijtihād* in the traditional legal schools of India.[35]

The introduction of the Ismā'ilis to the Yemen was largely as a result of the Egyptian Fatimid hegemony and conquests in

Arabia.[36] Fatimid ascendancy saw the establishment of a Ṣulayḥid Queen, Sayyidah Ḥurrah (c.1048–1138CE), as a monarch over large parts of the Yemen with special religious authority over the Ismāʿīlī communities of the Yemen and Gujarat.[37] Ismāʿīlī proselytizing in Gujarat is said to have begun in the mid-twelfth century CE and is attributed to a *dāʿī* (religious prosylitizer) named either ʿAbdullāh or Muhammad (depending on the particular tradition), who travelled from the Yemen. He was apparently burnt alive by Siddha Raja (d. 1143CE), the Brahmin monarch, after he was caught preaching Islam disguised as a Brahmin servant in the palace.[38] Annemarie Schimmel confirms the spread of Ismāʿīlī Bohoras in India but does not allude to the legends of ʿAbdullāh. Instead, she links them to the twelfth-century Mustaʿliyyah under Queen Ḥurrah in the Yemen.[39] The process of Ismāʿīlī proselytizing was further accelerated when the *dāʿī*, Sayyidinā Yūsuf ibn Sulāymān (d.1567CE), migrated to Sidpur after the Sunni Ottoman Turks conquered northern Yemen. It was under the Sayyid's patronage that the original Dāʾūdi faction of the Ismāʿīlī Bohoras was established.[40]

Yemenis were also established as *jamaʿdār*s ('commanders') in military service via the Arab army of the Nizam of Hyderabad well into the late nineteenth and early twentieth centuries. They were mostly of Ḥaḍramī origin from the two rival tribes of the Kathīrī and the Quʿaytī and as *jamaʿdār*s they were able to amass great wealth and extensive estates in Hyderabad. This wealth was later used to reinvest in the Yemen by acquiring port property, vast tracts of land and financing tribal conflicts between both tribes and rival sultanate struggles for control of Ḥaḍramawt.[41] The British, in their efforts to increase their influence in the region, sided with the Quʿaytī and both eventually signed a Treaty of Friendship, in 1882, after the British had supported the Quʿaytī possession of the port city of al-Mukalla a year earlier.[42] By 1888, the Quʿaytī signed a full Protectorate Treaty with the colonial occupiers under the rule of ʿAwaḍ ibn ʿUmar al Quʿaytī, succeeding his older brother ʿAbdullāh, who died earlier in the same year. Both brothers were born in Hyderabad and their interests in the Yemen and India were represented by their various successors in both tribal communities in Ḥaḍramawt and Hyderabad respectively.[43] Linda Boxberger quotes a translation of a poem that is said to have been recited by the Kathīrī sub-tribe, or clan, the Nuwwah, before a battle for the control of the town of Hajr then under their protection. The poem reflects the disdain for the Quʿaytī *muwalladūn*[44] and their 'foreign' take-over of the region, it begins,

> *Tell the Quʿaytī: so the souk (al-Mukalla) is not enough for you,*
> *And now you want Ḥajr, the protected.*
> *Tell him: it's impossible, the notion is rejected,*
> *You Indian, we don't even understand your language.*[45]

As the tribal conflict for control of Ḥaḍramawt continued the Kathīrī Sultan tried to internationalize the hostilities and made moves to enlist the help of the Ottomans, trying to bring them into conflict with the British. However, after appeals to the Zaydī Imām, Yahya, failed, the Sultan's politicking 'created [a] conflict of interests among different groups in Ḥaḍramawt and the Ḥaḍramī emigrant communities overseas.'[46] This came about because the Sultan's advisor, Ibn ʿUbaydillāh, a prominent member of the *'ulamā'*, wanted to see an Islamic ruler dominating the region rather than a non-Muslim European one. Ibn ʿUbaydillāh believed that the British had undermined the *'ulamā'*, and therefore Islam, by establishing secular legal and educational institutions. But most Ḥaḍramī Kathīrī communities abroad opposed their own Sultan and instead preferred to support the Quʿaytī-British rule of al-Mukalla. This choice was devoid of any religious ideological reasoning and was motivated purely by economic pragmatism. The transportation and communication systems between diaspora Yemeni communities in Europe, Indian and the Malaysian Archipelago were controlled by the European powers and opposing them would possibly result in the disconnection of the emigrants and the supply of much-needed remittances to their families and tribesmen back home.[47]

During the late nineteenth and early twentieth centuries, in the hostilities between Kathīrī and Quʿaytī tribes over sovereign claims to Ḥaḍramawt and the influence of tribal notables in the diaspora was a major factor in both the continued conflicts and the eventual peace negotiations and brokerage between the opposing Sultans.[48] The transnational tribal hierarchy and organization of both the Kathīrī and the Quʿaytī exemplifies the fluid nature of tribal identity and allegiance in the diaspora. Whilst emigrant Yemeni communities may experience both integration and hybridity in their new geo-cultural environs, maintaining a direct connection and interest into the political affairs of the tribe and homeland have remained a constant feature of migrant Yemenis. Linda Boxberger remarks, 'in 1939 there were about 80,000 Ḥaḍramīs in the East Indies whose strong ties with their homeland made them follow events there with the greatest attention.'[49]

Whilst the southern region of Ḥaḍramawt wrestled for tribal hegemony the northern regions of Bāb al-Mandab and Tihāmah were desperately trying to shake off the yoke of oppressive Zaydī Imāmate rule. The Zaydīs were a minority ruling elite who had ruled over the large parts of the Yemen for almost a thousand years. They emerged after the decline of the orthodox caliphate that had directly followed the Prophet Muhammad, a succession of his companions known as *al-khulafā' al-rashidūn* ('the rightly-guided caliphs'),[50] when the Yemen became an ideal haven and location for Islamic heterodoxy largely under the influence of the Ismā'īlī and Zaydī Shii sects. Al-Faruqi asserts that the Zaydī school of jurisprudence refers to Zayd ibn ʿAlī Zayn al-ʿĀbidīn (d.793CE), the third grandson of the Prophet Muhammad. Although Zayd was not the founder of this particular sect, the Zaydī adherents regarded him as worthier than his brother, Muhammad al-Bāqir, to succeed his father in the imāmate of the Shia. Al-Faruqi states that the rise of the Zaydīs in the Yemen is,

> a situational consequence of the political isolation, once they [the Zaydīs] took over power in Yaman [Yemen] and practically locked themselves up in its mountains for a millennium and a century.[51]

Yemen is the only place in the Muslim world where the Zaydī school has followers and as a minority sect it has influenced the whole Yemeni population.[52] However, in matters of *fiqh,* the Zaydīs largely follow the Sunni schools and only differ in particular issues; the negation of ablution when bare feet have been exposed but unsoiled, the killing of animals and preparing of food by non-Muslims, marriage to Christian and Jewish wives, and the concept of temporary marriage, or *muṭa*ʿ, practised by the majority of Shia but refuted by the Zaydīs.[53]

The Ismāʿīlīs historically settled in small enclaves throughout the secluded, rugged and difficult terrain of northern Yemen including Jabal Ḥarāz and Najrān. Although the Southern population are majority orthodox Sunni, following the Shāfiʿī school, a Zaydī Shii school eventually became a distinct minority and unique theological movement within the north Yemen originating from the ninth-century CE Zaydī state in Tabaristan.[54] The first Zaydī Imām of the Yemen emerged around the end of the ninth century CE and acceded after mediating between two opposing northern tribes.[55] However, despite eventually assuming power over the Yemen, the Zaydīs could not control the whole region and their influence was restricted to their strongholds in the northern highlands. Zaydī beliefs are nearer to the Sunnis than the Shia and their theology is largely devoid of the mysticism and occult beliefs of the Ismāʿīlīs and other Shia who subscribe to 'semi-divine' Imāms. Robert Stokey has commented on the theological pragmatism of the Zaydī school, saying,

> Its practical bent is reflected in its rejection of the idea of a 'hidden' [I]mam, expected to reappear with the prophets on the eve of Judgement Day. Rejected also is the notion of an occult exegesis of the Koran and the tradition accessible only to a few and its corollary, the systemic dissimulation practised by the Ismaʿiliya and some other shiʿa.[56]

Zaydī Imāms, although receptive to Sunni traditions, must be Sayyids, blood descendants of the Prophet Muhammad (also known in the Yemen as *al-sādah*), who are genealogically linked through ʿAlī, the Prophet's nephew. The Zaydī Imāms claim both Qaḥṭānī and Sayyid lineage, ensuring genealogical credence through Arab tribal purity and religious nobility. The Imām is freely elected by the Zaydī *'ulamā'* as both religious and political leader, and Zaydī control over the Sunni majority was often imposed through military prowess with occasional periods of peaceful détente. The later Imām, Yahya Hamid al-Din (c.1904–48), was able to exercise his power and increase his influence by presenting himself as a unifying nationalist leader and religious figurehead.[57] However, the Imām could not transform the ancient institution of Imāmate, known for its historical suppression of the majority Shāfi'ī Sunnis, into a modern manifestation – as a national leader of a unified nation-state. His reign witnessed the demise of Ottoman imperial rule in the northern region and his projected image as a popular nationalist leader was founded on his aggressive attempts to usurp Ottoman hegemony. Ironically, the Turks had found a friend in the Imām by creating a mutual enemy in the British, who occupied Aden and the surrounding areas in the south. The Ottomans confirmed Yahya as the legitimate Imām and conceded to his autonomous rule in the northern highlands. The Ottoman–Zaydī alliance may well have defeated the southern British-backed Idrīsī Amirate forces had it not been for the outbreak of World War One, which precipitated the Turkish withdrawal after massive Ottoman defeats elsewhere.

The Zaydī Imāmate was internationally recognized as the legitimate successor state to the Ottoman province of the Yemen, but its control was still limited to the northern highlands. When the Turks withdrew from the Tihāmah region, control fell into the hands of the Idrīsī Amirate and although the Zaydī State tried to re-establish sovereignty over the region in 1920 by ousting the Idrīsī Amir, the efforts of the latter were curtailed by a war with Saudi Arabia in 1934. The geopolitical boundaries defined as a result of the Zaydī–Saudi war assumed a permanent boundary that later led to the creation of the Yemeni Arab Republic after the revolution in 1962. After the war with the Saudis, the Imām set about consolidating Zaydī control where the Hamid al-Din family exerted most influence. In the process, Hamid al-Din's style of rule retrogressively transformed from that of a traditional Imām into one of an absolutist monarch.[58] This transformation provoked protests from both traditional conservatives and the-emerging nationalist modernists, which resulted in his eventual assassination in 1948. He was soon replaced by his son, Ahmad, after the brief rule of an Imām from another Zaydī family. Ahmad continued in a similar vein to his father, breaking with traditional principles of Imāmate rule in favour of monarchical self-rule, whilst at the same time resisting all efforts aimed at the modernization of the country. When Ahmad died in 1962, he was replaced by his son, Muhammad al-Badr, who survived an assassination attempt after a *coup d'état* within just one week of his succession. Muhammad fled the country and a protracted civil war broke out between loyal forces of the Imām and the newly-installed revolutionary Republic. In 1970, unification of the Sana'ai state was achieved and in the process the establishment of a genuine nation-state was undertaken in the north. Modern migrations from the Yemen were undertaken firstly by Ḥaḍramīs to the Ottoman-ruled Hijaz, and then by the 'Adenese' or southern Yemenis via maritime migrations to Britain and elsewhere. Later, in the mid-twentieth century, North Yemeni migrations to the oil-rich Kingdom of Saudi Arabia occurred. Paul Dresch has commented on the historical migration of the Yemeni people, stating:

> Throughout the country's history one finds accounts of famine, and in the twentieth century migrant labour funded ordinary people's lives, as first the Ḥaḍramīs, then Lower Yemenis then Upper Yemenis all worked elsewhere.[59]

The recurring droughts and famines throughout the history of the Yemen have made rural living and agricultural trade practically untenable. The social, political and economic 'push factors' in the modern period transformed rural peasants, reluctantly, into merchant seamen. The circumstances that precipitated the colonized Yemeni emigration experiences mirrored those of their Indian and Malay counterparts.[60] In the modern period, the Yemen has been a consistently poor country and according to UN statistics it is considered to be one of the least developed countries in the world.

The Creation of Two Yemens

Despite the creation of two communist states, the former northern socialist Yemen Arab Republic (YAR), and the former southern Marxist Peoples Democratic Republic of Yemen (PDRY),[61] moves towards unifying both independent modern states were established almost simultaneously.[62] However, genuine attempts at reunification were always a forlorn and half-hearted endeavour as both burgeoning republics vied against each other for the same Soviet economic and military sponsorship.[63] Effective civil war in the North between the traditional tribes, who were supported by Islamists and the Saudi government, against the new modernist and secular political elite was a serious distraction.[64] In the South, political in-fighting between Marxist purists and pragmatic socialists saw a string of political leaders continuously removed and replaced through a series of assassinations. Externally, Saudi forces were keen to restrain the communist influences streaming from the Yemen and employed both invasion through its regular army and insurrection by financing and arming the anti-communist ex-Sultana faction and other dissident groups in the North. The political precariousness of the PDRY in the South was due not so much to invading anti-communist forces, but largely through economic bankruptcy as a result of British colonial withdrawal and the temporary closure of the Suez Canal. However, despite both internal and external pressures and constant hostilities between the Northern and Southern states, the idea of reunification seemed to be the collective will of the people. In order to court the public mood, politicians and leaders from both the YAR and the PDRY tentatively kept reunification discussions on-going, albeit reduced at times to empty exercises in diplomatic rhetoric. However, two major events changed the political and economic climate of the region and in turn accelerated the reunification process: the collapse of the Soviet Union and the discovery of oil in both North and South Yemen.

Whilst outside influences fuelled the north-south division between the two Yemens, Ali Abdullah Salih, the then president of the

YAR, proved a skilful negotiator in adopting a pragmatic approach to re-establishing routes to reunification. Furthermore, when Israel invaded the Lebanon in 1982, both Yemeni leaders, Salih and Ali Nasser, toured the region's capitals in what Latta describes as a 'joint Yemeni diplomatic initiative to forge a common Arab position.'[65] Simultaneously, as the Soviet Union began to implode politically, its support for dependent states like the Yemen became less of a priority compared to the internal problems that arose after the introduction of Mikail Gorbachev's *perestroika* in Soviet Russia. Therefore, Soviet-inspired Marxist states were also forced to undergo their own liberalizing and democratic reforms in which free market economies and political pluralism quickly became the vogue.[66] The process of political reform was better accommodated in the North by the tactful initiatives of Salih who instituted a one-thousand-member General Peoples Congress (GPC) in 1982, with himself as the Secretary-General.[67] With the return of opposition leaders from exile and national stability established, Salih's political credibility was strengthened. Fortuitously, the North Yemen discovery of large oil reserves in 1984 had an almost immediate impact on the economy, further bolstering Salih's position to something equalling that of the former Imām Yahya.[68] Salih used his political muscle effectively to obstruct South Yemen from joining the Arab Cooperation Council (ACC), arguing that the PDRY's economic policies and Marxist philosophy were incompatible with the other member states.[69] Whilst Salih continued to exert his influence in order to exclude the PDRY from formal associations with the rest of the Arab world, boycotting its applications to all major inter-Arab political forums, economic development in the North was not as expedient as was politically required. With the discovery of the large untapped Shabwah oil fields in South Yemen, reunification once again became an enticing proposition.[70] However, hopes of massive oil reserves within the southern desert were also somewhat over-optimistic and whilst oil revenue today constitutes 60% of the state budget, 400,000 barrels per day spreads out thinly amongst a population of 18 million.[71]

1.3 – A postcard of the British-built water tanks at al-Tawāhī, Aden, which were built on the site of an extinct volcano crater, circa 1960.

In November 1992, a real breakthrough was reached in the drawn-out reunification process when both sides agreed to adhere to the Aden Agreement that was originally initiated in 1982. Basically, reunification had been achieved after agreements on the establishment of a new transitional government for a new Republic of Yemen within a 12-month period had been reached. The first six months saw a concerted effort by both leaders to win over the sceptics but, as developments 'snowballed' and increased fears of tribal factionalism loomed, both presidents hurriedly brought forward the reunification date to 22 May 1990.[72] The former president of Iraq, Saddam Hussein, was also instrumental in accelerating reunification and he was anxious for it to be concluded before the Arab League meeting scheduled later that year in Baghdad. Although it was widely known that Saddam wanted to upset the Saudis by facilitating a unified Yemen, his wider motives became apparent very soon afterwards when he invaded Kuwait in 1990.[73] On 1 May 1990, despite PDRY objections,[74] voting for the union was unanimous and the next day a triumphant Salih announced from Aden the birth of the Republic of Yemen.[75] Sana'a was to become the political capital and Aden was named as the economic capital of the new reunified state. Ali Abdullah Salih was to head the new Republic and Ali Salem al-Bidh was to be Vice-President. Haidar Abu al-Attas, an influential Ḥaḍramī and former President of the PDRY was to head the transitional government and his former Southern state faired well in political representations despite its small population.[76] However, in rushing through the reunification process a number of important issues including the role of religion, education policy, women's rights and the details of post-unity relations were not adequately addressed. And, whilst it may be true that to try to resolve these issues before reunification would have further delayed the process, resolving these central policy matters placed tremendous pressure on the interim government and even impeded economic prosperity and political harmony because of pervasive pre-unity political and ideological differences.[77]

Yemen Reunified

The Gulf crisis of the early 1990s, precipitated by the invasion of Kuwait by Iraq in August 1990, became a turning point in the history of modern Arabia. For just as the Suez War of 1956 stimulated the rise of Arab nationalism and solidarity, the Gulf War had direct reverse military and economic consequences on the relative unity of the Arab world.[78] In particular, the impact of the war on the political ideology and realpolitik of the Arab states resulted in a complete discrediting of Arab nationalism. The deep divisions created by the breaking of perceived Arab solidarity in favour of a Western-dominated alliance and security brought into question the validity of any inter-Arab solidarity based on forms of joint Arab security.[79] The retrogressive development of religious extremism propagated through Islamic fundamentalism, which had ironically originated from the austere scriptural literalism of Saudi-backed Salafiyyah and Wahhābiyyah movements, was becoming a threatening force to pro-Western Arab leaders. When the new Yemeni Republic refused to support the US-led coalition against Saddam Hussein, its oil-rich Gulf Arab sponsors and neighbours were angered by the Yemeni position, which they interpreted as ingratitude. The Yemen was precariously placed as the only Arab state among the 15 members of the UN Security Council at the outbreak of the Iraqi invasion and, whilst there was a unified condemnation from the other Council members, the Yemeni position was one of abstention.[80] As a result of its perceived pro-Iraqi stance, which in reality had been one of neutrality, virtually all aid to the Yemen by foreign donors was either suspended or drastically cut.[81] For example, US aid was cut from $23 million to three million and in addition to punitive measures by Saudi Arabia and Kuwait, who curbed billions of dollars of aid to the Yemen, the Saudi government revoked all the special privileges of Yemeni workers in the Kingdom in October 1990. The Saudis also began making arbitrary arrests, detentions, torture and general harassment of Yemenis living and working in the Kingdom.[82] The resultant mass exodus of some 800,000 enforced returnees to the Yemen was something the new government could ill afford.[83] Reliance on the remittances of migrant workers was a significant economic factor and its sudden curtailment would have further serious repercussions on the domestic economy. Furthermore, returnees from both Saudi and Kuwait brought back with them only what they could carry or salvage from the sale of their belongings, properties and businesses, rendering many of them virtually bankrupt. One deportee, Gadri Salih, described to me in some detail, briefly outlined in the Prologue, the trauma of leaving Riyadh during the first Gulf War, where he had lived as a boy after his original migration from the Yemeni community in Eccles, Greater Manchester, where he was born. After spending more than 10 years in Saudi Arabia, the contrast between his life there and the relative poverty of his father's native village forced yet another migration just two years after his return to the Yemen when his father had died. Using both his, and his mother's British nationality, he was forced to migrate back to Britain.[84] The Yemeni government lost further export revenues to Kuwait and Iraq estimated to be worth around $100,000 million.[85] The first Gulf War had a crippling effect on both the economy and international relations of the new Republic of Yemen, and reconciling itself with the major Gulf donors and the US became a political imperative for Salih. Paradoxically, the Yemeni display of Arab solidarity during the Gulf War would have probably manifested itself differently if it were not for the reunification. The PDRY had not traditionally warmed to Saddam's regime and it had remained consistently neutral during the Iran–Iraq War (1980–88). However, under Ali Abdullah Salih's leadership, the YAR had idealized Saddam's dictatorship. Salih was personally impressed by Saddam's Baathist rule in Iraq and he emulated a 'Republican Guard' and a nepotistic bureaucracy monopolized by kinship and tribal influence.[86]

After much protest and dissent from amongst certain sectors of the Northern shaykhdoms and questions concerning how the oil revenues were directed or, rather, misdirected, matters eventually came to a head and resulted in armed conflict. By March 1992, pro-GPC government troops and anti-government Yemeni Socialist Party (YSP) forces began to occupy strategic positions throughout the Yemen.[87] For some time, there was a stand-off as the ruling elite promised political concessions and economic reforms. However, for many these promises were simply political rhetoric and delaying tactics. In April 1994, fighting flared up again and the President's forces moved swiftly to crush the YSP militias.[88] Most of the conflict occurred in the north and the Islamists were also active in the fighting, justifying their involvement as a *jihād* against the YSP *kuffār* (lit., 'unbelievers') ideologies and forces. As the joint government and Islamic forces took control, local power amongst tribal shaykhs and political parties shifted. Aden was sacked and looted and although the war was not between the North and the South, but between political parties, Dresch notes that 'the effect was felt by Southerners to be a Northern invasion'.[89] As influential Northerners began to lay claims to land and real estate in and around Aden, it did appear to be a 'colonisation' of the South by the North. Further, the Islamists, largely Wahhābīs known to be backed by Saudi Arabia,[90] desecrated some of the tombs of Sufi saints buried in Aden and around Ḥaḍramawt.[91] The tomb chamber of Sayyidah Ḥurrah, the ancient Ṣulayḥid Ismāʿīlī Queen, was also partially destroyed in 1993 by extremist Salafīs who deemed the established practice of religious visits and pilgrimages to the site to be heretical.[92] The increased power of the Islamists had also inhibited progressive steps towards the implementation of women's rights in political participation and education. Protests against social reforms were usually led by female Islamists whose very public demonstrations were, ironically, to demand that women remain in the private domain. In addition, Islamic banking and the increasing numbers of Islamic *madāris* (plural of *madrasah*, meaning, 'school') augmented the Islamists' influence throughout the Yemen.[93] In the presidential kinship circles, inter-family and tribal marriages ensured a dynastic government prevailed in Sana'a, whilst, at the same time, the President and some of his close family members pursued control over many of Yemen's best known commercial and industrial companies. Other business ventures included multinational property magnates with interests in London, Paris and New York.[94]

As far as the national economy is concerned, 'the country is extremely poor, but how poor the [Salih] government may be is hard to judge and those attached to government seem extremely prosperous'.[95] The contemporary global concerns of market economy capitalism, modernity, terrorism and religious extremism, particularly the rise of Islamic fundamentalism or what is now more obscurely described as 'Islamism',[96] have in recent times appeared as 'flashpoints' in the developing new Yemen.[97] But the Yemen with its combined ancient biblical history and recent political struggles leading to reunification and the creation of the new Republic of Yemen is far more politically progressive and modern than many other Gulf States. In relation to the eventual outcome of its recent turbulent history, it is almost as if the dramatic events between the periods of Imām Yahya and former President Ali Abdullah Salih had never happened. But the hopes amongst some Yemenis of a revival of the Zaydī Imāmate tradition may have been dashed with the recent death of Al-Hassan Hamid al-Din (1908–2003), who died in his sleep whilst in exile in Jeddah on 13 June 2003.[98] He was the oldest son of Imām Yahya and was exiled in 1954 and spent most of his time between living in America and Saudi Arabia. During the 1962 revolution, the 'Prince' fought with 'royalist' forces in the far north based around Sa'dah which was occupied by the republican army. But his failing health saw him withdraw from the conflict in 1968.[99] A year later, his son was shot dead on his way to Friday prayers at the Hādī Mosque in Sa'dah. Al-Hassan Hamid al-Din had wanted to be buried next to his father's grave in Sana'a and the Yemeni authorities agreed to his request in principle. However, restrictions on which members of his family could accompany the bier, for his grandsons could but his sons could not, meant that he was buried instead in the cemetery of al-Baqī' in the Prophet's city of Madīnah.[100]

Tribes and Tribalism

For a traditional Arab society like that of the Yemen, tribal belonging offers a cultural continuity: a history and *aṣl* (literally, 'origin'), and provides an authenticity and rooting to a place and a people.[101] The structures of tribal societies are heterogeneous, traditional and pre-modern and the particular size and configuration varies from region to region, often determined by the historical socio-politics of the local people. In the Yemen, a tribe may be subdivided into many divisions, each ranging from a few thousand to a grouping as small as a hundred members.[102] Historically, the internal structures of tribes would derive ancestrally from the siblings of one family and its origins are geographically 'fixed' whereas individual men and families connected to the tribe need not be.[103] Tribesmen, regardless of their subdivisions, will usually locate themselves as descendants of 'one forefather' (*'min jadd wāḥid'*). In this sense, all subgroups belonging to a tribe are 'brothers' to each other in the same way that they are all 'sons' of one tribal originator.[104] Whilst tribal nomenclature has local variations for a number of reasons, each tribe also further identifies itself in contradistinction from other tribes, despite sharing the same dominant culture, customs and religious beliefs. Paul Dresch offers an informative insight and explanation into the contradistinction of tribal identity when he says,

> No village, section, or tribe by itself can properly be said to be a 'moral' community – none has sense without its opposite numbers; but the tribes none the less form together a society in that all are encompassed in the same values.[105]

This is because the relevance and unifying factors in tribal self-identification are based, primarily, on structural relations within a particular 'historical' context and social setting. 'History' in the pre-modern tribal sense can often include mythological and folkloric elements, which does not necessarily conform to a 'time and space' or 'factually accurate' understanding of history commonly held in contemporary or modern societies.

Patriachally constructed, Yemeni tribes share a sense of family honour, or *sharaf*, and within their concept of honour both the tribe, as a collective group, and the individual, as a tribal member, uphold the sense of honour and are bound by their shared bonds to protect and preserve tribal honour. For the individual, protecting one's personal dignity whilst simultaneously honouring the tribe is known as *wajh*, or 'keeping face' and to do otherwise is *'ayb*, or shameful.[106] In the collective context, it is the tribal shaykh who 'keeps face' on behalf of the tribesmen. The shaykh usually belongs to an 'original family' (*bayt aṣlī*) who through his family lineage has the honour of representing the tribe at a given period of time, although there is no set law making his leadership a permanent rule. Dresch comments, 'anyone of the shaykhly family may usually, in practice as well as theory, be chosen shaykh.'[107] Generally speaking, the shaykh acts as an intra-tribal reconciler and unifier and an inter-tribal representative and mediator. Through the respect and power invested in him by the tribe, the shaykh helps to maintain cohesion between community (tribe) and society (*waṭan*) via what Dresch describes as a 'structure of containment' – a system of codified arbitration.[108]

Within the ancient tribal customs and laws, collectively known as *'urf al-qabā'il*, the individual can expect the protection and support of the tribe, be it moral, spiritual, political, financial or otherwise, providing he has not contravened any customary laws, compromising both *wajh* and *sharaf*. The tribal *'urf* provides a system by which men recognize a collective set of rules that allows them to act in concert such as resolving how they may financially contribute to a mutual fund, or levy collective payments, or participate in cultivation partnerships.[109] Protecting both property (private and tribal lands and borders) and people (tribal kinsmen/women) is a priority and primary function of the tribe. Whenever the two are violated by an outsider then a recompense, or *fidyah*, mutually agreed by tribal leaders is paid. Through a detailed and often orally-transmitted system of tribal laws, the violation, protection, sale, travel, occupation and inheritance of land and family rights are codified through the *'urf*. But understanding tribal laws is complex and often compounded by local geo-cultural nuances as Dresch's detailed study highlights. For example, he notes,

> Sometimes one finds a killing between sections or tribes settled by a change of their common border, so that the victim's tribe acquires some of the other tribe's *faysh* [grazing 'wasteland'] or non-arable land; this is one of the few exceptions to the rule of border's explicit fixity.[110]

Dresch's research also details how methods for collective payments to cover *fidyah*, and even divisions of wealth, differ from tribe to tribe.[111] He also argues that without the shaykh and the symbolic office that he represents, 'there is no assurance that ties between equals will be any more than episodes in mutual contradiction.'[112] But even with the social structure of the tribe, which places the *wajh* of the shaykh vicariously and emblematically in front of other tribes, 'episodes in mutual contradiction' still frequently recur and often involve the shaykhs themselves.[113] Dresch observes that the marked distinctions and nuanced micro-cultures of individual tribes provide the most fascinating ethnographic element of this ancient culture. A society in which 'they are all equal and opposite, not in numbers or size, but as they divide up the moral world, the terms which all tribes share.'[114]

'The Remotest Village'

Yemeni communities in Britain and other countries of migration appear to transport a number of facets of their identity from their place and country of origin. The historical and cultural dimensions of their identity constructions seem to be rooted in their ancient custom of migration, tribal traditions, religious practices and Arabic civilization and language. But the socio-political reasons for migration, both ancient and modern are primarily those of dire economic need or political strife and even sometimes both. Theocracies, imperial invasions and secular dictatorships have all tried to impose their particular ideologies and systems on the Yemeni masses, who have continuously resisted all forms of hegemonic impositions through their tribal customs and bonds. Even in the diaspora, the tribe and the homeland remain important aspects of identity and exiled Yemenis have often organized aid and assisted resistance to support their political struggles back home. Ironically and somewhat sadly, whilst most Yemenis clearly have a great love and affinity for their homeland, the Yemen soil appears to conspire with conquering invaders and despotic rulers in uprooting and expelling them from their *qurā* (villages) and *bilād* (country). For many Yemenis carving out a living from tilling the soil is largely a fruitless endeavour. Migrations through drought and famine, occupation and strife seem to be an expectation, if not almost inevitability, for many Yemenis.

However, once in exile for whatever reason, the *raison d'être* for diasporic Yemenis becomes the preservation of their distinct identity in all its facets. This is largely achieved by maintaining strong physical and psychological links to the homeland through active communal ties between the exilic communities and the communities back in the Yemen. Although diaspora Yemeni communities will no doubt experience the gradual acculturation and integration of their progeny into the new societies and cultures into which they have migrated and settled, a history of generation after generation of migrations from the Yemen perhaps makes the migration process a familiar and somewhat undaunting experience. Further, in many ways migration might be said to be a cultural tradition for Yemenis, who seem neither dissipated nor displaced by the upheavals and unsettling processes of leaving one's family, community and country.[115] Today, as the new Republic of Yemen struggles for economic and political stability, ordinary Yemenis out in their fields or running their small shops, still rely on incoming wealth from migrant worker relatives. Migrations from the Yemen in modern times, are no longer part of a historic traveller/trader tradition – they are an economic necessity. The chief objective of the migrant workers from the Yemen in the twentieth and twenty-first centuries was, and is, to bring money home to pay off debts and secure landholding.[116]

This reality was personally observed after I was asked by one research respondent in Eccles, Greater Manchester, to forward a remittance to his relative in his village during a field trip to the Yemen. Whilst farming the land in one's *bilād* or *qurā* was a traditional means of sustenance, nowadays purchasing land, cultivating and producing crops, all require a massive investment. Besides, the only viable and sustainable cash crop of any value is the production of *qāt*, a particular social habit which consumes 30% of many families' gross weekly income. However, until the recent pro-democracy revolt that has resulted in the removal of President Salih, the unified government was able to encourage foreign financial aid with the promise of actively implementing 'democracy' and political pluralism in a far-too-slowly developing and progressing civil society in Yemen. Yet, while the recent emergence of the pro-democracy movement has seen hundreds of protesters killed and an assassination attempt on Salih, it appears to offer a glimmer of hope and ripples of excitement amongst the Yemeni population, even if the promise of a multiparty, democratic and united Yemen still hangs precariously in the balance.

FROM ADEN TO 'TIGER BAY', 'BARBARY COAST' AND 'LITTLE ARABIA'

Samuel Chew informs us that the first recorded Englishman to travel in Yemen was John Jourdain, a 'factor' or, representative, of the British East India Company who, 'leaving his ship *The Ascension*, at Aden, penetrated into the interior as far as Sana [*sic*].'[1] While Jourdain crossed through the mountain highlands to the ancient city of Sana'a, the remainder of the crew of *The Ascension,* under the command of Alexander Sharpleigh, passed through Bāb al-Mandab and entered the Red Sea to become the first recorded English vessel in that part of the world. Jourdain then rejoined the ship at the port of Mocha from where it continued to India. This expedition took place in the spring of 1609.[2] At the time Jourdain and his shipmates landed at Aden, its population was estimated to be around 60,000, consisting mostly merchants, traders and sailors. There is no further recorded contact until 1829, when the East India Company considered utilizing Aden as a coaling station to refuel the ever-increasing numbers of steam-powered merchant vessels sailing between British and Indian ports. In 1835, Captain Haines of the British East India Company opportunistically wrote:

> Aden ... might be the grand emporium for the export of coffee, gums, etc., as well as a channel through which the produce of India and England might be thrown into the

> rich provinces of Yemen and the Hadhramaut ... the trade would also be open to the African coast, the distance being so trifling; from thence, gums, coffee, hides, frankincense, myrrh, would be thrown into the Aden market and the trader thereby be enabled not only to return with the produce of the Yemen, but what of might return him [*sic*] a good profit from the African coast.[3]

A British Colony at Aden

By 1839, Aden was virtually reduced to a fishing village with a reported population of no more than 600 people. Captain Haines' report to the Bombay government optimistically described Aden's admirable strategic position, its fine harbours and natural defenses, as a 'must have' acquisition for the East India Company, which he concluded was poorly managed by the ruling Laḥijī Sultanate. The earliest relations between Britain and the Laḥijī Sultanate were based on a series of treaties and negotiated agreements that began in 1802 when a treaty of commerce was signed. This agreement eventually led to the British exerting their power and influence over the port and surrounding areas through the eventual imposition of the British Protectorate of Aden in 1839.

Initially, British efforts to realize Aden as a colonial entrepôt for tripartite trade between Asia, Arabia and Africa were slow and ineffective and the expected trade between British merchants and the interior coffee trade districts of the Yemen did not materialize immediately. Fortunately, trade with the northerly coast of East Africa prospered, largely due to the security for merchant ships in the region as a result of the establishment of Haines' garrison at Aden. Eventually, a growing trade between Indian and Arab merchants with Somali tribesmen was stimulated by the great annual fair held at Berbera in Somalia. In 1840, it was recorded that 300 native East African vessels and 21,000 camels were engaged in the great fair trade. However, as Berbera was abandoned during the annual monsoon season between April and October, the inland tribes moved to the African coast to prepare their huts for the expected trading vessels from Yemen, Muscat, Ras al-Khaimah, Bahrain, Porebunder and Bombay. The burgeoning British settlement at Aden soon capitalized on this trade by allowing Indian traders to build their storehouses in the port, unlike the nomads of Somalia who would not permit permanent and secure buildings at Berbera. This proved fortuitous for Aden which had, until this time, progressed little beyond being more than an offshoot of the Berbera trading centre up until the end of 1848. When Somali merchants gradually began to journey across the Gulf of Aden to conduct their business in the port, largely due to their own storage restrictions at Berbera, by 1878, the economic situation of Aden was radically changed.

From this period onwards the majority of African trade between Arabia and Asia was financed, supplied and controlled from Aden, drastically changing the fortunes of the port and the control and influence of the British in the region. American vessels had continued to use Mocha, loading 2.5 million pounds of coffee as early as 1805, and in the process obtaining very favourable terms from the Sharīf.[4] Yemen coffee exports still increased based in the northern ports of Mocha and Hodeidah despite Haines' attempts to entice the trade to Aden from as early as 1839. However, his increased efforts were continuously thwarted by the wily regional ruler Sharīf Hussain. But, as disputes between the Sharīf and the Zaydī Imām of Yemen began to intensify, the balance of mercantile power began to swing in favour of the British and their entrepôt at Aden. When the Zaydī Imām attacked the Red Sea coastal area in 1844, leading to the final capture of Mocha, by 1848 all business in the port was halted. As a result, within 18 months, all caravans at Ḥujariyah and Sana'a were bringing their loads of coffee to Aden. Yet, despite this development, American vessels avoided trading with the port, dissuaded by unfavourable custom rates and uncertainty over the availability of goods. In 1853, the East India Company declared Aden a 'free port', thus solving the problem and ensuring that from then on export shippers of all nations in the lower Red Sea directed their vessels to Aden.

By the time Haines departured as the first British Resident of

Aden for the EIC in 1854, a sizeable Arab and Indian trading community was consolidating its grip on the markets of North East Africa, Red Sea ports and the Yemen. In the same year, contracts for export coffee from the port were recorded at $184,000. However, as Aden grew the neighbouring ports of Mocha, Shuqrah and Bīr Aḥmad were seriously affected as increasing trade with American, French and German ships made Aden the primary focus of their trading activities. In his term of office as the East India Company's Resident at Aden, Captain Haines worked endlessly to develop and expand the port's commercial potential. In 1847, he recommended the construction of a second customs post at the port's main pass in order to register the trade from there and a pier was completed at Maʿallā in 1855, which allowed merchants to establish the main customs post there by 1864.[5] The rapid growth in the port's activities ensured that Arab, Indian and Persian traders in cotton goods, coffee, gums, spices and cloves, situated at the port of Zanzibar, quickly relocated their businesses at Aden. Although the port returns for 1855–6 reveal that the bulk of the port's trade was with India, particularly Bombay, 30% was with the United States. By 1856–7, France had surprisingly overtaken both India and the US in trading at the port, but it was predominantly British ships, providing the mail steamer service, that dominated Aden's traffic (29,000 tons/year between 1852–5 compared with 80,000 tons/year of non-British vessels).[6] Suprisingly, it was not until 1857, when Captain Luke Thomas began commercial operations in Aden, that a British trader was finally established at the port.[7]

British mail ships, largely P&O vessels after the termination of the government mail service, were given priority at the harbour and were provided with buoy berths. Until 1857, all other vessels were required to lie at anchor in the inner harbour and, where British mail ships had port company pilots, other merchants had to employ the services of Red Sea pilots until the establishment of the Aden Pilot Service in 1848. Steamships required an incredible amount of coal, all of which was shipped to the port by a fleet of colliers from the British ports of Cardiff, Newcastle, Liverpool and Hull – ports that were soon to see the settlement of Yemeni merchant seamen in the dockland areas. The draft limitations in Aden's Western Bay meant that the colliers were required to discharge their loads in the outer harbour to draft 17 feet before unloading the remaining coal in the inner harbour.

At the dockside, the labour required to handle all cargoes was mobilized and organized through the system of a *muqaddam*. The *muqaddam* acted as a 'foreman' or, 'leader' of small, freelance labour gangs for anyone wishing to employ them. The chief duties of the *muqaddam* was to recruit and employ local men individually, keep the labour gang together, fill the places of those who fell sick and provide sufficient men to meet the needs of the port employers. *Serangs* (Bosons) and *tindals* (Boson's mates)[8] supervised the actual work, with the *serang* accepting or refusing the services of the *muqaddam* as they saw fit. This degree of partiality was open to a system of small bribery, known locally as '*al-ḥaqq al-qahwah*' (literally, 'the right of coffee'), which meant that for a small 'service charge', usually set at a nominal fee – the price of a cup of coffee – an individual could buy his place on to a *muqaddam*'s gang, or a *muqaddam* could ensure work for his gang by greasing the palm of a *serang* or *tindal*. Ansari refers to the role of the *muwassiṭ* or *muqaddam* as:

> Serangs and ghat serangs – labour agents, moneylenders and lodging house-keepers rolled into one (and therefore very powerful men) – were already established in Calcutta and Bombay ... Yemeni and Somali maritime employment was organised and controlled in a similar way: *muqadams* (similar to serangs) were charged with supplying labour from their own tribes and negotiating contracts to the best advantage of the shipping companies and themselves. [9]

The *muqaddam* system was used by Haines from the earliest days of the British presence in Aden, specifically in the construction of the fortifications and the garrison erected around the port. Labourers not only found their way to Aden from the tribal highlands of Yemen, but they came from as far as Egypt and Iran. The overwhelming majority of labourers, however, were from Mocha or the hill-farming communities of northern Yemen. As a result of labour migration, Aden soon became a cosmopolitan community comprising of Arab, Indian, Somali and Persian workers and traders. It was through this very particular and effective employment process that Aden quickly developed a competitive edge over all the other coal bunkering stations and colonial ports. During the 1840s and 1850s, it was estimated that a third of Aden's population were hill farmers from the northern hinterlands, who would return to their mountain villages to sow their crops and then harvest them from June to October every year. This annual migration left the port with a serious shortage of labourers. Another third came from Mocha as the changing fortunes of the once-famous coffee port was slowly reduced to little more than a fishing village when the coffee merchants and traders relocated to Aden.

2.1 – A picture postcard view of British Colonial Aden, circa 1960.

In the early years of British control of Aden, migrant labourers usually settled in poor makeshift wooden huts along the dockside. However, by 1856, the EIC's Assistant Resident at Aden introduced a policy of tearing down the temporary huts at the same time that he was clearing the water tanks at al-Tawāhī. Hut occupiers were offered plots on which to build stone houses which meant that by 1867 there were 1840 permanent houses for a population of 17,564.[10] A survey conducted at Ma'allā in 1881 revealed that 15% of Aden's population was homeless, 60% were semi-settled in 'kutcha' houses, which suggests these were homes of Indian settlers, and the rest occupied stone houses. By 1870, the population of around 22,000 was dominated by migrant port workers who frequented the coffee houses in search of work, to take their recreation, eat food and, in many cases, collect their wages from the *muqaddam*, who was also often the coffee house owner. The size of Aden's population remained fairly constant until after the opening of the Suez Canal in 1869. Thereafter, steamers gradually began to replace the square-rigger ships, which made longer voyages around the Cape to China and India. More steamers inevitably meant more coal at Aden whose status was further boosted as an important refuelling and trading port when the triple-expansion engines for steamers were introduced in the 1880s accelerating the numbers of vessels passing through the port. Yet, as the port became increasingly busy, the facilities and harbour conditions at the docks had hardly improved. It was only after a parliamentary debate in 1885 and the subsequent formation of the Aden Port Trust in 1889 that the British government and the mercantile community at Aden arranged for a major dredging and reconstruction of the docklands, which enabled the mooring of the biggest ships of the day to berth at the port. The end result of the *muqaddam* system of employment and migration flow meant that many Yemeni lascar crews were discharged in Europe, and did not return to Aden; instead, a number of pioneer Muslim settlements around the ports of Marseilles, Amsterdam, Cardiff, South Shields, Liverpool and London emerged by the late nineteenth century.

Yemeni *Baḥriyyah* and Lascars

As a country at the heart of the industrial revolution and the subsequent manufacturing boom, Britain became a place of migration for many foreign emigrants and settlers. In the beginning, the Muslim presence was transient and temporary, largely facilitated by British imperial expansionism and commercial enterprise. But the empire slowly drew Muslims to its industrial centres by a number of means: firstly as oriental sailors, or lascars, and wealthy Arab merchants, then later as a large post-colonial labour force. The establishment of the Yemeni Muslim community in Britain is intrinsically linked to the historical legacy of British colonialism and imperialism, because Aden was ruled through imperial India until it was granted colony status in 1937. When Aden originally became a British Protectorate in 1839, the empire secured a vital strategic fuelling station for its merchant steam vessels sailing to and from British India and the Far East. Yemeni migration to Britain began with the formation of early nineteenth-century lascar settlements in Cardiff, Liverpool, London and South Shields. Humayun Ansari has asserted that 'the vital link in Yemeni emigration to Britain was the port of Aden.'[11] However, the burgeoning industrial docklands of imperial Britain were far removed from the remote highland village settlements from where most of the Yemeni lascars originated. The British colony at Aden was included in the Bombay presidency until 1932 when its control was then transferred to the central Indian colonial Government at Delhi, and the Resident at Aden subsequently became a Chief Commissioner. By 1937, Aden was finally separated administratively from India and it became a Crown colony.[12] This relatively late shift in the colonial politics of recognizing and ruling the Aden Protectorate as a separate entity from colonial India is perhaps largely responsible for the perceived 'invisibility' or, lack of any distinct recognition of an early to mid-nineteenth century Yemeni presence in Britain.

As colonized subjects associated administratively with British imperial India, the cultural and ethnic distinctiveness of Yemeni lascars was probably viewed as an insignificant detail in the larger scheme of colonial lascar employment within the booming maritime industry of imperial Britain. Hence, most of the contemporaneous accounts of lascar presence in eighteenth and nineteenth century Britain are largely absent of any specific cultural and ethnic details regarding the particular racial origins of Oriental lascars. Instead, general depictions and monolithic representations, as 'Indians', 'Arabs', 'Africans' and 'South Sea Islanders' are usually given. Occasionally, terms such as, 'Egyptian', 'Malay', 'Ottoman' or 'Soudanese' [*sic*] were employed, but how accurate these descriptive terms actually were is questionable. Fred Halliday has argued that the fluidity of identities in the reception and placing of Yemenis in the British colonial context accounts for one further striking characteristic of the Yemenis, namely their 'invisibility'.[13] He argues that the obvious reason for this was simply that there were not that many of them compared with South Asian Muslim settlers in Britain. He particularly notes that 'most of the time there was some larger identity into which they could easily be assimilated. In most cases there was an element of validity in this inclusion – lascars, Muslims, Arabs being cases in point.'[14] Richard Lawless' work also confirms a degree of identity confusion with regards to the Yemeni settlers in South Shields, noting that 'in the opinion of the people living in the district [East Holborn, South Shields] half of the Arabs were in fact Turks'[15] and that '[t]he Chief Constable of South Shields admitted in 1917 that he did not know the difference between a Turk and an Arab!'.[16]

SEAMAN

2.2 – The seamen's registration certificate of Ali Mohamed (b.1902) issued from Cardiff and dated 1929.

Like other sailors from the east India regions of Bengal and Bihar and those Far Eastern sailors from Malacca and Sumatra, the Yemenis of Aden and Ta'izz sought employment on merchant ships sailing to Britain. Humayun Ansari states that lascars were employed to overcome the maritime labour shortage created as a result of British seamen being inducted into the navy for war service against the French from the 1760s onwards and to address the reality that significant numbers of British seamen were 'deserting' at Indian ports.[17] Ansari also attests to the horrific treatment of lascars at the hands of ship masters that 'despite the better wages there is evidence that many of these Indian Muslim sailors were brutally treated on ships, which compelled many to try to escape such harrowing ordeals.'[18] Apart from London, many Yemeni lascars settled in Cardiff and South Shields, with smaller communities in Liverpool, Hull and later Manchester. He notes that by the last quarter of the nineteenth century a significant proportion of the lascars in Cardiff originated from Yemen and Somalia with the vast majority (95%) concentrated in the dock area and a small number in the city centre and other working-class districts. By 1911, it was estimated that the lascar population of Cardiff numbered around 700.[19] In Glasgow, a Sailor's Home was established in 1857 to cater for the ever-growing number of lascars settling in the city. A report by the Sailor's Home stated that by 1903 nearly one-third (approximately 5500) of the annual number of nightly borders were lascars:

> Among these Lascars were Yemenis and Somalis who, from as early as the 1850s, were recruited on steamers as firemen and stokers. In the East End of London, apart from Indian Lascar communities, Yemeni and Somali seamen together with Ottoman Turks represented some of the earliest Muslim communities in Britain.[20]

Ansari, like Paul Dresch, claims that many Yemenis were drawn to working on ships after a series of droughts and famines occurred across the villages of the northern highlands of Yemen during the latter half of the nineteenth century.[21] In the process, foreign remittances helped to support dependent families and for long periods prop up the ailing Yemeni economy. According to Joseph Salter's record, the arrival of large numbers of lascars was becoming a common occurrence in the nineteenth century and by the 1890s with around 500 lascars arriving at London's docks alone.[22] Peter Fryer informs us that Asian and Arab lascars were present among the destitute Black populations of London as early as the 1780s. Salter was an Anglican priest and evangelical missionary who devoted the larger part of his life as a cleric prosyletizing among mostly Muslim, with some Hindu and fewer Buddhist, lascars coming to British port cities through imperial and entrepreneurial vessels. The cleric's efforts produced two detailed contemporaneous published memoirs of his missionary efforts with the lascars. Salter's detailed account of his missionary work amongst the poor and destitute lascars of the nineteenth century provides us with a fascinating and startling account of colonial lascars in British docklands. The result is a unique pair of descriptive and ethnographic documents on the plight of Oriental lascars living in horrendously deprived conditions at the height of imperial Victorian Britain. His work also confirms the ill-treatment of the lascars and he comments that, 'In the 1850s Indian seamen, during their stay in Britain, were still enduring appalling conditions.'[23] The lascars were usually herded into lodging houses, often between six to eight to a room, without bedding, chairs or tables. Lascars who fell ill would find themselves suffering in a hospital or a workhouse without any means of communicating their ailments due to language problems. Between 1856 and 1857, eight lascars died of cold and hunger on the streets of London and a coroner reported that he had dealt with over 40 similar cases in the past few years.[24] Rozina Visram also attests that lascars were present in significant numbers by the late eighteenth and early nineteenth century, stating that:

> Although no direct evidence of Lascars in the [East India Company barrack] premises for the period 1795–1814 is available, the fact that a bill was rushed through Parliament without debate in November 1813, to compel the Company to provide for lascars, suggests the Company's own arrangements had failed. [25]

Lascar Destitution and Christian Mission

Missionaries became hypersensitive to the treatment that the colonial subjects were facing in the heart of the imperial metropolis and so Christian philanthropists established competing missions aimed specifically at aiding and proselytizing the stranded lascars. The Reverend Henry Venn, Secretary of the Church Mission Society, opened a 'Strangers' Home for Asiatics, Africans and South Sea Islanders in West Dock Road, Limehouse, catering for some 150 lascars. At the same time, the Reverend Joseph Salter was establishing his missionary works among the destitute lascars of Britain's burgeoning industrial cities. The overwhelming majority of black people in Britain by the late nineteenth and early twentieth century were lascars. Abandoned by steamers or attracted by the prospect of casual work, lascars had begun to settle around the docks at Cardiff by the early 1870s when Welsh coal was beginning to be exported rapidly around the globe as essential fuel for commercial steamers.[26] By 1881, a sailor's rest was established in the city to cater for the increasing presence of lascars working out of Cardiff, Newport and Barry. Fryer describes the plight of the lascars thus:

> Having spent the small sums they had been paid-off with, having pawned any spare clothes or other belongings, destitute seamen tramped from port to port, desperate for work. Their quest was endless and almost hopeless. Help form compatriots and parish hand-outs kept them from starving, but they often went hungry.[27]

The Colonial Office would often repatriate unemployed lascars, usually as a result of the intervention of the church missions. However, although an act of Parliament was passed in 1814 decreeing that no ship with a lascar crew was permitted to leave shore without a bond for their support until they were returned home, in practice very little changed on the ground.[28] In 1820, legislation had tried to limit the number of lascars present on British ships but the measures were short-lived as the growing demand for cheap labour in the maritime industry increased. An Act of Parliament in 1849 revised all existing restrictions and quotas, identifying all

Oriental lascars (Asians, Arabs, Africans and Malays) as 'British' for the purposes of shipping. This relaxation of the law allowed ship owners to exploit an endless supply of cheap labour.[29] By employing lascars, ship owners were able to keep their wage bills to a minimum by effectively hiring three lascars for the price of two European sailors.[30] Further, lascars were known for their sobriety and were seen as 'more manageable and amenable' in comparison with European sailors. Sydney Collins has also noted that Yemeni lascars were particularly valued for their loyalty as hard working crew members, 'They are reputed to be most obedient to their superiors, to cooperate as a work team, and to be willing to deputize for and indisposed workmate.' He also recorded further that due to their loyalty, 'Father and sons are often employed on the same boat. Thus for a period the son came under direct paternal supervision.'[31] Lascars did not usually belong to unions and were regarded, rather patronizingly, as docile, inferior, lacking in masculinity, self-reliance and initiative, although this image changed significantly by the early twentieth century. As a result of imposed racial stereotypes, largely framed by an inflated sense of colonial superiority, it was deemed that lascars, although quite competent sailors, could only make excellent seamen when led by European officers.[32] The false notion that, because of their tropical origins, lascars could withstand the heat of the engine rooms better than their white European counterparts meant that they were given the worst jobs on board ship: the engine stokers or so-called 'donkeymen'. This racial misnomer has also been highlighted by Grahame Davies who notes from the writing of Captain Jac Alun Jones, a former Welsh seaman and poet, who wrote:

> When Welsh coal exporting was in its glory, and every ship was burning coal to drive the engines, most of the firemen were Arabs, as they were famous as men who were able to withstand the great heat of the stokehold.[33]

This peculiar climatic discrimination also meant that lascars were deemed unable to work in colder climes and were, therefore, limited to sail in latitudes between 60 degrees north and 50 degrees south. Such racist imaginary meant that lascars were firmly placed at the bottom of the maritime labour hierarchy, a means of keeping their labour rates much lower than those of European sailors.[34]

As more and more ships docked in British ports, so the numbers of stranded lascars increased. The question of numbers arises in terms of trying to assess how many lascars were present in Britain in the late nineteenth century. Visram says that, by the 1850s, of the 10–12,000 lascars and Chinese seamen employed for service in British trade, at least 50% were brought to the UK every year and of these, 60% were Asiatic lascars.[35] This figure was dramatically increased with the opening of the Suez Canal, the introduction of faster steam-powered liners and the establishment of the British-controlled port at Aden. According to Salter's statistics (the source of which is not known) by the 1890s:

> an average of 500 Asiatics [Asians and Arabs] come to the docks every week, and more than 10,000 Asiatics and Africans – including East Indians, Chinese, Japanese, Persians, Malays and Africans of various races – visit London in the course of a year.'[36]

Whatever the actual figures, Salter's contemporaneous account gives us some idea of the huge numbers of Oriental sailors visiting Britain's ports in the nineteenth century, suggesting that their presence in the docklands was both highly visible and formidable. The Asiatic Mission, founded by Salter, was established with the intention of giving rest to:

> the bodies of the travellers who have reached us from the distant East, or inner Africa, strangers in a strange land, where their customs and language are so little understood, such a home is greatly needed.[37]

The evangelical missionary further asserts that 'England annually attracts to her shores from all nations those who come either as visitors to enjoy our civilization, or as adventurers to exhibit the manners and habits of heathendom for our amusement and information.'[38] Visram has observed that 'Christian missionaries and evangelicals saw lascars as a moral challenge. Like the *ayahs* (oriental nannies), they presented an opportunity for proselytizing.'[39]

As British imperial expansionism reached its zenith in the nineteenth century, the increasing numbers of colonized others became a familiar presence throughout the country's rapidly developing industrial docklands and cities. However, we are told by Salter that, 'the prejudice against bringing foreign labour under any circumstances into the east of London was very great.'[40] Perhaps proving that even then, as now, migration to Britain by significant numbers of visible ethnic and religious others was fraught with political and cultural tensions. The majority of the mission's clientele were Muslims and Salter rather disparagingly comments, 'those who visit the Rest [Home] are mostly Mahommedans [*sic*], varying from the bigoted Afghan and Arab to the semi-fetish worship of Africa.'[41] The Asiatic Rest was located 'opposite the walls and near the gates of the East India Docks', and a plaque in both Persian and Bengali was mounted on the front door of the mission.[42] Inside copies of the Qur'ān in Arabic and the Bible, translated in various languages, were available to visitors. The walls of the mission were decorated with hand drawings of both Makkah and Madīnah, donated by various sailors who had visited the holy sites, along with Biblical verses translated into numerous oriental languages. One in Arabic 'tells the wanderer from the Nile, "Whoever believeth in the Lord Jesus shall be saved".'[43] Salter established the Asiatic Strangers Home, under the auspices of the London Christian Mission in 1856 specifically to provide welfare and proselytize among the destitute lascars. Although the Emancipation Act of 1833 had effectively abolished slavery across the British colonies, plantation owners and British merchants introduced a form of indentured labour that simply provided a 'legal' means of enslaving by signing up colonial subjects to a lifelong employment service to British coffee, tea, sugar and cotton plantations across the colonies. Other less permanent forms of employment allowed the recruitment of *ayahs* and lascars to suit the particular needs of those hiring. Subsequently, many *ayahs* and lascars, employed at the ports of Bombay and Aden, were immediately dismissed once they had reached the shores of Britain.

This unscrupulous form of employment left thousands of 'Orientals' stranded across British ports with no guarantee of returning to their homeland. Lascars simply had to try to buy their way onto the crew of a ship using the same *muqqadam* system that they had used initially to gain employment in their country of origin. A lack of funds to pay *'al-ḥaqq al-qahwah'* or opportunity for employment on the right ship meant that lascars often took to begging on the streets of British port cities. Salter makes reference to the many 'Asiatics' and Arabs begging in east London around 1856 and recounts the number of unfortunate 'Oriental lascars' buried in pauper's graves in London cemeteries. The favoured locations for congregated lascars in London appear to have been Westminster, Whitechapel and Shadwell, and Salter comments, 'Westminster has always had its contingent of Asiatic mendicants, with the usual undergrowth of half-caste children.'[44] Salter also informs us that the presence of the lascars was neither confined to the imperial capital 'nor were those resorts restricted to London: similar ones were to be found in Birmingham, Manchester and Liverpool.'[45] Amongst the lascar beggars and street entertainers that Salter encountered was a lascar, who he met in both London and Manchester, suggesting that lascars often adopted a vagrant existence to ensure their income. 'Monkey Abraham', Salter tells us:

> was another [lascar] who issued daily from the 'Black Hole'. He earned his title from the queer attitudes he could assume. His head was some distance in advance of his body; his elbows kept crookedly afar from each other, while his boney knees sought closest acquaintance. His dress and cap were bedizened with spangles, and he wore a necklace, in four rows, of beads and strange seashells.[46]

As an evangelical Christian missionary Salter was extremely critical of what he described as 'telescopic philanthropy', the process of sending Christian missionaries to all corners of the empire without addressing the reality of thousands of destitute colonial 'heathens' roaming the streets of British cities.[47]

2.3 – The old British Port Authority building at Steamer Point, Aden, now a museum and known by Yemeni sailors as Dār al-Sayyūn ('Place of Travel'), taken in December 2004.

Salter's justification for Christian mission among the colonial subjects in Britain was based on the fact that there were men of every race and creed, speaking a multitude of different languages and living in the burgeoning industrial centres of Britain; he comments that, 'if you want to convert Mahommadens [*sic*], Turks, Chinese, men from Bengal, Java or Borneo, you may find them all here.'[48] He also places his religious proselytizing squarely in the context of the British imperialist project, stating:

> [with] Turkey crumbling, Persia helpless, Egypt Anglicised, Indian conquered, and Bokhara, the city of learning, taken by the Russians – all proving that when the sword is struck out of Islam's hand [*sic*], the Koran was weak and useless. [49]

He appears to hold a particular distain for Islam, largely due to the fact that most Muslims were unaffected by his religious call and 'Mahommadanism', he writes, 'is as cold as cast iron in winter.'[50] Salter mentions an occasion when he had tried to proselytize to an unimpressed Muslim lascar, recalling that, 'we tried to interest him in the story of Calvary but he and an Arab lying by his side expressed their resolve to abide by their trust in God and Mahommed.'[51] However, Salter does give accounts of a number of Muslim conversions to Christianity. Allah Baksh was a lascar who deserted his ship,

Flintshire, and came into contact with the Asiactic Mission as a result of his destitution. Salter describes him as 'foul' and constantly engaged in 'impure talk'. The mission claims to have converted the lascar to Christianity and, in the process, reformed his character into almost that of a saint's. Baksh explained his new habit of donning a bright red overcoat thus, 'I was a sinner, dyed in sin, but I was doubly dyed in the Saviour's blood, and I wear this coat in memory of it.'[52] Allah Baksh was baptized in London and was later engaged to preach the Gospel to his own people in India. Another interesting individual aided by the mission was the lascar Syed Abdoollah of Lucknow, known to the mission for over 35 years and originally a committed Muslim who apparently eventually professed himself Christian and was baptized in London. Although self-educated, he is said to have become 'Professor of Persian, Hindustani [Urdu] and English'. Salter claims that Abdoollah was 'passed over' for the East India civil service but he was eventually appointed as government inspector of schools in Calcutta.[53] Clearly, the dividends of conversion to Christianity provided real opportunities for a number of desperate lascars. His account gives other examples of a significant conversions to Christianity by Muslim lascars, for example, 'two other once well-known characters – Mohammed and Hussein – were baptized in St. Annes' Church, professing their faith.'[54]

Muslim Rites and Rituals

Salter also recalls an interesting missionary visit one Sunday afternoon to a group of '30 noisy Mahommadens' who had occupied the shuttles room at the back of *The Royal Sovereign* public house on High Street, Shadwell, for the occasion of celebrating Eid al-Fiṭr. What appeared to Salter as a chaotic and noisy spectacle was the joyous celebration of a religious festival accompanied by hand drums and choral singing by the lascars. The celebration must have presented itself as a happy distraction from the misery of their destitution. The predominantly Yemeni lascar settlement of Cardiff, which later also became known as 'Tiger Bay', a means of portraying its imagined, exotic 'Oriental' settlers, shared its 'othering' nomenclature with Salter, who describes the earlier London dockland areas around Shadwell also as 'Tiger Bay'.[55] Adding to the descriptive 'exoticization' of the destitute lascars appears to have helped to reinforce their non-Christian 'heathenness' and Salter perpetuates this image by suggesting that most of the lascars he visited were stricken by an addiction to opium; 'one celestial had become so deformed by vice and age as to receive particular notice for the support he seemed to give to the popular idea of the Darwinian theory.'[56] He even informs us that one of the opium dens frequented by 'Malays and Arabs' was opened as a mission-room![57] However, most of the proselytizing actually took place on board the moored steamers and square-rigged ships in the docks. Salter described the steamers and their crew as 'beautifully fitted with every possible accommodation. Each steamer has on board, including saloon servants, deck and fire crew, about 100 men of various nationalities.'[58]

Observing a mealtime on the deck of a ship full of lascars, he disparagingly comments, 'knives, forks and spoons are mere encumbrances here: your Oriental is very pliant in the fingers, and not particular.'[59] Although Salter tries to make distinctions between the various ethnic, cultural and religious lascars he encounters, the overriding effect of his descriptive accounts present a monolithic representation of the 'Oriental' other in which the cultural distinctiveness of the various lascars was subsumed into a broader subjugated colonial homogeneity. Through his imperial and evangelical Christian vantage, the lascar 'other' is little more than a pitiful spectacle of unfettered heathenism ripe for civilizational and spiritual enlightenment through religious conversion. In another account, he recalls how nine Ottoman warships, mostly manned by Sudanese sailors, came to British docks for servicing and repairs, thus:

> 'The Turk is Coming', and this time he was anxiously looked for. He had no intention of invading our peaceful shores, but a small fleet of Turkish war vessels was on the way to England for repairs, and on board each of them were reported to be about 800 men.[60]

The missionary takes great delight in recounting the tale of how he boarded one of the ships and distributed translated Bibles to the crew without the permission of the captain. Subsequently, the captain came on deck only to angrily admonish Salter and his fellow missionaries before ordering them ashore. However, Salter is keen to inform the reader that despite the embarrassing encounter, he was still able to proselytize to one of the sailors, saying:

> He was found to be no bigot, for his ear was open to the truth. He was too tolerant perhaps for the country to which he belonged, and indeed to which he never returned, for the adjacent cemetery, about half-way along the centre path, a little to the left, is the grave of Mustafir [Muṣṭafā], with a headstone and inscription in Turkish.[61]

Whilst there appears to be a stark contrast for the lascars between their lives on board ship and their lives of destitution on British shores, Salter's record provides us with some unique information about the religious observances of Muslim lascars on board ship. He offers us a detailed account of a *jumū'ah* (Friday congregational) prayer he observed on board a moored steamer;

> All the men were in uniform, with bared feet, and took up their positions in military order, in companies [rows] of about fifty each, and facing the east for mecca [Makkah]. There was an interval between each company, and sufficient space between each line to admit of prostration, the Khatib appeared on an elevation [minbar] prepared for him. He wore flowing robes and a white turban. Devotion began in a standing attitude by recital of the prayer. The position of the audience constantly changed, sometimes erect, then stooping with their hands on their knees, and then prostrate on the ground. The military precision with which this large company moved, dropped on their knees, or fell on the ground was very impressive, and suggested severe discipline. At times there was such silence that even breathing seemed suspended. A portion of the Koran was read from one of the shortest suras at the close of the book:-

> 'Say He is God Alone:
> God the eternal.
> He begetteth not
> And is not begotten:-
> And there is none like unto him.'
>
> The whole gathering fell on their knees, and in a few minutes more were prostrate, with their foreheads pressed against the bare deck. Then they sat on their heels reciting another prayer, and resumed the standing attitude as the Khatib cried:-
>
> 'And God hears him who praises Him'
>
> And hundreds of voices sent back the response:-
>
> 'O Lord, Thou art praised!'
>
> Many of the words they uttered were repeated several times in different attitudes, and the attitudes were constantly changing, and were again resumed. At one time the whole assembly seemed affected with something in the mouth, for they all spat or blew off to the left, and then immediately turned their heads over the right shoulder and repeated the action. [62]

The accuracy of Salter's account is open to question, particularly given that he concludes his *jumu'ah* experience, stating:

> The ceremony ended with a short address from the Khatib, while he held an inverted sword! A bishop of the Christian church assumes a shepard's crook as his insignium, but this bishop of Islam assumed a sword! The crook and the sword are very fitting emblems of Christ and Mahommed [*sic*].[63]

In terms of the general well-being of lascars on British shores, Salter informs us that one of Admiral Nelson's battleships, *Dreadnought*, was moored at Greenwich and was used as a seamen's hospital, specifically for the treatment of Oriental lascars, most of whom, Salter says, were Arabs, most likely Yemenis. However, after the decommissioning of *Dreadnought* it was replaced, but only temporarily by the warship *Caledonia*, and thereafter the lascars were treated at the naval college in Greenwich. Salter compassionately reflected:

> It is a pitiable sight to see an able-bodied Lascar leave the hospital on crutches. His wife and children, in many cases depending on his hard earned rupees, receive him from his long journey a cripple for life.[64]

Beyond the accidents and many fatalities lascars experienced at sea, a large number occurred as a result of imprisonment in British jails. Salter mentions that out of eight cases he was involved with through the London Christian Mission only one lascar survived his imprisonment. Five died before completing their sentences, one was freed but later committed suicide, and another died sometime after as a result of mental illness.[65]

The missionary recalls a typical prison visit recounting that a man named 'Akbar' came from the ship *Moghul* and was sentenced to two weeks for assault on a man who tried to rob him. Another lascar named 'Feroz', an 'old mendicant' with 'no desire to work' whose wife and family lived in St. Giles', was arrested for begging. 'Khuda Baksh' was also arrested for begging and had another week to serve but his ship had already left the port. 'Sheikh Mohammed', the proprietor of one of the opium smoking rooms, was arrested for robbery and had two more months to serve. Another lascar, 'Allah Baksh', whose ship was still in dock, was sentenced for 'passing bad money, of which he was unable to give any account', had eight more days to serve.[66] Lascar offenders were often put into the care of the Asiatic Mission before being deported. Perhaps the misdemeanors they had committed did not warrant a custodial sentence and by placing such individuals into the care of the mission, the judge was effectively monitoring the unwanted lascars, a form of Victorian 'tagging', so that they could not disappear before their eventual deportation.

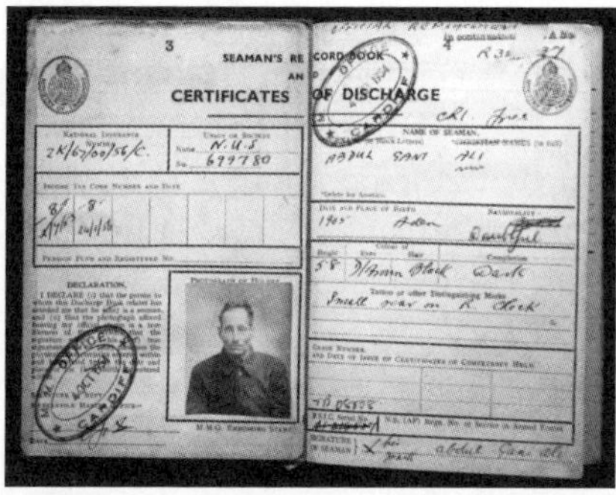

2.4 - The seamen's record book and certificate of discharge of Ali Abdul Gani (b.1905) issued from Aden in 1929 and discharged in 1954.

In addition to dealing with male lascars, the mission also occasionally took up the plight of deserted *ayahs* and Salter relates the particular case of a young woman from Madras who was found destitute, wandering the streets of west London in 'native attire'. The Hindu *ayah* had been dismissed for allegedly refusing to undertake her duties, but when questioned she simply stated that she was missing her children. Salter employed the skills of the Rev. Mr. Bilderbeck, 'a native of the Presbyterian Church at Madras', who was visiting London at the time, as an interpreter. As the *ayah* was a Hindu, she could not take an oath in the orthodox way – 'with Ganges water administered by a Brahmin' – so she was required to 'speak the truth, and only the truth, or you will be done to as the cow was done to on the banks of the Ganges.'[67] No explanation regarding the specific details of what happened to the cow at the banks of the Ganges is given, but the oath produced the desired effects in terms of the accused producing a true testimony about her absconding from her employers. One of the most interesting meetings held at the Rest is an occasion that recounts the meeting of 24 female Indian *ayahs* who responded to an open invitation from the mission. Salter informs us that among them were Ceylonese, 'Madrassis' and Bengalis:

> They were Hindus, Mahommedans, Roman Catholics and Protestant Christians. Their arrival and departure stirred considerable attention, for they came in their gay eastern attire to celebrate the occasion, with bangles, nose jewels and other native ornaments, to take tea at the Rest with their new English 'mama' and the Padre.[68]

The strange and farcical case of 'Mohammad Ali Khan' is also worthy of mention in the context of the unfortunate lives of many lascars who ended up in Britain. Khan made his way to London in an attempt to petition the British government through the India Office as a means of putting pressure on his former employer, an independent Indian Raja, who had sacked Khan after succeeding to the throne on his father's death. Khan insisted that not only could he not be sacked, but that as his employment was on the basis of being a servant in perpetuity, he should also have his salary continued, regardless of his employment status. In order to put pressure on the British authorities, Khan employed a tactic known as *dharnā baithnā*, a process by which the plaintiff resolves to starve and die at the door of the offender until and unless justice is done. If not, the cause of death is transferred to the 'account' of the person on whose door he dies. Unfortunately for Khan, he chose to hold his ancient ritual protest during the cold and inhospitable British winter and almost became a victim of pneumonia in the process. As a result, he postponed his protest until the summer where, after having restarted his protest, he was taken to a local police station for refusing to move on. But Khan was persistent and he eventually ended up in court at the Old Bailey, after being held on remand, where he was consigned by the judge to Hanwell Lunatic Asylum. However, Salter tells us that

> after years of painful experience he resolved to abandon the contest and became a pilgrim. He left for Juddah [Jeddah] en route for mecca [Makkah], the spot where sin and sorrows are ever lost to the fullest satisfaction of every pious Moslem.[69]

Salter's account further recounts the harrowing abuse suffered by a group of lascars by whom it was alleged that nine members were killed and thrown overboard and the others were seriously wounded at the hands of ship's captain. One of the lascars knew about the Mission and approached it for help. On visiting the ship, Salter claims that he witnessed 'six emaciated Asiatics huddled over an iron crane, moaning, groaning and surrounded by a crowd of wondering English.'[70] A lascar named 'Fujeer Alli' was chief witness to the event, but he died of his wounds just a few days after the Mission interceded. The Captain and his officer crew were prosecuted for their crimes with the Mission bringing the case before the law courts. The account of the mistreatment of the lascars is graphically brutal and truly disturbing. The trial lasted for four days and the Captain was convicted of manslaughter for the three cases on which he was tried. The Mission was commended by the judge for its efforts in seeking justice for the defenceless lascars. On another occasion, the Mission was approached by the police to help locate a missing lascar crew that had jumped ship at London. After checking the usual opium den haunts, the lascars could not be found. However, it was reported that a party of lascars had boarded a train for Sunderland. The mission then sent one of its staff to follow the crew and the next day the lascars were discovered and handed over to the police and then to the port authorities in Sunderland.[71] Salter's monograph also provides us with an early occurrence of a Muslim burial in Britain after a lascar named 'Suffar Ali' died in hospital. With the help of the Mission his body was retrieved by a *serang* called 'Mir Jan' and another 50 lascars, all dressed in white robes. Salter recounts in some detail witnessing the Muslim burial,

> A gaudy shawl served the purpose of a pall, and the remains of Suffar Ali, borne on the shoulders of his shipmates, were followed by a long line of mourners in their white attire ... The Arabian prophet has suggested two reasons for a hasty burial: 'should the deceased be a righteous man, he may the sooner enter paradise; and should he be wicked, the sooner he is off their shoulders [pall bearers'] the better [*sic*].' So they followed the remains of Suffar Ali almost at a trot,

singing a melancholy dirge as they hurried on – melancholy, for it was at low pitch, and never varied beyond four notes. ... Before entering the cemetery the coffin was deposited on the grass in an adjacent field, for there they had intended the ceremony to take place. The remains were guarded by the *Serang*, while the other mourners repaired to the clear stream to wash off the dust they had gathered during the journey, the more important purifications having taken place before starting in the morning. ... The men then formed three straight lines equidistant from the coffin, between which the first line stood the officiating priest ... suddenly, with a clear and distinct voice, the priest shouted 'Akbar' [sic], and the shout was repeated by every Mahommedan ... Audible prayers followed, sometimes by the priest alone, and sometimes in response. The whole ceremony lasted about fifteen minutes. The coffin was then removed, and they proceeded to the grave, making a melancholy wail of the Mahommedan *Kalima*:

> 'La Allaha illa Allaho Mahommed rasul Allah [*sic*]'
> 'There is no God but Allah, and Mahommed is His prophet.'

The coffin was then lowered to its final resting place, and after the English fashion, earth was thrown onto the grave, as a sign of the body's return to its original element. A portion from the *Kalam Ullah*, as they call their Koran, was read, and *fatias* [*al-Fātiḥah*] repeated for the departed, in the benefit of which all Mahommedan dead are said to share. ... We note the fact that everyone who took part in the ceremony retired to a respectable distance, that those two black angels with blue eyes, whose names are *Munkir* and *Nakir*, might not be interrupted while they examined the departed Suffar Ali respecting his faith, and when the mourners were quite satisfied that these angels had effected their commission, they closed around the grave, repeated another portion of the Koran, and retired.[72]

In contrast, it is interesting to compare Sydney Collins' 1950s study of Yemenis in South Shields, which also includes a description of the burial of an Arab lascar in 1939 and was reported in the *South Shields Gazette*:

> The funeral of Alawin [possibly a reference to the deceased's affinity to the 'Alawī *ṭarīqah*] Ahmed who died while at prayer was observed here yesterday. The Moslems [*sic*] standing around the grave had the peaks of their cloth caps turned to the rear and palms uplifted in front of them. Prayer around the grave was led by the Imam ... while the mourners responded, starring into their cupped hands. The coffin arrived on the shoulders of eight Arabs and the prayer service began with the Imam intoning in Arabic, 'God is great, there is no God but Allah, and Mohammed [*sic*] is his prophet.' Near the end a handful of earth was scooped by the mourners into the grave.[73]

Occasionally, lascars would die on board ship and would be given a full *janāzah* (funeral prayer) at sea. Davies quotes a passage from W. E. Williams' seafaring memoirs published in 1977, which recounts one such incident:

> This was a black man, one of the children of Mohammed. Losing him was a bereavement for us all, as the ship family is a small and tight-knit one ... In his funeral the captian did not take the burial service. One of the Lascars was a religious leader for the others, and it is he who would always lead them in prayer and recitation of the Koran [*sic*]. We could hardly understand a word, but the feeling was as clear as though it had been said in the first language of each of us. One of the family has gone.[74]

In another account, Davies cites how after the prayer a sign would be given by an officer and a trip line would be raised allowing the deceased lascar's body to slip from the cradle into the sea, with one writer saying, 'I had prepared many bodies in this manner before I was twenty-one years old.'[75]

2.5 – Mohammed Sayaddi, a community elder (muqaddam), *offers advice in the last Arab boarding house in South Shields, circa 2005.*

In 1853, Salter and his fellow missionaries met with the Nawāb of Surat, Mir Jaffer Ali, who was in London on a private visit. The missionary took the opportunity of visiting the Nawāb regularly as a means of improving his knowledge of 'Hindustani'.[76] As a result of his acquaintance with the Nawāb, Salter was also introduced to the upper echelons of India's indigenous ruling elite, including the 'Queen of Oude', who was in Britain to petition Queen Victoria on behalf of her imprisoned son at the hands of the British in India. The impact of the so-called 'Indian Mutiny', the revolt against the British colonial occupation of India in 1857, seriously effected British imperial perceptions of the Oriental Muslim other. The revolt was a huge threat to British political rule and mercantile activities in India and, in the immediate aftermath, the British exacted a brutal revenge upon the Muslim *'ulamā'* (religious scholars), whom they blamed for inciting a Muslim-led *jihād* against them. In the process, the image of Muslims, and their beliefs and practices, were transformed from docile and placid 'heathen' subjects into threatening and unpredictable bloodthirsty menaces.

Conversely, Sikhs were largely held up as loyal subjects who had defended their colonial masters against the treacherous and 'Jihādist' Muslims. When Russaldar, a Sikh military officer, who had assisted the British officers during the 'Indian Mutiny', visited London a short time after 1857, he was met with great excitement by Salter and the Mission who had some unexplained difficulty finding lodging for the Sikh officer. After a great deal of searching and refusal, possibly on the grounds of the Sikh's colour, culture and religion, Russaldar was eventually, and somewhat ironically, secured lodgings at 'an eating-house kept by a Mahommedan in North London'.[77] The year 1876, Salter tells us, was prolific for foreign visitors to Britain: 'at the Royal Albert Palace, Battersea, "Indian Villages in India" were exhibited ... Here were Mahommedans and Hindus drawn from the various parts of India, all willing to listen to the Gospel theme.'[78] The influence of the Asiatic Rest is further attested to by the arrival of 37 discontented lascars who had ended up in London after signing at Bombay to join a ship at Aden. However, after they arrived there three days too late, they were assigned to another ship but declined to serve in it, apparently without giving 'satisfactory reason'. After finding their way to London, presumably by serving on yet another steamer, it appears the lascars were likely to be left destitute in London. The Mission successfully interceded and an agreement was made allowing the lascars to work their passage back one way to Bombay.[79]

Another intervention by the Mission on behalf of a hospitalized lascar who had been working on the P&O line, involved a dispute in which the Captain claimed the lascar was fit for work after his illness, but was simply refusing to do so. The Mission took the case to a local magistrate who issued an official confirmation of the lascar's continued ill health. Upon receipt of the written court order, the Captain simply tore it up, but the mission forced further proceedings and eventually the captain was forced to accept the lascar on board, but still in a condition of recovery. In 1893, *The Crescent* published an article highlighting the plight of what it termed 'Muhammadan sailors' entitled 'Lascars Adrift', which detailed the destitution, racism and discrimination faced by Oriental Muslim sailors in Britain.[80] It referred to placards calling on ship owners and their agents to boycott Indian sailors and it claimed that sailor's mission homes would not take 'foreigners' unless they could pay.[81] According to the periodical, it appears that only the Turkish Consul in Britain had tried to address the sailors' problems, despite the article claims, him having 'no concern with the Indian subjects of the British Most Christian Queen'. The publication urged the British government to respond to the problem asking 'could not an Anglo-Indian Consul be established at each of the British ports visited by steamships plying between Hindustan and Great Britain?'[82] The following issue of *The Crescent* carried a small item reporting a disturbance between Muslim lascars and locals at the port town of Barrow, Cumbria.

> Sunday last, the Lascar sailors belonging to the steamer *Clan Macdonald* were holding a Muhammadan festival at Barrow, and were parading the streets with tom-toms, &c., [*sic*] and, on the way back to the docks, by some means a man's hat was knocked off, and a fight ensued between the coolies and the white men, fists and sticks being freely used. And many on both sides were badly handled and bruised.[83]

Whilst the plight of the nineteenth-century Oriental lascars in Britain witnessed many of them becoming victims of poverty, deprivation and racism, they appear to have faired much better compared with other Muslim communities in the imperial metropole.

Lascar Settlement in Manchester

Manchester's development as a production centre of cotton was aided by its damp climate and its traditional skills in wool production. Manchester cotton traders were also adept in the purchase and import of large quantities of raw material from both the Levant and America.[84] In 1838, the Anglo-Turkish Commercial Treaty was signed at Balta-Liman, near Istanbul, after which the Ottoman Sultan was soon importing more 'piece goods' from Manchester than the rest of Europe put together. But cotton exports to the Levant were often hindered by inadequate transport facilities.[85] The production boom drew in many migrants to the city not only from rural Lancashire, but also entrepreneurial travellers and wealthy merchants from the Orient. Among the many oriental sojourners were wandering lascars, many of them poor and destitute who were seeking refuge in the burgeoning industrial cities beyond their transitory British docklands settlements. And, although Joseph Salter's early reference to a few destitute lascars in Manchester does not constitute a community, it is interesting to note that even as a small band of individuals somehow brought together in adversity, they appeared to him as a micro-community. Salter records an 'Asiatic lodging house' that he stumbled across as he surveyed the 'human sewers of Manchester and Salford' during his missionary work amongst the lascar communities.[86] Of the 20 lascars he found in Manchester, six were lodging in Salford with 'Jan Abdoolah', a Muslim of possibly Turkish or Indian origin.[87] According to Salter, Abdoolah's lodgers, all of whom were also Muslim, were composed of 'a Javanese and five natives of India'.[88] The Christian philanthropist and missionary further mentions a famed lascar known locally as 'Monkey Abraham', whom he had previously encountered in London, describing him as a tall and skinny man who wore a strange multicoloured coat with silver-ringed earrings and a large silver ring around his neck. Abraham's name was, Salter claims, 'not chosen but earned, and anyone who saw the ape-like attitude he assumed, with his ridiculous ornaments, would never doubt how well he merited the appellation'.[89] It would appear that becoming an 'exotic' spectacle by 'cashing-in' on his 'otherness' was a desperate but profitable means of sustenance for the starving lascar. However, the fortunes of stranded and landlocked lascars in late nineteenth-century Manchester may well have been transformed when the industrial and economic boom experienced by Manchester in the eighteenth and nineteenth centuries brought two historic communication systems to Manchester that exported the city's economic output to the world.

2.6 – The seamen's registration certificate of Ali Mohamed (b.1902) issued from South Shields and dated 1924.

The Duke of Bridgewater's canal, opened in 1761, from Worsley to Manchester, had been inspired by the man-made inland navigation at Sankey Brook near Liverpool, then Britain's second port after London. Originally the Bridgewater canal, with its tunnel and aqueduct at Barton, was built by Francis Egerton (1736–1803), the third Duke of Bridgewater, to transport coal from his colliery at Worsley to the factories in the city centre of Manchester at a cost of nearly £250,000, quite a considerable amount at the time. The canal is connected to the Manchester Ship Canal, a 36-mile river navigation, which starts at the Mersey estuary, near Liverpool. Construction began in 1887 and it was completed six years later at a cost of around £15 million. Hedley Churchwarden organized preparations for the official opening of the canal by Queen Victoria in 1894 under a special commission. Churchwarden was a Victorian convert to Islam who was also known by his adopted Muslim name, Mahmoud Mobarek Churchwarden. His efforts in the canal's opening ceremony were a great success which brought him an official thanks from the Lord Mayor and Councillors of Manchester, although according to his biographer he appears to have been mistreated by the company that subcontracted him.[90] The completion of the Manchester Ship Canal opened up the city and its manufactured products, particularly in finished cotton goods, to the world. In the process, Manchester Docks became a gateway to settlers from around the globe. Factory workers, dockers and seamen were all drawn to Manchester's docklands in search of employment. Trafford Park, the huge dockside industrial estate, employed thousands of people who, together with the local community and visiting seamen, created a thriving cosmopolitan centre that not only became home to a newly-forming Yemeni community but also to many other ethnic, cultural and religious subgroups that were settling in the area. As a result, much like the 'Tiger Bay' area of Butetown, Cardiff, and the Holborn area of South Shields which was called 'Little Arabia' because of its large Yemeni population, the area became known locally as the 'Barbary Coast' due to its perceived 'exotic' African, Asian and Arab populace.[91]

FIRST WORLD WAR: FROM SACRIFICE TO SUFFERANCE

LIFE IN THE late nineteenth and early twentieth-century industrial docklands of Britain was a precarious affair for the transient Oriental lascars. As a result, lascars preferred to congregate within their own ethnic and cultural subgroups: Indian, Arab, African, Malay, etc. This in turn facilitated a small industry for seamen's rest homes and lodgings, usually established by *serangs* and *muqaddam*s who had settled in the various ports and had usually married local, indigenous wives. For the newly-arriving lascars, urgent matters needed to be attended to: registering with the local police, finding work on another ship and refurbishing their kits and stores, all of which was no easy task for someone new to the country and usually with little or no English. All of these necessary tasks required a degree of liaison with the local community and competency in speaking English. Mashuq Ally notes 'it should be borne in mind that many of the Muslim seamen were drawn from the least literate sections of their society and as a consequence were subjected to the most appalling conditions.'[1] In order to avoid misunderstandings and possible mistreatment, lascars often sought advice and surety from someone they could trust and communicate with in their own language, which usually meant their trusted boarding-house keeper. As a consequence of the maltreatment many lascars suffered, a large number abandoned their vessels by literally jumping ship. Jake Abram, a former tug boat operator on the Manchester Ship Canal, records in his published memoirs that the Strick Line Shipping Company had many vessels docking at Salford sailing to and from the Middle East and the Persian Gulf. The ships were known locally as the 'Baghdad Boats' and Abram recalls pulling a drowning lacsar from Eight Dock after he jumped ship from a platform where he had been painting the side of a 'Baghdad Boat'.[2] He recounts his conversation with the retrieved and soaking lascar, thus:

> 'What are you doing?' 'No like Sarang [*sic*].' That was the name of the head lad. 'Sarang no good, I'm not going back on ship.' I said, 'I'll take you back to the ship.' 'No, no! Please don't take me back.' 'You're going back.' But I put him on the quay and whether he went back or not, I don't know.[3]

This situation resulted in many lascars in British ports seeking better and more secure employment within the docklands and newly-founded associated industries at the turn of the twentieth century when many of the docks became hugely prosperous:[4] the establishment of an efficient network of rail and dock amenities developed in the early 1840s at Cardiff; shipbuilding and heavy engineering industries developed rapidly at Tyneside by the 1890s; the large-scale import of raw cotton and export of finished cotton goods from the ports of Liverpool and Manchester, aided by the completion of the Manchester Ship Canal in 1894; and the creation of the East India Docks and the increased flow of goods meant that more labour was required for the manning of warehousing and additional unloading crews in London – all were markers of Britain's mercantile and economic dominance.[5] The majority of lascars who sought employment in shore jobs were illiterate and unskilled and, therefore, largely directly unemployable within the docks and shipyards.

3.1 – In the centre on board ship is Fireman Muhammad Abdul Aziz, also known as 'George', who was born in Britain to Egyptian parents, circa 1940s. Muhammad later married Sadia, the daughter of al-Hubabi.

Alternatively, some lascars opened small businesses such as cafés and restaurants, others ran seamen's rests and boarding houses and some swept the roads and streets. Fortunately, however, for many of the unemployed lascars, dockland employment prospects increased significantly at the beginning of the twentieth century. In Cardiff, for example, the registered net tonnage of vessels cleared from the port with cargoes and ballast increased from just over one million tons in 1857 to 12.6 million tons in pre-1914 days, far exceeding those of other British ports like Liverpool and London.[6] K. L. Little asserts that it is most probable that the conditions of the British shipping industry were the deciding factor in the settlement of seamen regardless of their racial and ethnic origins throughout the ports in the UK. Added to the ever-growing shipping trade at the docks in Cardiff was a particular form of maritime employment known as the 'Tramp trade', which secured longer voyages than those of traditional liner voyages, but it did not offer permanent employment. Liner routes, Little notes, were less casual in their employment needs and therefore offered securer jobs for lascars.[7]

Trade Unionism and Lascars

In 1911, the great national strike of seamen took place inspired by Havelock Wilson and his colleagues who founded the movement for a national union. The strike was as a result of a growing collective consciousness amongst merchant seamen of their right to industrial recognition in a working culture of poor wages, deplorable working conditions and social deprivation. Among the seamen's grievances was the employment of foreign (lascar) sailors working on British ships.[8] The union argued that ship owners were deliberately discharging indigenous British sailors on 'trumped-up' charges, thereafter replacing them with cheaper foreign labour, leaving the white sailors to either accept the lower wages or else seek employment elsewhere. Another accusation against the ship owners was that, by employing crews of mixed nationalities, they were forestalling any opportunity for their crews to work towards collective rights in pay and working conditions and were, in effect, union-busting.[9] However, British seamen, spurred on by Wilson and his comrades, succeeded in stemming the employment of coloured lascars. Between 1890 and 1903, the numbers of lascar seamen on British ships had increased from 27,000 to 40,000, while in the same period the number of indigenous white seamen had actually decreased by 10,000. However, by 1912, there was an increase of 30,000 white seamen and a reduction of foreign seamen by 9000.[10] After the First World War (1914–18), the unions were able to ensure that foreign sailors must be paid at British rates, a rule that was then enforced by the National Maritime Board. However, the rule only applied to crews signed on at British and European ports. In respect of lascar sailors boarding ship at Calcutta, Bombay, Suez and Aden, 'the gap was left wide open for manipulation of the wage situation in other ways'.[11] As President of the newly-formed National Sailors' and Fireman's Union (NSFU), Havelock Wilson openly exploited racial tensions between lascars and indigenous sailors to further the employment prospects of his overwhelmingly white union members.

Beyond the politics of British working-class employment rights through the development of the trade union movements of the late nineteenth and early twentieth centuries, racism and discrimination still played a huge part in the marginalization of the settling Yemeni lascar docklands communities. Peter Fryer tells us that 'most white seamen rejected them as shipmates; white dockers too, refused to work along side them'.[12] In John Jones Williams' maritime memoir, published in 1983, he openly stated his hatred of Arabs, recounting:

> The thing I hate most is seeing their dirty faces and their little red caps [*ṭarbūsh*]. My forefathers must have fought the Turk and the Arab [*sic*], and the hatred must be in my blood. [13]

Many lascars either sold off or pawned what few belongings they had and tramped from port to port searching for work. By 1910, a Parliamentary enquiry was established to assess the plight of the abandoned lascars. The Committee on Distressed Colonial and Indian Subjects compiled a report that captured a catalogue of unfortunate lascar tales of poverty, rejection and destitution. A witness from the Colonial Office's West Africa Department, who reported that Africans who called at the offices for help were generally, 'time wasters' and people who would prefer to be on the streets, 'to sponge upon anyone they can'. The witness went on to recommend that 'it might be a useful thing to have some compulsory power of repatriating people like that'.[14] Racial discrimination against the lascars was further increased through Government legislation introduced between 1854 and 1894 designed to prevent their settlement in Britain via a series of amended poor and destitution laws which placed the onus on British shipping companies to regulate and monitor the whereabouts of their lascar crews while docked in Britain.[15] In 1854, ship owners were fined £30 for leaving a lascar behind in Britain and by 1871 the Board of Trade appointed Lascar Transfer Officers at all major British ports with powers to escort lascar crews to London for deportation back to their place of origin.

However, by far the most draconian and discriminatory measure was the Merchant Shipping Act of 1894, Section 125, which empowered ship owners to contractually oblige lascars, once docked in Britain, to proceed to any other UK port and there sign up for another crew sailing back to India via the port of Aden. Any lascar failing to honour his contract fully was liable to criminal prosecution. This Act was supposed to protect lascars from becoming destitute in Britain, but in essence it simply forced more to jump ship.[16] State laws with respect to lascar sailors were deliberately ambiguous in order to ensure the regular flow of cheap maritime labour from the colonies whilst at the same time racist and discriminatory legislation continued to kerb lascar settlement in Britain. In 1905, the Aliens Act was passed and it reflected a growing xenophobic sentiment across the country. Objections to the migration of large numbers of Eastern European Jews, fleeing persecution from Czarist Russia and the employment of indentured Chinese labour in colonial South Africa lent themselves to the mounting tensions of lascar employment in the British shipping industry.[17] Despite union pressure to 'scapegoat' the lascars and limit their numbers on British ships by demanding a language test – that one in every five lascars of any given crew on a British ship should be fluent in English – the amended Act of 1908 exempted lascars, unlike the Chinese, from the test. Rozina Visram asserts that the reason for this exemption was that lascars had 'special privileges and exemptions' under specific lascar legal articles.[18] However, when a national strike by the sailors' unions broke out in 1911, in which the lascars remained largely neutral, union antagonism against the lascars erupted once again. In order to avoid any charges of being racially motivated, despite one of the main union grievances being that there were 'ten times more Eastern labourers on British ships', union representatives argued that their objections were not because of race and colour 'but because they lowered the standard of life for white men'![19] The union issued an open declaration 'to have one of the biggest fights that the country had ever known' if the government did not act to curtail the collusion between the shipping owners and the Board of Trade attempting to lower the standard of life secured by years of trade union effort.[20]

World War One

The fortunes of Yemeni lascars were changed dramatically by the outbreak of the war in 1914 when Yemeni settlement in Cardiff and South Shields represented the two largest Muslim communities in Britain.[21] Lascars numbering around 51,000 constituted 17.5% of the total number of seamen employed on British registered ships and the average pay for lascars in 1914 was approximately £1.30 for deckhands and £1.20 for firemen a month, compared to approximately £5.50 a month paid to their white counterparts. Added to this severe disparity in wages, lascar crewmen employed from the colonial ports of Bombay, Calcutta, Suez and Aden were further exploited through inadequate and inferior food quality and crew quarters through reduced accommodation sizes on board ship.[22] Further, non-unionized lascars meant a relatively trouble-free ship, provided that the lascar sailors and their white counterparts were kept separate. By 1914, issues of equality, race and religion became somewhat of a problem for British troops during the 'Great War' when it was then believed that white soldiers would refuse orders from 'coloured' officers. Britain had to rely upon its colonial subjects to aid the war effort and India alone volunteered 1.3 million soldiers with many fighting on the front lines. As merchant sailors, Oriental lascars from the Muslim communities throughout the country's docklands shipped vital supplies from British ports. More than 3500 lascars lost their lives, with 1000 coming from the Yemeni community in Cardiff alone. Davies cites Captian Jones' memoir, which recounts the incredible bravery of a Yemeni sailor named 'Ali Mohamed', who was awarded the British Empire Medal (B.E.M.) for his efforts:

> After realising the ship was sinking ... who appeared at my side on the bridge, but one of the Arabs ... he said 'I stay with you, sir', and refused to go to the boat with the rest of the crew. Between us we were responsible for saving two of the crew who had been badly injured ... in my official report to the authorities about the disaster, I gave the little Arab his due and it was to my great satisfaction that I found he had been rewarded by the king and had been given the B.E.M. [23]

Ansari says that 'during the First World War migration from those parts of the empire that had traditionally provided cheap labour accelerated'.[24] Yemeni lascar participation in the First World War was both incredibly dutiful and loyal, given the amount of racism and discrimination they faced as subjugated colonized settlers at Britain's ports. Had Britain not claimed Aden as a colonial Protectorate in 1839, then perhaps Yemeni volunteers would not have readily made such huge sacrifices in defence of the imperial motherland. Whilst it is difficult to attain specific numbers for the amount of Yemeni lascars who lost their lives in the First World War, a government report put the figure of 3427 lascars killed while sailing out from Bombay and Calcutta, with a further 1200 imprisoned in enemy countries.[25] It would appear somewhat unlikely that Yemenis would have featured in these figures in any significant number, but it cannot be ruled out completely given that Aden was still governed by the colonial India Office until 1937, which made ethnic and cultural distinctions between colonized Arabs of Aden and their Asian counterparts of Bombay and Calcutta often indistinguishable.

In addition to the 1000 Yemeni men from the Cardiff community lost at sea during the First World War, a further 400 men were rescued at sea after their ships were sunk with many then being left helpless on the beaches of British ports to die of the effects of exposure.[26] The increased demand for labour to replace the British men called up for military service changed the fortunes of the settling Yemeni lascars away from their maritime employment. Peter Fryer claims that Tyneside's Black population was increased fourfold during the war and in Cardiff the population rose from an estimated 700 in 1914 to over 3000 by April 1919.[27] Added to the settling lascar communities were large numbers of stranded crews of merchant ships that were requisitioned for transporting troops back from the front lines of Europe and for shipping vital supplies and munitions. A number of Yemenis found their way into the munitions and chemical factories in Manchester and others sought unskilled employment either in the shipbuilding industry or in auxiliary industries like the timber yards or manufacturing industries. It is claimed that within 48 hours of the war declaration 8000 British merchant seamen had joined the armed forces and 900 enemy seamen serving on British ships, which would have included significant numbers of Ottoman Turks and subjects, had lost their jobs.[28] This huge labour hole was filled by colonial lascars and as a result the existing settled communities of Cardiff, South Shields, Liverpool and London underwent rapid expansion. However, this migration wave did not go unnoticed by the local press who were quick to express their concerns over the unusually high numbers of 'Arab seamen' settling in their midst. In a letter to the *Shields Daily Gazette* in May 1916, submitted by 'True Briton', it ranted:

> it seems rather strange that whenever a set of Arabs sign on a particular ship, they are all from the same boarding house. Of course I am aware that they are all members of the Seamen's Union, but still some of these men's relatives maybe conspiring in the desert at this present time. Even C.T. boats are engaging Arabs in preference to Britishers. I was under the impression that vessels under Admiralty orders were not allowed to ship aliens. Now I would like to see our ship owners give orders to their captains and engineers not to engage an Arab whilst there is a Britisher wanting a job. Talk about patriotism why, it makes me sick when we see the way our men are being treated.[29]

By 1916, due to the demands of the war, all lascar maritime contracts were extended to 18 months, but the growing need for manual labour and the higher wages offered in the factories away from the ports enticed many lascars to either desert or jump ship. In May 1916, the Anchor Line shipping company reported several cases of desertion to the India Office, complaining that 'certain parties were canvassing eastern crews'.[30] In a letter to the Board of Trade in July 1916, the influential Liverpool Steam Ship Owners' Association also blamed the increase in lascar desertions on 'organised attempts' to lure them to more profitable employment on shore. The Association warned the Board of Trade of the serious consequences to the shipping industry in trying to fill the labour gap during wartime and insisted that the 'growing evil' be stopped. The Board of Trade acted swiftly with the help of the India Office and by August 1916, a public warning was issued against enticing and harbouring lascar deserters.[31] After the war colonial soldiers were discharged and many were left stranded in Britain. The economic recession meant that employment was scarce and for the ex-servicemen racial discrimination further lessened their job prospects. In the interwar years, only industrious migrants would find a place in Britain where unemployment and destitution meant the likelihood of deportation.

The 1919 Mill Dam Riots

As the shipping industry employment opportunities declined with modern, faster oil-powered ships replacing steam vessels the lascars, formerly employed as coal stokers, rapidly became redundant. The seamen organized themselves in an effort to protect their jobs, despite government legislation limiting the number of 'coloured seamen' employed on British ships. Dr Khalid Sheldrake of the Western Islamic Association made representations on behalf of the Yemeni Arabs to South Shields City Council and the Port Authorities as early as 1919 in an effort to establish racial equality rights in the shipping industry after employment discrimination and race riots. The riots were fuelled by racist comments often made by union officials. John Fye, a seamen's union official, encapsulated the feelings of white sailors towards the Arabs when, in 1919, he said to Yemenis trying to sign on for a ship in South Shields, 'You black bastards, this ship is not for you.'[32] Similar race riots also occurred in Liverpool and other British ports as white sailors increasingly believed that the 'coloureds' were taking their jobs and, therefore, should be repatriated. The press inflamed the situation and the *Liverpool Courier* claimed that 'one of the chief reasons of popular anger behind the present disturbances lies in the fact that the average Negro is nearer to the animal than is the average white man.' As the riots spread to London, the national press absolved the aggressors and blamed the lascars, implying that interracial marriages and associations between 'black sailors' and white women were the 'reason' for the riots. In south Wales, three people were killed, dozens injured and large-scale damage caused to property. One rioter told the *South Wales Argus*, 'we are all one in Newport and mean to clear the niggers out.'[33] The Cardiff Yemeni community faced fierce attacks and the army was brought in to restore peace. But when colonial Australian soldiers drew their rifles to fire on the Yemenis, shots were returned by lascars from a minority armed with revolvers. The infamous and misnamed 'Arab riots' that broke out among Yemeni communities during the spring and summer of 1919 across the British docklands of South Shields, Cardiff, Liverpool, London and Hull were precipitated by the demands of indigenous white sailors for the limitation, control and repatriation of 'Arab' (majority Yemeni) seamen.

The broader context of the race riots was raising unemployment and economic recession as a direct result of the First World War.

3.2 – Yemeni seamen arrested during the disturbances at the Mill Dam, South Shields 1919.

However, the wider economic factors only brought to the surface the existing undercurrent of racial tension and hostility towards non-white sailors. In South Shields, where the first of the so-called 'Arab riots' took place, tensions had slowly developed as the settlement of Yemenis, Somalis, West African and West Indian sailors began to form a sizeable community around the docks from as early as the 1860s.[34] The spark that finally ignited the flames of racial hatred occurred in February 1919 when a small group of Yemenis, all British subjects, paid £2 each to clear their union books (updating all outstanding union subscriptions) in order to allow them to 'ship out' but they were then refused work. When the Yemenis raised their objections, John Fye, an official of the Stewards' and Cooks' Union, incited a crowd of white sailors by using foul and racist language against the Arabs, one of whom he then struck. The Yemenis hit back and the crowd then chased the Arabs to the Holborn district of South Shields, where most Yemenis lived and lodged. At Holborn, Yemenis came to the aid of their compatriots and a few individuals, armed with revolvers, fired warning shots over the heads of the pursuing mob. The mob then about-turned and hastily retreated, with the Yemenis chasing them back to the Shipping Offices at Mill Dam. A huge fight then broke out, leaving the offices wrecked and the protagonist, Fye, and a fellow union official severely beaten. Fye was later convicted of using language likely to cause a breach of the peace, but in the affray, army and navy patrols were called in and a number of Arabs were duly arrested. At Durham Assizes, the sentencing magistrate expressed a degree of sympathy for some of the Yemeni defendants, acquitting three, but 12 were sentenced to three months' and two more were given one months' hard labour.[35]

The riots in Wales began on the evening of Saturday 7 June 1919 in Newport, but they quickly spread to nearby Cardiff and Barry. In Cardiff, a crowd of around 2000 white people gathered around the Canal Parade Labour Exchange and began attacking a small group of Yemenis and Somalis. The mob then moved to Bute Street and started attacking the homes of non-white sailors, wrecking an Arab boarding house in the process to frenzied cries of 'Lynch the bastards!' and 'Kill the bastards!'.[36] The mob continued their onslaught by attacking the home of a resident *imām*, 'Hadji Mohamet' from Somalia, who was married to a local white woman who urged her husband to escape. The *imām* took refuge by climbing up the drainpipe on to the roof of his house from where he helplessly watched the angry mob ransack his home before the police arrived to disperse the aggressors.[37] In the escalating violence that spread across several nights, the Yemeni and Somali communities bravely attempted to defend their lives and properties from the racist thugs. A small number resorted to armed defence and a number of shots were fired above the heads of the racist attackers in a bid to scare them off. Around 15 people were injured, one seriously and another white man was killed. In the aftermath, of the six people who were charged in court for the violence, one was a white man, four were Yemenis and one was a Somali. Two of the Yemenis, Ali Abdul and Mohammed Khaid, were charged with shooting at people including a policeman. The following consecutive nights witnessed repeated violence and even further arrests. Again, shots were fired at the attacking mob and again, it appears that a disproportionate number of Yemenis and Somalis were arrested for a series of offences relating to firearms, affray and public order. As is all too often the case, the victims were portrayed as the aggressors and comments made after the events by the Cardiff branch of the National Union of Railwaymen, who passed a motion crystallizing the racist hostility towards the racial minorities who were, after all, the victims of mob violence, called on the government to 'do their duty by the coloured men in this country and send them back to their homeland.'[38] The sentiment was echoed in the 13 June 1919 issue of *The Western Mail*, in which the editorial stated, 'The Arabs ... are mainly seamen and their repatriation should be a simple matter.'[39] The rioting became so widespread and feelings ran so high that the deportation of some 600 lascars was instituted to pacify the white sailors. But the deportees were not volunteers and for many their status as British citizens was effectively revoked. The Colonial Secretary, Lord Milner, issued a memorandum headed 'Repatriation of coloured men', referring to the bitter resentment and injustice suffered by the colonial seamen, many of whom had served in the armed forces during the war. But more importantly, he feared that repatriations would have a direct effect on white British minorities living in the colonies. Whilst deportation was seen as the solution to the race riots, the policy failed to protect the lascars and their families as legitimate permanent settlers and British citizens.

'Mixed Race' Marriages and 'Mongrol' Children

Much to the horror of late Victorian and early Edwardian British society, settling lascars were establishing intimate relations with white women across the UK's docklands communities. Despite the imposition of a cultivated racial and social order, which placed the subjugated colonial Muslim 'other' at the bottom of the imperial social hierachy, and a relentless negative portrayal and reception of 'oriental' men as lustful, sexual predators with a particular penchant for white women, many encounters led to permanent relationships and lasting marriages.[40] Whilst British society positively frowned on all such relationships, it usually explained them away as being the result of white women of a 'certain class' and 'ill-repute', giving in to the wanton and unbridled desires of exotic foreign men. Such women and the resultant liaisons were viewed as an inevitable by-product of the dangerous and unruly environments of the dockland areas of imperial Britain. The celebrated Welsh novelist, Howard Spring (1889–1965), in his two-volume autobiography, *Heaven Lies Above Us* (1939) and *In the Meantime* (1942), recalls his early life working as an office-boy at an accountants in Cardiff Bay, before going on to become a messenger-boy at the *South Wales Daily News* and eventually a war correspondent and journalist for the *Manchester Guardian* and the *Evening Standard* respectively. Spring's vivid account of 'Tiger Bay' at the turn of the twentieth century captures both the exoticism and fixation of the multicultural docklands of Britain:

> There was a fascination in the walk through Tiger Bay. Chinks, Dagoes, Lascars and Levantines slippered [*sic*]

> about the faintly evil by-ways that ran-off Bute Street ... The flags of all nations fluttered on the house fronts, and ever and anon the long bellowing moan of a ship coming to the docks or outward bound seemed the very voice of this meeting place of the seven seas. It was a dirty, rotten and romantic district, an offence and an inspiration, and I loved it.[41]

Spring's dangerous and nostalgic description of the Butetown area of Cardiff's dockland captures both the horror and attraction of the burgeoning British maritime communities at the turn of the twentieth century. Cardiff's 'Tiger Bay' like Manchester's 'Barbary Coast' and South Shield's 'Little Arabia' existed in contradistinction from the inland cities and towns of late imperial Britain. To a large extent, their very existence was viewed as a window into Britain's vast empire which, ironically, by the late Victorian and early Edwardian periods had more Muslim subjects than Christian. This uncomfortable reality was perhaps never better realized than in the cosmopolitan and multicultural spaces of Britain's port cities.

The exotic 'Otherness' of the docklands communities was further pronounced by their geographic isolation from the cities to which they belonged. Both Butetown and Trafford Park were cut off from their respective cities by a series of communications networks: canals, roads and railways vital in the transporting of raw materials and finished goods endlessly flowing to and from the harbours of industrial Britain. As a result, the settling Yemeni, Somali and South Asian communities had little reason to visit the centres of their respective cities and, likewise, the local indigenous communities kept well clear of the docklands for fear, often misplaced and irrational, of being robbed, molested or stabbed. This apparent danger lurking amidst the multicultural British docklands is reflected in an account of a former resident of Trafford Park's 'Barbary Coast':

> M'grandmother used to say, 'It's not a nice place to go down passed [*sic*] the [Trafford] park.' She was a lot better off than most of them down there and she used to say it was the

> lowest of the low, that area. There was a street they used to call 'the street of a thousand nations', Monmonth Street was the name of it. They used to say there wasn't a same nation lived next door to each other.[42]

'Arab-Only' Boarding Houses and Cafés

A major contributing factor in the gradual settlement of the transient Yemeni lascar communities across the port cities was the establishment of a growing number of Arab seamen's homes, run largely by settled Yemeni sailors, often married to local wives. These early entrepreneurs were able to offer suitable and friendly temporary accommodation to Arab sailors whilst at the same time facilitating their urgent needs and affairs, such as supplies and liaising with the local police, port authorities and ship owners – effectively becoming a British *muqaddam*, similar to the *muqaddam* prospective sailors encountered in Aden. In South Shields, Arab boarding houses allowed a number of individual settler Yemenis to become both extremely influential and quite prosperous. By the late nineteenth century, stringent legislation and strict regulations were introduced to protect vulnerable sailors from being exploited by private persons accommodating sailors. Instead, sailors were required to lodge in licensed seamen's boarding houses in which the owners had to faithfully adhere to limited numbers of guests, health and general hygiene standards and open inspections by the Medical Officer of Health, the Board of Trade and the police.[43] In addition, boarding-house keepers had to acquire a certificate of good character from the Chief Constable testifying that the keeper was fit and proper and without previous convictions. Yet, despite the tightening of laws and standards for Arab boarding-house keepers enforced by both local and national authorities, the boarding-houses became embroiled in other matters relating to their lascar lodgers.

As the number of Arab boarding houses increased, so did the competition amongst the boarding-house keepers to become a *muwassiṭ* and *muqaddam* between their guests, the port authorities and ship owners. The dividends for the boarding-house keepers in acting as middlemen were both financial and prestigious. By acting as an employment broker between their lodging lascars and the maritime industry, the boarding-house keepers would earn a small 'fee' from both the lascars and their employers. Additionally, the more successful the boarding-house keepers became at brokering employment, the more lascar lodgers and clients they would attract and, therefore, in turn, the more labour they could supply to the ship owners, thus increasing their personal incomes. In this particular form of lascar employment, South Shields emerged as the UK's centre for lascars seeking maritime jobs. Thus, regardless of where Yemeni lascars docked in Britain, large numbers would make their way to South Shields as a means of bettering their chances of work and thereby avoiding a lengthy period stuck at port awaiting employment.

3.3 – Retired Yemeni 'stoker', Obeya, relaxes in the boarding house in South Shields, circa 2005.

As a result of this inward migration from other British ports to South Shields, the links between the various Yemeni docklands communities were strengthened. Because of the pivotal role the boarding-house keepers (or 'masters', as they were often referred to by the port authorities and shipping companies) assumed, the lascar seamen's homes became important institutions in the Arab seafaring communities. Lawless has stated that, 'The Arab boarding house master was a man of substance who wielded considerable influence over the seamen lodging with him and indeed within the wider Arab community in the town.'[44] The lodging houses not only ensured future employment through the house keeper's established connections with both the port authorities and the ship companies, they also provided food that was *ḥalāl* ('lawful' according to Islamic law) and often a space was set aside where men could pray and observe their Islamic liturgies. Many Yemeni lascars remained faithful to their religion and devotedly kept their obligatory prayers even on board ship. Some lascar crews prayed in congregation in designated areas, above deck or below in the engine rooms:

> If there was enough rooms to be had, they would set one aside especially for worship and would decorate the walls and floor with special carpets ... when on their knees worshipping and kissing the floor [*sic*], they would always make sure that their heads were towards Mecca.[45]

As late as the 1960s, Badr ud-Din Dahya had noted that little had changed in the single-male Arab boarding houses across Britain, observing that Yemenis spoke the Arabic dialect of the northern highlands tribesmen and wore their traditional Yemeni dress; the *fawṭah* (sarong) and *shawāl* (headdress). Dahya's research also highlighted the importance of prayer in the lives of the Yemeni migrants, stating:

> Most migrant houses have a private *masgid* [*masjid*] or room set aside for prayers. The *masgid* [he observed] is furnished with red carpets and is equipped with copies of the Holy Qur'an, books on catechism ['*aqīdah* or 'doctrine'], *maulid* books, hymn (*qaṣīdah*) books, rosaries and joss sticks.[46]

In addition to operating as a functioning congregational prayer room, Dahya states that the *masjid* fulfilled the same function as the traditional *maqṣūrah*, a recreational and social room usually connected to village mosques in the Yemen highlands, to which, he says, 'the migrants bring their visitors, who may be kinsmen, villagers or fellow-countrymen, to exchange news, recite the Qur'ān and pray as a congregation.'[47] The relationship between the lascars and their 'masters' was founded on mutual trust and often lodging lascars would leave their belongings and money with the 'masters' as safekeeping. Equally, when employment was scarce, house keepers would loan substantial amounts of money to their lodgers or would allow them free board until they eventually secured worked. Some boarding-house keepers even established links with other *muqaddimūn* in Aden, acting as agents, recovering debts, sending remittances to families in Yemen, forwarding letters and arranging passage for lascars who wished to return home. Even Yemenis who had settled and married local British wives would seek assistance and advice from the boarding-house masters. For example, when a Yemeni lascar named Ali Nagi committed suicide in Durham Prison whilst awaiting deportation in 1935, Mohamed Dowa, a boarding-house master from South Shields, organized a collection from the lascar community to pay for Nagi's funeral.[48]

As individual boarding-house masters became increasingly important to the success and future of the lascar communities, many of them were favoured and patronized by their own tribesmen from Yemen. Lascars inevitably felt both culturally and socially better catered for by someone from their own tribe. Further, should any difficulties or misunderstandings occur, tribal belonging and loyalty (*'aṣabiyyah*) assured that trust and honour would be maintained and respected. This is not to say that the Arab lodging houses were exclusive spaces, catering only for compatriots and tribesmen, as they also took in seamen of other nationalities. Lawless records, for example, how Muhammad Muckble's East Holborn boarding house took in both Indian and Malay lascars, while Somali lascars preferred to lodge with Hassan Mohamed at his boarding house in Chapter Row, South Shields.[49]

The majority of the Arab lodging houses in South Shields were located in East and West Holborn, close to the Shipping Federation Offices at Mill Dam. A variety of Arab lodgings had been established in the area for a number of years, with some establishments having changed ownership a number of times over. The premises also varied in size and capacity with some lodgings having no more than a couple of rooms where others could easily accommodate as many as 60 or 70 lodgers. Owners would also sometimes reside with their families within private quarters or would live in separate houses close by to their businesses. Usually, the boarding houses would have a common area where the lascars could congregate to take their meals, relax and converse or play cards and dominoes. This space has been compared by Dahya to that of the traditional *maqṣūrah* associated with the village mosques of northern Yemen. Occasionally, Yemenis would recite their own Arabic poetic compositions whilst others might play a reed pipe or even an *ʿūd* (an Arabic lute-like instrument). Most lascars appeared to prefer their own company, avoiding the local pubs and ale houses, so often frequented by their non-Muslim sailor peers. In times of low maritime employment, lascars could wait for weeks and sometimes months for their next commission and this meant that lascars needed some place other than their lodging houses to while away their time.

The pressing need for a culturally conducive, alcohol-free environment soon saw the establishment of Arab-run cafés that, like the boarding houses, became important features of the developing Yemeni docklands communities. The cosmopolitan mix and racial diversity of Britain's late nineteenth- and early twentieth-century port cities were catered for by a variety of 'ethnic cafés' which, in addition to the Arab cafés, included Chinese, Indian and Malay eateries. 'Abdul's', a Yemeni café established in Trafford Park, Manchester Docks around the 1940s, was apparently famous amongst Arabs and non-Arabs alike for his tasty cabbage rolls. In addition, the café also offered traditional fish and chips and a Yemeni dish known as *miḥshī* (stuffed vegetables with rice and meat). Collins' study on integration among the burgeoning multicultural docklands communities of the early to mid-twentieth century found that even as late as 1940s, cafés were the de facto community centres of the growing Yemeni communities in Britain. This was certainly true of the Yemeni community in Eccles, Greater Manchester, that later developed where community member, Aziz Bugati, described his visits to one of the Yemeni-run cafés:

> They were like a social place, y'know, they [Yemenis] would get together and it used to be great. We used to go in and because my friend's father owned it, we used to get free drinks [laughs]! So that was good! ... The odd Yemeni used to do a bit of gambling as well, so er ... [laughs], that wasn't so good! I remember that there used to be all Yemenis, they used to all ... our fathers ... play cards there, cards was [*sic*] very popular [laughs]! They used to drink tea and you could buy food ... you could buy *ḥalāl* meat there. But I remember not many used to spend their money [laughs]!'[50]

The cafés not only provided Yemeni food but also a means of relaxing and socializing in a friendly setting and cultural space that belonged to the Yemenis and was therefore less hostile and threatening than the local pubs or seamen's bars. Recreation and work were both arenas of limited social and cultural interchange for Yemenis who worked in the ships' boiler rooms or on the factory floors, usually with their compatriots. The Arab cafés provided an important meeting point and congenial environment that was not only open to Yemenis, but was also frequented by the indigenous population, sometimes even groups of local girls:

> The first [Yemeni] café was [established by] Mohammed Kasseum ... so we had to stay together and we go to Brook Lane café [in Eccles] and look out for the girls [laughs]! I tell you the truth. We were young then, all of us! [51]

No doubt the cafés did provide a convenient and safe environment in which to meet local girls. Another female British Yemeni respondent spoke of how her Yemeni father met her mother, who was of 'mixed race' from a Yemeni father and a Yemeni-Liverpudlian mother, in her grandparent's Arab café back in Liverpool:

> Well, apparently my dad was 25 years older than my mum and my nana [grandmother] used to own a café in Liverpool, and a lot of the Arabs went there. It was a bit like the [Arab] cafés in Eccles. Most of the Arabs met there.[52]

Collins' research further noted that 'cafés and boarding houses provide recreational centres for the [Yemeni] men, who meet daily for conversation or card games, while they drink cups of coffee, tea or milk.'[53] However, many Yemenis preferred to socialize among themselves, largely avoiding mixed social gatherings, instead grouping together with other Yemenis usually from the same tribe. The Arab cafés, like the Arab boarding houses dotted throughout the locales, remained a feature of British Yemeni communities up until the 1980s. A Yemeni who frequented the Arab cafés in the 1960s and 1970s described the atmosphere thus:

> We were all together every Saturday, one day all the men there are not working. On Sunday they all came on there [*sic*], play cards – not for money! We used to play friendly games and we stay there all night until twelve o'clock, dancing to Arabic and Yemeni music and then they tired [*sic*] and they want to go home.[54]

In terms of preserving Muslim identity, religious observances and collective worship, the Arab boarding houses and, to a lesser degree, the Arab cafés facilitated prayers and liturgies within specially allocated spaces in their establishments, as observed by Dahya in his ethnographic research amongst the British Yemeni communities conducted in the 1960s. Collins' study surveyed the number of cafés present in the South Shields' community in the latter half of the twentieth century;

> In the summer of 1950 there were thirteen Moslem [*sic*] cafés and five boarding houses in Tyneside, but as some boarding houses also have cafés, the numbers may be duplicated. Three of these [cafés] were owned by Somalis and one by a Pakistani, while others were owned by Arabs.[55]

Collins observed that the cafés usually opened around nine in the morning and remained open until 11 at night with the clientele usually consisting of single-male Arabs. They would often group together for informal chats, discussing current topical issues or gossiping over cups of tea or coffee. He also noted that card games were often played that in turn gave way to gambling, which often lasted several hours. Collins also recognized the important role the Arab cafés played 'like the mosque or zoaia [*zāwiyah*], the Moslem [*sic*] café is one of the institutions introduced by the immigrant to perpetuate his native way of life.'[56] But whilst evidence of religious practice in the daily lives of the migrant seamen was faithfully maintained by many Yemeni lascars in the docklands, few references were made to their religious identity in public.

Humayun Ansari explains that most Yemenis developed the opinion that the less they were noticed, the more they would benefit and in comparison, they established rather closer ties with the indigenous population than other Muslim subgroups.[57] Although Yemenis are the oldest established Muslim community in Britain, researchers like Fred Halliday have consistently defined them as an 'immigrant community' for two given reasons: they have worked in the UK as opposed to merely residing in it and, they have established and maintained social structures and networks with fellow emigrants from a particular country of origin through residence in a common urban area.[58] British Yemeni communities have largely developed, as we have seen, through the process of economic 'chain migration'[59] and community social institutions like the Arab boarding houses and Arab cafés provided vital nuclei for establishing social cohesion and community identity. The importance of 'feeling at home' while physically being 'away from home' was facilitated in the Arab cafés and was explained by a respondent, Tariq Mahyoub, who was born in the Yemen but was brought to Britain along with his mother to join his father in the early 1970s, and recalled his first experience of a British Yemeni café:

> When I was a kid my dad took me to the café, on the second day, I think it was, when I'd just arrived [from Yemen] and, erm ... it was really nice to see about 50 old men in the café [which was] facing the mosque. Y'know, they were just playing cards and stuff like that and they were just interested in you, y'know ... like, 'Oh! Who are you?' It was nice really but I didn't see no kids ... erm, then that was it really. We stayed

> and we got some help. We lived about 10 minutes away and everyone was asking me about the Yemen and that.[60]

The cafés soon became a regular feature of the British Yemeni communities and many second- and third-generation British-born progeny fondly remember the cafés as places they would often frequent during their early years.

A British-born Yemeni from Eccles, who was brought up in the 'Barbary Coast' area of Trafford Park, Manchester Docks, recalled affectionately:

> Er, they [the Yemenis] all lived in this area [Trafford Park] but some other places [in the UK], I don't even know. And, erm, they were very good people and there used to be a coffee bar and an Arab restaurant down there [near the docks]. Our house used to be on the same street and I used to go there for a coffee all the time, and there was another one [Arab café], Ali Saeed [was the owner].'[61]

After the creation of Arab boarding houses, the Arab cafés came into their own as places that did not just facilitate recreation and socialization for Yemeni lascars, but became institutions where transient single-migrant Yemenis could catch up with news and events from the Yemen. In the beginning, this was achieved through shared stories of individuals recently arrived from back home and news written in personal letters from relatives in the Yemen. But as communications networks improved, newspapers and magazines began to arrive from the Yemen and then later, as modern technology developed, radio news via the BBC's Arabic Service or Egyptian radio would become a permanent feature of the Arab café experience. A second-generation member of the Eccles Yemeni community reminisced on the demise of the cafés that were once the lifeblood of British Yemeni community socialization:

> We used to go to the Arab cafés, I remember the Arab cafés, I remember three. There was Hadi's [International Restaurant] that used to be across the road [from the mosque] and

> 'Happy Days' [now a takeaway, formerly, 'Freda's Café'] that used to be a café. And there was one near the bingo [hall], now that's just open land.[62]

As an example of how important the cafés were in the formation of British Yemeni community identity it is worth noting that in the small town of Eccles, in Greater Manchester, a location that witnessed a relatively late settlement of Yemenis, starting in the late 1940s. The total population of Eccles is currently around 11,000, at the peak of Yemeni settlement and migration in 1972 the Yemeni population was estimated at 2500, around 20% of the total population. In the same period, there were no less than five Yemeni-owned cafés; one located at 126 Church Street, another, the Tudor Café, at 226 Liverpool Road along with the International Restaurant and Freda's Café, also on the Liverpool Road. The fifth, Mohammad Kasseum's café, was relocated from nearby Monton to new premises facing Eccles Town Hall in 1969.[63]

Muwassiṭ Rivalries

Whilst the bygone era of the Arab cafés appears to evoke an instant nostalgia for many British Yemenis, the reality of regular friction and hostilities seems to be conveniently forgotten. In the same way that the Arab boarding-house masters became community linchpins as a result of their employment-brokering services, the Arab café owners equally came into their own as quasi 'social workers', who would often be required to settle skilfully arguments and disagreements that erupted in their cafés as a consequence of political or religious disagreements or a falling out over a game of cards or dominoes. The cafés also became the first port of call for Yemeni lascars who left one British port city for another in the arduous search for maritime employment known as the 'Tramp trade'. On this journey the cafés were both convenient stops, providing a *ḥalāl* snack and refreshment as well as being places that could, more often than not, refer lascars to a particular boarding-house master or *muqaddam*. In the process, a referring café owner could expect a commission for directing customers to particular boarding houses. Occasionally, the problems that arose within the British Yemeni communities were more serious than a simple misunderstanding or a disagreement over a game of chance. As Lawless' study on the South Shields Yemeni community during the early twentieth century attests, 'Some boarding house masters were bitter rivals and their rivalry sometimes led to confrontations, even death.'[64] Frequent disputes between the boarding-house masters and their boarders over money resulted in violent incidents. A particular example is the court case for assault between Salah Survie, a ship fireman, who was charged with attacking and wounding Ali Said, his boarding-house master of 72a East Holborn, South Shields, after Survie lunged at Said brandishing a knife in an argument over a debt. After lodging with Said for three weeks without paying, Survie was then thrown out by Said. However, Survie claimed that Said had a large amount of his money in safekeeping but refused to return it. A fight broke out and Said attacked Survie aided by two other men. In self-defence, Survie pulled out a knife and struck at Said.

In another similar case, Abbas Heider, also a ship fireman, was charged with the attempted murder of café owner Ali Hassan, whose premises at 75 East Holborn was a few doors up from Ali Said's boarding house. Heider who had apparently boarded with Hassan, claimed he had left £100 in safekeeping with the café owner to be forwarded by Hassan to Heider's family back in Aden.

Unfortunately, it appears that none of the remittance was ever received. Hassan's defence lawyer explained to the Durham Assizes that the money had not been forwarded because Hassan had used it instead to support a number of unemployed Yemeni lascars who were without any financial means. The judge apparently accepted Hassan's misplaced act of charity and duly sentenced Heider to six months' imprisonment.[65] Whilst a number of other similar disputes and offences came before the courts, there is also strong evidence to suggest that many disputes were amicably settled within the community through the custom of arbitration. It is in this particular context that tribal loyalties (*'aṣabiyyah*) and cultural customs and traditions (*'urf*) may often have worked to the advantage of the Yemeni lascars. Avoiding the dishonour and inconvenience of a lengthy and sometimes costly court case, the custom of tribal arbitration would allow the problem to be resolved swiftly and satisfactorily, with all parties maintaining *wajh* (literally meaning 'face', but understood as 'personal dignity').

Boarding-house keepers were regularly entrusted with large amounts of cash in their position of trust and as 'honorary bankers' for their lodging lascars. In addition to the safekeeping of large amounts of cash in their trust, the masters would also have extra cash on their premises generated by the nature of their business and enterprises. This left many of them vulnerable to robbers and thieves. Lawless cites a number of individual Arab boarding-house keepers who were murdered by robbers, some as a result of opportunist thieves who struck during the race riots at Mill Dam, South Shields, in 1919.[66] However, some masters refused to leave themselves open to villainy and took matters into their own hands. In December 1924, Ahmed Alwin, a café owner of 42–3 Commercial Road, South Shields, along with his English wife, Kate Amelia, were jointly charged with possessing four revolvers and 179 rounds of ammunition without a firearms certificate. The couple claimed in their defence that they had simply confiscated the weapons from lodging seamen and then forgot to report the matter to the police. They were fined £10 each after a lascar who owned one of the confiscated pistols reported them to the police.[67]

The profession of boarding-house keeper and café owner, although prestigious, was precarious for those operating in the Yemeni lascar communities. As described, there were occasional conflicts and disagreements with their lodgers and clients, issues relating to entrusted belongings and monies, the constant threat of robbery and the thankless task of securing employment and a constant supply of labour for lascars and shipping companies respectively. In addition, Arab boarding-house keepers and café owners were expected to become philanthropists whenever a lascar fell on hard times due to the lack of employment opportunities. This expectation placed a heavy burden on the masters because for almost every individual residing, albeit temporarily rent-free in their establishments, there was a dependant extended family back in Yemen awaiting receipt of much-needed remittances from their male relative in the UK. This generous provision offered to struggling unemployed lascars was often overlooked by the port authorities, shipping companies, seamen's union officials, police and local councillors, who instead targeted a high degree of adverse criticism and abuse towards the Arab boarding-house keepers. The main allegations were that the boarding-house keepers, as *muwassiṭūn*, were committing corruption and bribery in the employment of Arab seamen on British ships and the illegal entry of Yemeni tribesmen into the country.[68] The general charge aimed at the *muwassiṭūn* was that they actively encouraged, and in some cases even physically and financially aided, the illegal migration of Yemeni sailors into the UK.

3.4 – Retired Yemeni seamen socialize in the boarding house in South Shields, circa 2005.

Sailors unions went even further and asserted that the *muwassiṭūn* were supplying false documents to sailors and facilitating the harbouring and passage of individuals between the British Yemeni communities both to avoid detection and provide maritime employment by illegal means. Inevitably, there was 'no smoke without fire' and a small number of Arab boarding-house keepers were found and charged and, in specific cases, deported, along with the illegal Yemeni lascars they smuggled into Britain, back to Yemen. Unsympathetically, the accusers blamed the increasing high rates of lascar unemployment on the *muwassiṭūn* themselves, claiming that had the illegal importation of Yemeni lascars not been so readily aided by the Arab boarding-house keepers, they would not be in the position of 'obligation' to their unemployed lascar lodgers. The sailors unions further charged that the increasing numbers of Arab seamen, who were willing to undertake more duties for less pay, were putting indigenous 'white' sailors out of work. By the end of the 1920s, as the onset of the 'Great Depression' gripped industrial post-World War One Britain, the Arab boarding-house masters found themselves having to maintain even greater numbers of unemployed lascars. And, as more and more newcomers continued to arrive at the British docklands looking for work, the masters felt obliged to accept them. By May 1928, a Home Office memorandum reported that:

> It is known that boarding-house keepers are now beginning to feel the pinch of having to keep idle seamen whose irregular landing they have encouraged or connived at; and that this indirect pressure ... is one of the means of checking irregular landing.[69]

In response, the masters kept up the pressure by writing to the government through its colonial India Offices to plead their case. When other Arab boarding-house keepers wrote directly to the High Commissioner of India complaining that their livelihoods had been ruined by providing free food and accommodation to Arab seamen who were penniless and unemployed, Dr Khalid Sheldrake, an English Muslim convert and representative of the Western Islamic Alliance, offered the following explanation:

> The position of the boarding house masters is, I am well aware, desperate. As a matter of fact, I know one whose mortgages on his property are taken up. The reason the boarding house keepers have continued to maintain these men is that there is an unwritten Mohammadan law [*sic*]

> that whatever you have you share with a destitute brother. Therefore, these men have been maintaining the Arabs all along, and have ruined themselves by their kindness.[70]

In an effort to aid the failing Arab boarding-house businesses, the British and Foreign Sailors' Society agreed to offer temporary financial assistance to unemployed lascars in South Shields. In 1921, an agreement was signed between the Society and the masters to pay a weekly allowance for the destitute lascars' upkeep, to be paid directly to the boarding-house masters. This local scheme offered some temporary relief but, as the depression worsened, a far more drastic step of repatriation was discussed between the Society and the lascars. Furthermore, legal restrictions of Arab seamen to Britain in the early 1920s were extended to include all 'coloured sailors' in 1925. The Special Restriction (Coloured Alien Seamen) Order, issued by the Home Office, required all 'coloured alien seamen' to register with the local police within a limited number of days. Initially, the order was implemented to limit 'Adenese' Arabs (Aden Protectorate subjects) only and was restricted to a small number of ports.

Restricting Lascar Settlement

By 1926, the order was applied to all British ports and all 'coloured' sailors, effectively introducing a 'colour bar' into Britain, and thus defining 'British' and 'alien' racially. In Scotland, a number of seamen sought other means of employment away from the racism experienced in the docklands. A 'little Asiatic colony' of Punjabi Muslims referred to as 'steady and industrious' took up employment in the Lanarkshire steel industry but were resented by local (white) trade councils who made representations to the Ministry of Labour requesting their repatriation. In addition to the racism and xenophobia manifest in the infamous riots across the British Yemeni docklands communities in 1919, Yemeni lascars had to further endure a constant restriction on the number of non-white seamen working on British vessels as a result of tightening legislation. The passing of the Aliens Act 1923 was one measure in a long line of new laws aimed at curbing lascar employment. Blatant discrimination in the job market against non-whites was somewhat innocuously referred to as a 'colour bar'. Fryer says that in industry during the interwar period in twentieth-century Britain 'the colour bar was virtually total'.[71] The 'colour bar' exclusion of non-white British subjects from the job market did not really abate until the 1940s when extra labour was needed for the war effort and Black workers could then find employment in British factories, even if their white colleagues, workers' unions and employers were resistant. Yet, whilst the pressing need for more labour in the wartime factories allowed a degree of job opportunities for non-whites, refusal of admittance to lodgings, service in cafés and restaurants, entrance to dance halls and cinemas and refusal on public transport etc., were all areas of public life from which non-whites were excluded by virtue of the continued 'colour bar'.

At ports across the country, the unions would not allow a coloured man to sign on for a ship while there was a white applicant for the job, as the 1919 so-called 'Arab riots' at Mill Dam, South Shields testified. By the end of the 1920s, when the 'Great Depression' had totally gripped the British economy, devastating the manufacturing industry, 'Tramp shipping', the phenomenon of unemployed lascars moving between port cities in search of maritime work, was hit hardest. Where British ships were given government subsidies to literally keep them afloat, a condition of payment was that British (white) only labour would be employed on subsidized ships.[72] Due to the Aliens Act 1923, all coloured seamen were now registered as 'alien' and were thereby were automatically barred from all subsidized ships. Further laws introduced, such as the Special Restriction (Coloured Alien Seamen) Order 1925, were interpreted by local authorities and police forces to mean that every non-white was an 'alien' regardless of any documentary proof showing that one was British. When indisputable evidence of British citizenship was produced in the form of a passport, the police would simply confiscate it from the lascars without issuing a receipt and any coloured seamen refusing to hand over their passports were threatened with arrest and imprisonment. Equally, shipping companies would refuse to pay lascars until they produced an alien's certificate of registration, regardless of their British nationality. As 'alien' seamen were usually paid around 20% less than that of their white British peers (a practice that continued in the shipping industry until the 1970s), ship owners could make a considerable saving on labour costs by insisting that non-white sailors registered as 'aliens'. The Yemeni lascar communities were hit badly as a result of these draconian and discriminatory laws. Ethnicity and race were determining factors in how minorities, particularly colonial subjects, were seen and placed within wider British society during this period in Britain's history when the country's imperial power was at its zenith.[73] As a result, colonial subjects, including British Yemenis, were actually seen as inferior and as such, 'deserved' to be treated as less than equals.

Across the job market whether on shore or at sea this pervading colonial attitude resulted in a 'whites first' policy in employment. Whilst maritime labour conditions for British, European and US sailors improved steadily from 1919 onwards, progressed by the founding of the International Labour Organization (ILO), in real terms, working conditions for colonial lascars actually worsened. By 1936, the Convention of International Labour Conference recommended the regulation of lascar sailors working hours after years of exploitation which had established a working practice in which lascars worked for longer hours than their white European counterparts on the same ship for considerably less pay. In response, Black seamen in Cardiff formed the Coloured Seamen's Union in an effort to unite and counter the racism and discrimination they continually faced. In 1935, they sent their leader, Harry O'Connell, to London to liaise with the League of Coloured Peoples and in April of the same year a two-man investigation team travelled to Cardiff for a week to assess the plight of the lascars there. The team later reported that they found a:

> settled, orderly community, trying with desperate success to keep respectable homes under depressing conditions ... We met men as British as any Englishman, forced by fraud to register as aliens, after living here since the [First World] war; charges and countercharges; misleading newspaper reports; men in authority bellowing 'repatriation'; muttered resentment against British children called 'half-castes'; and dominating everything, an imminent danger that deliberate trickery would mean for these men and their families expulsion from British shipping and ultimately from Britain.[74]

The investigation undertaken by the League of Coloured Peoples proved beyond doubt that the lascars, many of whom had fought gallantly as voluntary British servicemen in the First World War, were all forced to register as 'aliens' despite the indisputable proof of their British nationality.

INTERWAR PERIOD: SHAYKH ABDULLAH ALI AL-HAKIMI AND THE 'ALAWĪ *ṬARĪQAH*

By the end of the First World War, British Yemeni communities had been established across a number of port cities in the UK including South Shields, Cardiff and Liverpool for over a generation. In South Shields, Yemenis numbered around 4500, most of whom where single males catered for by some 60 'Arab only' boarding houses. These apparently exclusive lodging places were not established out of a sense of isolation but rather were a response to the exclusion of 'black and coloured' sailors from the boarding houses in which white European and indigenous sailors lodged.[1] Racial discrimination also took the form of legislation when, in March 1925, the Home Office implemented a Special Restriction Order, under Article 11 of the Aliens Order 1920, which required the registration of all 'coloured seamen' in the UK at local police stations. Ironically, many 'coloured' sailors, particularly Yemenis, were actually British citizens. The plight of the Yemeni, Somali and Indian lascars in Britain caused much consternation amongst Christian charities and missions in the latter part of the nineteenth century when their acute destitution and deprivation was recorded in the two published works of the Reverend Joseph Salter.[2]

By 1919, the Western Islamic Association, based in London, and the Islamic Society, affiliated to the Woking Muslim Mission, had both made representations on behalf of the Yemenis of South

Shields to the local City Council and the Port Authority after there were increasing race disturbances and employment discrimination which deliberately targeted Yemenis. As the Yemenis were largely a transient community, at that time there was no permanent religious centre such as a mosque where the Yemenis could collectively offer their prayers. However, after the docklands disturbances, Dr Khalid Sheldrake, an English convert to Islam and a representative of the Western Islamic Association, made efforts in August 1929 to establish a purpose-built mosque for the South Shields Yemeni Muslim community. He collected some donations from the Ismāʿīlī Shiite ruler, the Aga Khan, and the wealthy Niẓām of Hyderabad, India, and purchased a plot of land in the city, but the scheme never came to fruition.[3] It was not until the appearance of Shaykh Abdullah Ali al-Hakimi, one of British Islam's most important figures, that British Yemenis were able to establish themselves firmly, through their particular expression of Sufism, on to the UK's religious landscape, as the oldest settled Muslim community in Britain.

Shaykh Abdullah Ali al-Hakimi

In the 1930s, Shaykh Abdullah Ali al-Hakimi (c.1900–54), a Yemeni religious scholar and merchant from al-Hakim, a Dhubḥānī village near Taiʿzz, and adherent of the North African ʿAlawī *ṭarīqah,* a branch of the Shādhilī Sufi order, was given permission by his Shaykh, Aḥmad ibn Muṣṭafā al-ʿAlawī, to begin a Muslim mission amongst the Yemenis in Britain. As a part of his Sufi proselytizing, he established a number of *zawāyā* (Sufi centres)[4] among the Muslim communities in Britain.[5] Al-Hakimi met Shaykh Aḥmad Muṣṭafā al-ʿAlawī in the early 1920s, most probably in Morocco and then later studied Sufism with the Shaykh at Mustaghanem, a Mediterranean port on the coast of Algeria and the birthplace of al-ʿAlawī. After initially becoming a *faqīr* ('initiate'), al-Hakimi was eventually appointed a *muqaddam* (a representative of a Sufi shaykh) of the ʿAlawī *ṭarīqah* before first moving to Marseilles and then later Rotterdam to establish *zawāyā* in both locales amongst the migrant Yemeni sailors. In 1936, al-Hakimi moved to Britain after previously obtaining the Shaykh's *ijāzah* (permission) to begin his mission amongst the British Yemeni communities in Cardiff, South Shields, Hull and Liverpool. Under al-Hakimi's guidance, the British Yemeni communities underwent a dramatic religious transformation, introducing new rituals and practices in accordance with the teachings of the ʿAlawī *ṭarīqah*. As a result, the communities became highly visible where previously they had been practically unnoticed. Richard Lawless states that al-Hakimi's arrival in Britain 'brought about what can only be described as a religious revival among these small Yemeni seafaring communities. Religious life was regularised and dramatized.'[6]

Shaykh Aḥmad Ibn Muṣṭafā al-ʿAlawī

The Grand Shaykh of the ʿAlawī *ṭarīqah* Abu'l-ʿAbbās Aḥmad ibn Muṣṭafā al-ʿAlawī, was born in the coastal town of Mustaghanem, near Oran in Algeria in 1869. The town was quite conservative in that it had barely been affected by French colonialism. His great-great-great-grandfather was given the title 'al-Ḥajj' (denoting someone who has made the pilgrimage to Makkah) and his name, al-Ḥajj ʿAlī, lent itself to the diminutive, 'Ibn al-ʿAlawī' – the name given to his descendants.[7] Although his ancestors were local notables and his great-grandfather, Aḥmad, was a renowned Islamic scholar, the Shaykh was born into a poor family as the only son with two sisters. He received no formal education apart from learning the Qur'ān from his father and memorizing nine-tenths of its contents. As a young man, he appears to have drifted through a number of different trades before becoming a cobbler. At the age of 16 his father died and he took up trading and opened up a small shop in partnership with a close friend. At this relatively young age, the Shaykh was already frequently visiting *majalis al-dhikr* (Sufi devotional gatherings) and initially his mother was resistant to him leaving the house to attend such gatherings in the evenings, but she eventually gave her blessings as she continued to live with the Shaykh until her death in 1914.

As the Shaykh became more involved in his spiritual path, aided by frequent home visits from a local Islamic scholar, his newly-married wife became so perplexed that she filed for divorce on the grounds that the Shaykh was not fulfilling her rights. However, she was dissuaded when the Shaykh reluctantly abandoned his home tuition. Al-ʿAlawī founded his *ṭarīqah* in 1918 after he was granted *ijāzah* (permission) from his own Shadhili *ṭarīqah* shakyh, al-Būzaydī, to do so as a result of displaying extraordinary spiritual prowess. Thereafter, he soon established a *zāwiyah* in his hometown where after his demise the Shaykh was then buried. His *ṭarīqah* quickly spread across North Africa and the Middle East and, perhaps aided by Muslim sailors, there were also a small number of adherents in France and Holland. In his biography of the Shaykh published in 1961, Martin Lings opens his preface stating, 'The Shaikh al-ʿAlawī is almost entirely unknown outside the precincts of Islamic mysticism [Sufism].' But, Lings also acknowledges the Shaykh's scholarly contribution to Islam through his publications and travels. Lings also mentions that the Shaykh was briefly celebrated amongst his contemporary French Orientalists such as Dermengham and Massignon, with the former noting that al-ʿAlawī was 'one of the most celebrated mystic shaykhs of our time'.[8] However, beyond these passing references it is not really until Lings' own biography, published some 30 years after the death of the Shaykh, that any serious academic study of his life and work becomes noted by western scholars.

In terms of his spiritual path, al-ʿAlawī first became an adherent of the ʿĪsāwī *ṭarīqah*, a Shādhilī branch of Sufism which appears to have been a form of cultic-charismatic Sufism from which the Shaykh soon disassociated himself in preference for litanies and invocations based on the Qur'ān and *aḥādīth*. Although, al-ʿAlawī recounts how he slowly withdrew from the *ṭarīqah*, he admits to continuing the practice of snake charming, a particular speciality of the ʿĪsāwī *ṭarīqah*, until he eventually met with Shaykh Sīdī Muhammad al-Būzaydī. Shaykh al-Būzaydī had established a local reputation as a saintly scholar but also as one who did not seek to gather initiates to his order. However, after the Shaykh had made many frequent visits to al-ʿAlawī's shop, during which many profound discussions concerning faith had taken place, both al-ʿAlawī and his business partner, Sīdī al-Ḥajj Ibn ʿAwdah, took *bayʿah* (allegiance) with Shaykh al-Būzaydī. As a *faqīr* of al-Būzaydī, al-ʿAlawī was carefully guided by his master, who instructed him to abandon his informal studies in Islamic theology in preference of his Sufi litanies (*dhikr*). Al-ʿAlawī admits to conceding to his Shaykh's request with some considerable reluctance. Cited at length in Lings' biography, al-ʿAlawī gives a wonderfully detailed account of the step-by-step initiations (*maqāmāt*) he was guided through by his Shaykh. Once he had reached a certain *maqām* (spiritual station), he was then instructed to restart his theological classes. In the ensuing studies, al-ʿAlawī began to understand the literal texts of Islamic theology through the prism of his intense meditation and the spiritual teachings of his Shaykh. The resultant affect was a flurry of esoteric philosophical writings which included *Miftāḥ al-Shuhūd* (*The Key of Perception*), a book on astronomy that sought to explain cosmological phenomena through a spiritual understanding of the Divine.[9]

4.1 – Shaykh Aḥmad Muṣṭafā al-ʿAlawī, Grand Shaykh of the ʿAlawī ṭarīqah, circa 1930s.

As al-ʿAlawi reached higher levels of spirituality, he was eventually taken to Morocco to aid his Shaykh in proselytizing the *ṭarīqah* amongst the masses. He remained in Morocco for some 15 years and it is most probably during this time that Shaykh Abdullah Ali al-Hakimi first came into contact with al-ʿAlawī. After the death of Shaykh al-Būzaydī, al-ʿAlawī returned to Mustaghanem after first stopping off at Tlemcen, where he had previously sent his wife to stay with her parents. Unfortunately, within a few days of his arrival, his wife, who had been seriously ill for some time, passed away. On his eventual return to Mustaghanem, it was claimed by his devotees that al-ʿAlawī was 'divinely' selected through the process of 'inspired' dreams experienced by a number of *fuqarāʾ* (initiates) of the *ṭarīqah*. Lings' monograph gives us a few accounts of such dreams as recounted by various adherents.[10] The biography also includes a chapter that is largely a translation of an autobiographical account of al-ʿAlawī's life in which the Shaykh makes reference to a number of his marriages that had ended in divorce. The Shaykh's explanation of the divorces avoids any blame on the part of his ex-wives but, rather, attributes the failed marriages to his own neglect. He recalls, 'In a word, any shortcomings that there were where on my side, but they were not deliberate.'[11] Lings' publication is laced with the esoteric philosophy of Sufi teachings and doctrines. As an adherent of al-ʿAlawī, Lings describes with great ease and beauty the concepts and hierarchies of the Sufi *ṭarīqah*, particularly the idea of unbroken chains of transmission (*silsilah*) as a mystic path to inner knowledge of the Divine. In doing so, he labours at some length to establish the validity of al-ʿAlawi's *ṭarīqah* as a new branch or pathway in the ancestral tree of the Shādhilī and Darqāwī spiritual orders. He comments that:

> The Shaikh al-ʿAlawī's decent from Abu'l-Ḥasan ash-Shādhilī through the chain of the ʿĪsāwī Ṭarīqah is not included [in al-ʿAlawī's 'spiritual chain' offered in his Appendix]. Moreover the ramifications of all the different branches, even if they were known, would be far too complex to be reproduced in one tree.'

He continues,

> The economy of this tree may be measured by the case of Ḥasan al-Baṣrī (AD 640–727) who on his long life must have

> received various transmissions from many Companions of the Prophet, whereas he is set down as the spiritual heir of one Companion only.[12]

In terms of the British Yemeni connection to the ʿAlawi *ṭarīqah* via Shaykh Abdullah Ali al-Hakimi, Lings' work offers only a passing reference, reduced to a footnote, relating to the spread of the *ṭarīqah* beyond North Africa. He says:

> The Shaikh had many disciples, mostly seamen, who established zāwiyahs at various ports of calling including not only Cardiff but also subsequently, after his death, at Liverpool, Hull and South Shields, and inland at Birmingham.[13]

Unfortunately, Lings' concise account of the spread of the *ṭarīqah* amongst the Muslims of Britain does not give an informed view of the spread of the *ṭarīqah* as a result of al-Hakimi's missionary efforts.

The ʿAlawī Ṭarīqah in Britain

Perhaps the earliest recorded study of the ʿAlawi *ṭarīqah* established in Britain amongst the burgeoning Yemeni Muslim community was that undertaken by the renowned Arabic philologist, Professor R. B. Serjeant of the University of Cambridge, published in 1944.[14] His short paper was based on a fieldtrip to Cardiff and South Shields conducted in 1943 in which he also made a reference to about 20 Yemeni families living in South Shields, which would translate as a conservative estimate of around 100 people.[15] Serjeant also notes that Yemeni communities had existed in both Cardiff and South Shields before World War One. He tells us:

> Cardiff town is not unknown in Arabia ... for in the interior of the [British] Aden Protectorate, I have more than once met Arabs who had lived there at one time or another. Anyone who would see a small corner of Arabia in England [*sic*] I can only advise to stroll down from Cardiff station to

> Butetown; by their finer features and slight bodies he will easily distinguish the Yemenis from the polyglot population which contains nationals from all parts of the world.[16]

Accounting for the Yemeni families settled in South Shields at the time of his visit, he poignantly notes that 'nearly every one ... has lost a relative at sea during the present war'.[17] This bleak reality is a startling admission of the sense of duty and loyalty British Yemenis had for their adopted country. Serjeant's paper also reminds us that smaller communities of Yemenis, or what he describes as 'colonies', were to be found in Hull, Liverpool, Birmingham and Sheffield, confirming Fred Halliday's later study of a British Yemeni 'second wave' or inward migration from the port cities of original settlement to the industrial cities of Britain. Serjeant is particularly enamoured by the 'mixed race' children of Yemeni-British parentage, noting 'their children, alert and intelligent, hardly distinguishable in complexion from their English schoolmates are carefully brought-up in the Moslem [*sic*] faith.'[18] Commenting on the 'Alawī *ṭarīqah* in Cardiff, Serjeant explains,

> The community is organised in the form of religious confraternity of the type known as *tariqa* or 'spiritual path'. The initiate, entitled *faqir*, passes through various grades of spiritual attainment until he reaches that degree of understanding which entitles him to be called a *Sufi*, explained by the Arabs as 'one who has purified his heart'.[19]

He goes on to inform us that very few reach the higher station of *murshid* ('one who guides') or Shaykh.[20] The *ṭarīqah* to which the British Yemenis belong, Serjeant writes, 'is the *'Allawi tariqa'* – an offshoot from the great Shādhilī order that has spread across the Muslim world. Describing the spiritual aptitude of the founder of the 'Alawī *ṭarīqah*, Shaykh Aḥmad ibn Muṣṭafā Al-'Alawī, he writes, 'on the manifestation of his own saintly powers, his professor [Shaykh] placed himself under the 'Allawi who founded the tariqah which is called by his name'.[21] Al-'Alawī's spiritual *muqaddam*, Abdullah Ali al-Hakimi, after some years spent under the Shaykh's guidance, was thereafter responsible for establishing a number of ʿAlawī orders in Britain, whilst 'Yemenis belonging to this sect were to be found in Marseilles, Rouen and Le Havre before the [Second World] war.'[22] In addition to the *ṭarīqah*'s primary spiritual function, Serjeant points towards the social functions undertaken, stating:

> The sheikh [al-Hakimi] looks after the sick, and at its own expense, the society sends ill or aged members back to Arabia. A school is maintained in Cardiff, attended by about fifty boys and thirty girls.[23]

The article further explains that in addition to the Islamic education provided for the children through the establishment of the school, which drew British Yemeni families to the city from the other port city communities across the UK, a select few older boys were sent abroad to undertake traditional Islamic learning:

> at the beginning of the war, three Yemeni children, by English [*sic*] mothers, were sent to study at the famous ancient university of Al-Azhar in Cairo, all expenses being bourne by the confraternity.[24]

In fact, one of the boys sent to study was the young Shaykh Said Hassan Ismail, who was later to become one of the longest serving British imāms, who sadly passed away in 2010.[25] Shaykh Said's father was tragically killed during the war whilst serving on a British vessel shipping vital supplies when it was sunk by the German Luftwaffe. The young orphaned Said was then adopted by Shaykh Hassan Ismail, who was at the time the assistant to Shaykh Abdullah Ali al-Hakimi, and he raised him as if he were his own son. Under the patronage of Shaykh Hassan Ismail, Said was given the traditional Islamic learning which led to him being chosen to study abroad along with the two other British Yemeni boys.

4.2 – Shaykh Abdullah Ali al-Hakimi, muqaddam *of Shaykh Aḥmad Muṣṭafā al-'Alawī, Shaykh of the 'Alawī* ṭarīqah *in the UK and Free Yemen Movement political activist, circa early 1950s.*

After completing his formal Islamic education and then spending a few brief spells in the Yemen, Shaykh Said Ismail eventually became the Shaykh of the Cardiff Yemeni community and a lifelong adherent of the'Alawī *ṭarīqah*. Serjeant's brief study of the *ṭarīqah* offers us a unique glimpse of the wartime British Yemeni communities of Cardiff and South Shields, providing particular details of the activities of the 'Alawī *ṭarīqah*. Serjeant states that he attended the annual *mawlid* festivals at both Cardiff and South Shields, describing the contrast between the grey, drab and bombed-out British docklands in which the Yemenis resided, against the 'colour, the costume and the warmth of Southern Arabia, so you might be in Aden or one of the little market towns of the interior.'[26] The learned professor should be forgiven for his exoticization of the religious observances he witnessed and his ethnographic account should be understood in the context of mid-twentieth-century imperial Britain, a period when Muslim settlement was not as pronounced as the post-World War Two settlements became. Instead, Muslim community formation, certainly in terms of a visible Muslim presence, was indeed limited to the exotically-named dockland areas of 'Tiger Bay', 'Barbary Coast' and 'Little Arabia'. This disconnection occurred because the docklands Muslim communities were essentially, geo-culturally 'cut-off' from the cities to which they belonged and, as a result, they and their locales were perceived as 'strange', or even slightly dangerous and intimidating places for any white Briton to be. This sense of spectacle and 'otherness' is quaintly, if not now somewhat anomalously, captured and expressed through Serjeant's informed and academic observations as one of Britain's foremost scholars of Arabic. His privileged observations of the *dhikr* sessions informs us that:

> Zawiyas (oratories) for prayer and meditation are set-up whenever a number of 'Allawi's settle, and an annual festival is held which last three days. During the festival there are processions, prayers, addresses, the chanting of *nashids* or praises of God, and the performance of the curious ceremony known as the *dhikr*, or the 'mentioning' of the name of Allah.[27]

Serjeant rather patronizingly describes how he managed to locate the Yemenis amongst the drab and decaying houses of South Shields' dockland, stating,

> I found our friends at a small house in the sea-faring quarter ... easily identified by the number of Arab and Somali seamen going in and out. Most wore cap and suit, but some had already changed into bright coloured clothing from Arabia.[28]

He then describes his encounter with Shaykh Hasan Ismail, 'rosary [*subḥah*] in his hand, and clad in white as befits the spiritual head of the community: for white, they say, is the best of all colours.'[29] After meeting the Shaykh he was then escorted to another room in the same building, from which he could hear on approaching 'the sound of chanting [*dhikr*], and many little children were to be seen in holiday dress'.[30] He noted that the men and women were segregated and that the women were 'only visible from a distance', but two women wearing the headdress of the Yemen asked if it were possible for Serjeant to 'get a message to their sons then serving [as British soldiers] in the Middle East'.[31] After visiting the house, Serjeant was then taken along with the *mawlid* procession to the *zāwiyah*, a place he describes as:

> a large room in a kind of seamen's lodging house, carpeted and garnished with lovely Yemen blankets spread side by side with our shoddier machine-made European carpets.[32]

He observed that Shaykh Hasan Ismail was stood at the centre of the procession,

> grave, stately and kind, the elders by his side, and the green banners inscribed with the legend *la ilaha illa 'llah* ('there is no God but the God'), a white crescent and stars, borne aloft before him.[33]

He witnessed the children taking pole position, at the front of the procession, flanked on either side by Yemeni seamen wearing 'European clothing', extended along both sides of the whole procession, 'each holding the hand of his neighbour'. Clearly, safety and security during the *mawlid* procession was a real concern given the hostility that British Yemeni communities had suffered in the UK's docklands. Serjeant accompanied the procession explaining,

> as they moved slowly along they chanted 'Allawi *nashids* with an intense sincerity, watched by the English, who with curiosity and disinterested friendliness were attracted by the novelty of the bright colours in this heavily industrialised area.[34]

Once the procession had reached the *zāwiyah*, those who had marshalled it, discarded their European dress in preference for their *fawṭah* (a cotton sarong, indigenous to the Yemen, South Asia and the Far East) and their *shawāl* (a particular style of turban associated with the men of Yemen). Serjeant informs us that the *dhikr* session he witnessed comprised at least 100 adult males who formed a huge circle with Shaykh Hasan Ismail at the centre. Throughout the day he observed a number of *dhikr* sessions, recounting,

> Sometimes as many as five or six are performed on these occasions, for as it is said in the mystic language, 'Mention the name of God until they say you are mad.' Another form of *dhikr* as practised by the Mevlevis in Turkey has been described by European travellers who know the sect as, 'Dancing ['whirling'] Dervishes'.[35]

After the *dhikr* sessions Serjeant tells us that a lavish meal of mutton was served 'in Arab style as prepared in the Yemen', in which 'condiments brought from Arabia mingled richly with the perfumes with which the South Arabs anoint themselves on festival days, and my senses were gladdened with the very smell of that far country.' His attentions are then once again drawn towards the women, whom he says had been 'onlookers only at the procession, and were perhaps celebrating the feast in their own way'. However, he goes on to note that it is 'strange' that English wives seemed willing to 'so readily adopt the customs and manners of the Moslem [*sic*] women of the Yemen'.[36] He says that in the Yemen even the name of a female relation 'cannot with propriety be mentioned in the presence of other men'. Serjeant further observes that, on marriage, the majority of British wives appear to convert to Islam and that one wife had even 'learned Arabic, and, even stranger, to perform the *dhikr*', which he actually saw as an admirable achievement. He also identifies a degree of cultural displacement experienced by the majority of settler Yemeni lascars which appears to contrast starkly with their particular cultural practices in the Yemen:

> In their native land, most of the Yemenis are agriculturalists, tribesmen, speaking the common language of the country used by nobles and people alike: by contrast their English is the unpolished speech of sea-faring folk, and this gives them a strange dual personality.[37]

The prescriptive *dhikr* employed by the *ṭarīqah* has been described in some detail by Serjeant who also attended a *dhikr* gathering at the Yemeni *zāwiyah* in Cardiff during his visit in 1943.[38] At this period, the *ṭarīqah* was at its zenith with large numbers of adherents from the Yemeni communities throughout Britain. Experiencing the intense fervour of the *majlis* (ritual gathering) as their vocations and swaying increased, Serjeant observed,

> The action is so vigorous that I consider it nearly impossible for anyone to perform of his own accord. When the Sheikh perceives that the participants have had enough, he makes the dhikr stop; were he not to do so, they would continue until they dropped on the ground with exhaustion.[39]

Like Serjeant, Sydney Collins also witnessed a *majlis al-dhikr* during his fieldtrip observations amongst the South Shields Yemeni community in the 1950s. Collins noted that many of the *ṭarīqah*'s religious processions and *mawlid* celebrations were attended by Yemenis and Somalis who were not initiates of the *ṭarīqah*. As a result, they would join the celebrations and activities but would exclude themselves from the *dhikr* sessions:

> Most of the worshippers then dispersed, leaving the Sufis to continue the ritual act called by them the 'Steps'. A ring was formed around one member of the group usually the Imam, but not necessarily. They held hands, swaying their bodies from the waist in an inward and outward movement, keeping time to deep, guttural rhymic beats. The sounds developed into a crescendo as the floor creaked beneath the thumping sounds made by their feet. This continued for about five or six minutes until the participants appeared to be exhausted. The act was explained as a special expression of praise to Allah, imitating the steps leading to the deliverance of Isaac.[40]

Although the only participants of the *dhikr* were initiates of the *ṭarīqah*, Collins noted that 'visitors and non-Moslem [*sic*] friends are also welcome'. Food was often prepared and was then shared with all present as a means of both distributing the *barakah* (spiritual blessings) and proselytizing through *da'wah* ('invitation' of non-initiates to the *ṭarīqah*).

The Establishment of *Zawāyā*

In the process of explaining the specific origins of the ʿAlawī *ṭarīqah*, Serjeant offers us a single tantalizing reference to the man solely responsible for introducing this particular form of Sufism to the British Yemeni community, Shaykh Abdullah Ali al-Hakimi. Although in the brief reference Serjeant acknowledges al-Hakimi's pivotal role in bringing the *ṭarīqah* to Britain, his claim that al-Hakimi is 'from the town of Dhubḥān in Southern Yemen'[41] is erroneous. Dhubḥān is in the province of al-Ḥujariyyah, near Taʿizz. However, Serjeant must be forgiven for his unintentional mistake as it is often wrongly assumed that the majority of Yemenis in Britain originate from the former British Protectorate of Aden established in 1839, in what eventually became part of South Yemen, a separate state from North Yemen until reunification in 1990. Halliday notes that the Yemenis who came to Britain in the twentieth century were erroneously referred to as 'Adenis'.[42] In reality, of the Yemenis coming to Britain pre-1967 through the British Protectorate, only a few would have actually been 'Adenese', with most coming from the rural northern highlands around Taʿizz or the southern hinterlands of Tihāmah. The migration of Shaykh Abdullah Ali al-Hakimi, as the community's spiritual and religious leader, coincided with a major change in the shipping industry, when coal-powered steam ships were replaced by oil-fuelled vessels, and the first transformation of the British Yemeni community from all-male, transient docklands communities to an urbanized industrial workforce began. After the First World War, in which around 3000 British Yemeni sailors died in defence of Britain, the introduction of faster and more efficient oil-burning vessels saw many of the Yemenis without work. The labour intensive boilerman or 'donkeyman' duties often allocated to Yemenis, Somalis and South Asians were no longer needed, and this forced many to seek work beyond their traditional maritime employment. A large number left the seaports for the industrial heartlands, and larger communities began to form in cities like Manchester, Birmingham and Sheffield. The competition for jobs, not just at sea, had sparked off a number of race riots, and the

Yemenis, like the other South Asian and West Indian migrants, were easy visible scapegoats and targets for racism and discrimination. The influx of other migrant communities to the docklands area in Cardiff, where the Yemenis were concentrated, became known somewhat exotically as 'Tiger Bay', and the visible 'otherness' of the Yemenis has throughout their history in Britain been the irrational cause for racial violence against them. The origins of the Birmingham Yemeni community date back to the late 1920s when lascars were forced by both legal restrictions and a decline in jobs from the dock areas into the industrial heartlands. Further, when the race riots of 1919 spread throughout the port cities of Britain forcing the deportation of over 600 Yemeni lascars, many sought other means of employment away from the racism experienced in the docklands.[43] By the late 1940s the early Yemeni settlers in Birmingham, influenced by the teachings of Shaykh al-Hakimi, soon established a *zāwiyah* on Edward Road, Balsall Heath, and by the 1950s and 1960s, the community experienced a further migration of single males coming directly from the British Protectorate of Aden.

The original Shaykh of the Birmingham *zāwiyah* was Muhammad Qassim al-'Alawi, a Shamīrī tribesman who was raised in a village near Ta'izz where he spent his youth receiving a rudimentary education and raised his family's goat herd before travelling to Cardiff as a sailor in 1925 at the age of 15.[44] After sailing around the globe as a result of his commissions on merchant vessels sailing from Cardiff, he joined the local branch of the 'Alawī *ṭarīqah* and soon after travelled to Mustaghanem to meet Shaykh al-'Alawī who granted him the title of 'Shaykh', but Muhammad always preferred '*muqaddam*'. In 1941, Shaykh Hassan Ismail suggested that Shaykh Muhammad move to Birmingham as a *dā'ī* for the *ṭarīqah* among the local Yemeni community.[45] Shaykh Muhammad then established the city's first *zāwiyah* at his home in Edward Road and for almost 60 years he served his local community as a teacher, prayer leader and spiritual guide. He was seen as a father figure within the sizeable Birmingham Yemeni community. When Shaykh Muhammad passed away in 1999 aged 90, he was buried in Birmingham at the request of his family and in accordance with the expressed wishes of the Shaykh himself.[46] Amongst the many mourners at his funeral was the brother of the former president of Yemen, Ali Abdullah Salih, General Muhammad Abdullah Salih and Dr Abdullah al-Shamiri.[47]

In South Shields where Shaykh al-Hakimi first settled, the Muslim community was mostly Yemeni, numbering around 4500 and catered for largely by Arab-owned boarding houses. Shaykh al-Hakimi noticed that many Yemenis had taken English wives and a significant number of them had converted to Islam, but educational provision and religious instruction for convert wives and their 'mixed race' children was absent. In 1936, the Shaykh established Islamic studies classes and within two years the community purchased *The Hilda Arms*, a former public house, on Cuthbert Street, South Shields, converting it into the 'Zaoia Allaoia Islamia Mosque [*sic*]'. The establishment of this Islamic centre and other *zawāyā* throughout the British Yemeni communities transformed their religious identity, from one that had previously been somewhat peripheral, if not invisible, into a networked community with local religious centres and nationally coordinated activities such as the *ṭarīqah*'s religious processions and political activities of the Free Yemen Movement. After the Second World War, growing opposition to the Zaydī Imāmate rule in North Yemen was gradually spearheaded by Shaykh al-Hakimi. A failed revolt in 1948 meant that al-Hakimi became the focus of the Free Yemen Movement among the Yemeni diaspora in Britain, Europe and the United States. Al-Hakimi's prolific organizing skills, previously manifest in the establishment of a number of ʿAlawī *ṭarīqah zawāyā* throughout Britain and Europe, were now employed in the political struggle to modernize and reform the Yemen from the clutches of the tyrannical Imām. In the process, al-Hakimi tried to counter the traditional neglect of women in Islamic education, as witnessed by his efforts to teach the British convert wives of Yemeni sailors in South Shields.[48] As a result of his observations of life in Britain, Halliday asserts that al-Hakimi, 'began to stress the importance of a more open attitude to other religions and to emphasize how Muslims could learn from societies and beliefs other than their own.'[49] Just as he had mobilized the British Yemeni community towards the path of spiritual revivalism through the introduction of the *ṭarīqah* across the docklands communities, he attempted to rally the community in opposition to the Imām in North Yemen. However, al-Hakimi's efforts to educate the large number of British convert wives was not appreciated wholeheartedly by many Yemeni settlers, as Sydney Collins' published work on the post-war South Shields Yemeni community of the 1950s recalls:

> The attitude of the sheikh towards women with regard to the Moslem [*sic*] religion was a deviation from the normal pattern to which the immigrants were accustomed. Consequently, they reacted unfavourably to this departure, opposing the practice of women having a room in the Zoaia [*zāwiyah*] for their religious meetings. Ultimately, the women were deprived of this room and along with the privilege of holding their meetings, and if there were prospects of a restoration of these privileges, hopes faded with the departure of the sheikh to Cardiff. [50]

Al-Hakimi in Cardiff

Why exactly al-Hakimi left South Shields is not clear but it could have possibly been due to the growing demands for his services amongst the burgeoning Yemeni community in Cardiff as much as the setbacks he appears to have encountered with his religious reforms in South Shields. Whatever the reason, the Shaykh's arrival in Cardiff did not go unnoticed by the local press and the *Western Mail* reported that the stated reason for al-Hakimi's move to Cardiff was to 'direct a scheme for the erection of a mosque'. Presumably, this was to become the Peel Street *zāwiyah* later to become the Nur al-Islam Mosque, which during the Second World War took a direct hit from a German bomb. The incident was considered by the local Muslim community to be a 'miracle' as al-Hakimi's then deputy, Shaykh Hassan Ismail, was leading congregational prayers at the time of the bombing and although the *zāwiyah* was devastated, no one was injured as a result. The newspaper report of al-Hakimi's arrival notes that Shaykh Hassan Ismail was among those eagerly awaiting al-Hakimi, who told the journalist: 'It is my ambition to found a mosque in Cardiff, and I shall remain here, with my wife, until my ambition has been realised.' He further claimed that there were 5000 Muslims in the city and that the only place they could worship was the 'Zoaia 'Allawi Friendship Society in Bute Street'.[51] The mosque was eventually constructed, despite al-Hakimi's lengthy and intermittent absences, which included a number of visits to the Yemen where in 1943 he made contact with the Free Yemen Movement. In an effort to mobilize support for the war effort among colonial subjects, the Colonial Office agreed to fund the rebuilding of the newly-established Nur ul-Islam Mosque, Peel Street, after the German bombing in the early 1940s. The reconstructed mosque was gifted £7000 by the Colonial Office and its grand reopening in 1943 was witnessed by the distinguished academic, R. B. Serjeant.[52] In the newly-rebuilt mosque, al-Hakim, fresh from his meeting with the Free Yemen Movement in the Zaydī Imām-ruled North Yemen, immediately began the production and publication of his political anti-Imāmate propaganda. He established a fortnightly Arabic newspaper, *Al-Salam*, which is probably the first of its kind to be produced in the UK.

The printing press at Peel Street allowed al-Hakimi to take the Yemen revolt to a global diapora Yemeni community that stretched from the Far East, India, and Arabia to Western Europe and North America. Yet, he was unable to obtain the support of the majority of Yemenis from the British docklands communities. Steeped in a very traditional and conservative understanding that the Zaydī Imām was both a legitimate religious and secular leader who conformed to their cultural loyalties and Islamic ideals, they generally believed it was irreligious to criticize him. Ironically, their romanticized notions of Islamic fidelity, through their support for the Imām, ran contrary to the dire economic reasons that had forced them into exile from the Yemen in the first place.[53] Further, their reluctant migration had resulted in their disconnection from a rapidly growing opposition to the Imām back in the Yemen. Halliday has also suggested that the reforms connected with the Free Yemen Movement, were 'drawn from urban, educated sectors, different from the peasant background of the migrants'.[54] Whilst the force of the Imām's reaction to the reformers concentrated on the *al-minṭaqah al-wusṭā* ('middle region') of Yemen, the place from which the majority of British Yemenis, as Sunni Muslims, originated, it took some time for the British Yemeni community to realize the severity and brutality of the punishments and policies meted out on their fellow tribesmen by the Zaydī Imām, Ahmad. There is little doubt that al-Hakimi miscalculated the response of British Yemenis to the Free Yemen Movement and the devastating consequences upon his personal status, religious reforms and spiritual development of the community through his establishment of the 'Alawī *ṭarīqah* across the country. In the local context, Halliday has argued that al-Hakimi effectively 'cut himself off from the Cardiff community by attempting to win support for the Free Yemen Movement'.[55] And, whilst al-Hakimi proved himself to be a great spiritual teacher and prolific organizer, he was certainly not a skilful politician. He even failed to gauge the reaction of his political activities on his closest aid, Shaykh Hassan Ismail, who adamantly and consistently upheld the view that all Yemeni Muslims owed loyalty and allegiance to the Zaydī Imām and that the *'ulamā'* (religious scholars) in particular, should not concern themselves with what he considered to be political meddling. Furthermore, to al-Hakimi's detriment, Shaykh Hassan Ismail had a greater influence over the majority of the Cardiff Yemenis by virtue of the fact that he had had a longer and more consistent presence in the community. Many members had personally witnessed his 'miraculous powers' after the bombing of the Nur ul-Islam mosque during the war. However, by far the most important consideration for the majority of Cardiff Yemenis was that Shaykh Hassan Ismail was 'one of them' by virtue of the fact that he was a Shamīrī, unlike al-Hakimi, and the Shamīrīs were (and still are today) the dominant tribe in Cardiff and the UK. Hence, the overwhelming majority of Yemenis sided with Shaykh Hasan Ismail and thus allied themselves with the Zaydī Imām.

Interestingly, the non-Shamīrī Yemenis and Somalis remained

loyal to Shaykh al-Hakimi and, therefore, presumably to the Free Yemen Movement.[56] The political tensions played out within the locales of the British Yemeni communities and, at one point, Shaykh Hassan's followers actually attempted to oust al-Hakimi and his sympathizers from the Nur ul-Islam mosque. As events came to a head in February 1951, officials from the Islamic Cultural Centre (Regent's Park Mosque), London, were asked to try to settle the on-going dispute at a meeting attended by over 500 Yemenis from both sides.[57] *The Western Mail* (2 February 1951) carried an article covering the climax of the clash between the two opposing sections of the community and the final overthrow of Shaykh al-Hakimi's authority over the British Yemeni community:

> With a number of policemen inside and outside the building 500 (Moslems) [*sic*] were on their feet shouting and waving at a stormy meeting. The meeting was called in an attempt to settle a long-standing dispute which has split Moslems in Britain into two camps. In the one are the members of the Ismail Allowaia Religious Society led by Sheikh Abdullah Al Hakimi. In the other are members of the Allowaia Shadilia Sofieya [*sic*] Society led by Sheikh Hassan Ismail, Imam of Nur-el-Islam Mosque. Both societies have powerful followings in centres throughout the country, the adherents of Shiekh Ismail being the majority. The followers of Sheikh Ismail seek to install him in place of Sheikh Al Hakimi whom they allege is more interested in politics than religion. But Sheikh Al Hakimi's followers deny the allegation. They say that for certain reasons Sheikh Ismail is trying to divide Moslems in Britain – a charge which Sheikh Ismail in turn refutes. High ranking religious leaders came from London yesterday to act as arbitrators. They were a doctor of the Islamic Cultural Centre in London and a Pakistani barrister. The doctor told the meeting he had come to hear both sides of the case, and to make a decision impartially as to whether Sheikh Al Hakimi was to remain Imam. The Assistant Secretary to the Nur-el-Islam Mosque and Sheikh Al Hakimi's right-hand man, said it is impossible for the

> arbiters to hear both sides of the meeting because it had been called by Sheikh Ismail's followers without the support of the Imam's side. Consequently, the Imam was represented by only a few. Nearly half an hour of uproar followed.
>
> The meeting was brought to a close when the doctor stood up and replaced documents in his brief case. He said it was clearly impossible to reach a decision without consulting both sides and spent the rest of the afternoon talking in private to Sheikh Al Hakimi in the Mosque and Sheikh Ismail in his registered religious premises. He said that 'the position is too delicate for us to make an immediate decision and we may have to call a higher authority'. The barrister said that the dispute could be settled with a compromise if Sheikh Ismail handled the religious side of the affairs of the Mosque and Sheikh Al Hakimi carried on with the political side.[58]

Despite a series of meetings and a few physical clashes, the differences between both sides remained unresolved and instead of trying to take over al-Hakimi's mosque and political base, Shaykh Hasan instead withdrew his followers from the Nur ul-Islam mosque and established a separate *zāwiyah*, which today is represented by the purpose-built South Wales Islamic Centre, Alice Street, Butetown, Cardiff. Whereas, al-Hakimi's followers retained the name, if not the original building, of Nur al-Islam Mosque, now situated on Maria Street, Butetown, Cardiff.

As early as the 1950s, a number of Yemenis in Eccles, Greater Manchester, had associated with the *ṭarīqah* introduced by the Shaykh. They later established a *zāwiyah* at a house owned by Hassan al-Haidari, one of the earliest Yemeni migrants to Eccles, and he later became the first *imām* of the present Liverpool Road mosque. The *zāwiyah*, located at 49 Peel Street, Eccles, was also al-Haidari's home and the front room of his house was used for congregational prayers for about 20 years.[59] In 1982, a local newspaper feature referred to the *zāwiyah* stating, 'prayers were held in a room of a house but as the numbers attending public [congregational] prayers grew so people looked for a bigger place'.[60] It appears that as the community expanded the pressing need for a fully-fledged mosque and Islamic centre became a priority. Another account that also refers to the original *zāwiyah* states that, although it initially served the burgeoning community, 'still there was a need for a proper mosque'.[61] However, in addition to the genuine need of a larger and more multi-functional religious centre, there may also have been theological objections within the community to the usage of the *zāwiyah* and growing reticence to its continued use appears to have been threefold. The primary objection was related to the 'ownership' of the mosque building because, according to the Qur'ānic text, a mosque should not be ascribed to anybody or owned by a particular individual, rather it belongs to the Muslim community *per se*. The verses that form the basis for this opinion according to the commentary of Abdullah Yusuf Ali are:

> And who is more unjust than he who forbids that in places for the worship of Allah, His name should be celebrated? – whose zeal is (in fact) to ruin them? It was not fitting that such should themselves enter them except in fear. For them there is nothing but disgrace in this world, and in the world to come, an exceeding torment. (2: 114)[62]

And,

> And the places of worship are for Allah (alone): so invoke not any one along with Allah. (72: 18)[63]

Although the above-cited verses refer specifically to the prohibition of the early Muslims praying in the holy precinct at Makkah imposed on them by the pagan Arabs, the translator asserts that the inferred meaning establishes the principle of public or community 'ownership' of mosques. This is because Islamic law dictates that public places of worship must be dedicated exclusively to Allah for worship and this is a recognized canon amongst the consensus (*ijmāʿ*) of Muslim jurists.[64] This religious ruling rendered the exclusivity of the *zāwiyah*, as a building owned by Hassan al-Haideri and dedicated to the *ṭarīqah*, somewhat problematic for more orthodox Muslims. Secondly, the religious observances of the *ṭarīqah*, its ascetic leanings, influences and practices, particularly the method of *dhikr* within the *zāwiyah*, may have had a limited appeal amongst the growing community. More orthodox and conservative Muslims from the community began voicing their dislike of what they believed to be heretical practices. By this time, large numbers of Yemenis were migrating directly from the Yemen, many of whom were influenced by modern reformist movements such as the Wahhābiyyah[65] and the Salafiyyah.[66] The ultra-orthodox reformists believed that Sufism and Sufi practices are religious innovations (*bid'ah*) and are, therefore, prohibited. As a result, they were averse to offering prayers in the *zāwiyah* as a place they might associate with polytheism (*shirk*). Thirdly, the *zāwiyah* was restricted to the ground floor of a terraced house and it could not accommodate all the necessary functions of a mosque, which would include a large space for congregational prayer, a communal kitchen, adequate ablution facilities, a space for children's Qur'ān, Islamic studies and 'mother-tongue' or Arabic language teaching, washing facilities for the deceased, and living quarters for the *imām* or caretaker. The limited space of the *zāwiyah* also became impractical in a number of other ways as the community began to increase in population, diverse ethnicities and Islamic expressions.

Manifestations of Religious Identity

In terms of public manifestations of Yemeni religious identity, religious processions were held regularly through the city streets of Cardiff and South Shields on the occasions of Eid al-Fiṭr and Eid al-Aḍḥā in which Yemenis would don the apparel, not of their native Yemen, the *fawṭah, shawāl* and *jambiyyah*, but rather the adopted dress of North African Arabs and Berbers, in respect for their Algerian Grand Shaykh, Aḥmad Muṣṭafā al-'Alawī. Other processions were held to celebrate the birthdays of the Prophet Muhammad and the Grand Shaykh in which the indigenous English and Welsh convert wives and their 'mixed race' children all paraded in their oriental Islamic garb. The *mawlid* of Shaykh al-ʿAlawī was established after his death in 1934 and was most probably initially commemorated within the first year of al-Hakimi's move to Britain in 1936. Al-Hakimi's work amongst the Muslim convert spouses and progeny of Yemeni sailors was particularly developed, establishing Qur'ānic and Islamic instruction classes along with Arabic language studies for mothers and children alike. In fact, al-Hakimi published a number of Arabic books including, *al-As'ilātu wa al-Ajwibātu Bayin al-Masīḥayyatu wa al-Islām* (*Questions and Answers Concerning Christianity and Islam*), to aid Arab husbands concerning theological questions regarding Christianity and Islam that they might be asked by their wives, children or native British acquaintances. In another book, *Dīn Allāhi Wāḥid* (*The Religion of God is One*), al-Hakimi emphatically states:

> In it [his book], to the best of my knowledge, I endeavour to bring closer together the religious Moslems and Christians, and others, but as regards Religion, God's religion is one. For those of the past age and those of this present age, and on the tongues of all the Prophets, was one religion and no other.[67]

Richard Lawless' work further informs us of the importance placed on the shaykh's Sufi missionary work amongst the indigenous wives by offering the following quote,

> Before the shaykh came, we felt we were only Arab's wives, but after we felt differently. We felt better, we had our own religion and priest [*sic*] and we were proud of it.[68]

Conversely, Fred Halliday asserts that al-Hakimi faced fierce opposition to his pro-women stance from a number of Yemeni and Somali men who perhaps felt threatened by his reformist religious empowerment of their converted Muslim wives. Halliday even suggests that al-Hakimi's move from South Shields to Cardiff was precipitated by the controversy and dispute over the women being given a space to pray and hold religious activities within the recently established *zāwiyah*.[69] However, the British authorities appeared to be pleased with the Shaykh's religious activities and he was also able to forge good local political contacts in both Cardiff and South Shields. Furthermore, at the international level, he also developed close relations with senior British officials in Aden, including Sir Bernard Riley the then Governor of Aden and Tom Hickinbotham who later became the Governor of Aden in 1951.[70] In the UK, al-Hakimi was able to redress spiritually the physical abuse and discrimination that many Yemenis faced as a result of the employment struggles and unrest experienced across the maritime communities throughout the British docklands after the First World War. The claim levelled at the Arab seamen was that they were taking the jobs of white indigenous sailors by working for less pay. However, legislation introduced under the Aliens Order in 1920 had already restricted the movement of Arab sailors by enforced registration with the local port authorities and the police. Further, by the 1930s, the National Union of Seamen (NUS) was employing wholesale discrimination against the lascars, which eventually forced a punitive rota system on Arab seamen operating from the ports of Cardiff, South Shields and Hull. Effectively, the rota system limited the number of coloured and Arab seamen registering on individual vessels sailing from British ports.

In response, a number of violent demonstrations and riots between Arab and white sailors previously referred to across British ports ensued. Al-Hakimi's religious activities seemed to steer the Yemeni sailors away from radical trade unionism and communist politics, focusing instead on spiritual self-reform. This point was later publicly acknowledged by both the Police Chief Constable and Deputy Lord Mayor of Cardiff during a dinner given by Shaykh al-Hakimi in the city in July 1950. Lawless asserts that as unemployment became more acute amongst Yemeni seamen in British ports, al-Hakimi's efforts to strengthen the religious organization of the communities did not challenge the political *status quo* and, therefore, 'as far as the British authorities were concerned, the energies of the seafarers were better spent in pursuing their religious ambitions than associating with radical political movements such as the Communists.'[71] However, al-Hakimi was not himself devoid of political activism as witnessed by his fiery and outspoken criticisms of the ruling Zaydī Imām Yahya of Yemen, and, in the subsequent developing anti-Imāmate struggles, he eventually became one of the leaders of the Free Yemen Movement.

The Free Yemen Movement

His publication of *Al-Salam* printed the Free Yemen Movement's manifesto which called for political and material reforms including an end to the Yemen's isolationist policy and the building of roads, schools and hospitals across the Yemen. Although it is not certain when Shaykh al-Hakimi became involved with the Free Yemen Movement, when he visited the Yemen in the summer of 1943 travelling through the northern mountain city of Taʿizz, he was arrested and duly deported by the then Crown Prince, Ahmad, probably for his involvement with the promotion of the Free Yemen Movement throughout the diaspora Yemeni communities in Britain and Europe. Al-Hakimi eventually established a centre for his political activities based at the Nur ul-Islam Mosque at 16 Peel Street, Cardiff. He had originally established the 'Zaouia Allawi Friendship Society' from a house in Bute Street, Cardiff, that had previously been used as a small *zāwiyah* by his former deputy, Shaykh Hassan Ismail.[72] The Shaykh continued with his political activities as President of the Yemen Union by announcing the formation of the Grand Yemeni Association (GYA) in Aden, January 1946, and by publishing a book, *Daʿwat al-Aḥrār* (*A Call to Freedom*). By November of the same year al-Hakimi formed the Committee for the Defence of Yemen which pledged its support of the GYA and sent representatives to diaspora Yemeni communities in Europe, USA and Africa to:

> Set up a permanent delegation to visit Arabs and Islamic capitals so that the leaders of the Arabs and Muslims will understand the need to solve the Yemeni problem.[73]

The Committee for the Defence of Yemen continued to function for a number of years gaining support from Yemenis in Cardiff, Liverpool, South Shields and Hull. Al-Hakimi stepped up the anti-Imāmate political pressure by writing to Ernest Bevin, the then British Foreign Secretary, claiming to speak for the whole Yemeni nation via the auspices of the GYA. His letter graphically spelled out the gross atrocities committed against the Yemeni people by the Imām, stating that it was time to 'smash the bonds of tyranny and injustice which has burdened her [Yemen] for the last thirty years.'[74] Shaykh Abdullah urged the British Government to support the Aden-based GYA against the Imām, concluding that if Yemenis could not live under the rule of a democratic government then they would 'face a glorious death for the sake of justice'.[75] By December 1948, al-Hakimi he had launched his publication of *Al-Salam* from the Nur ul-Islam Mosque in Cardiff. Although produced in Britain, the majority of the magazines were posted overseas to North Africa and the Middle East, with a small number of copies smuggled into the Yemen. Al-Hakimi used *Al-Salam* to publicize an international Islamic conference held in Cardiff in 1949 and attended by delegates from 11 Muslim countries. The conference discussed key issues facing the Muslim *ummah*, which included the independence struggles of the then colonized Arab and Muslim world such as Kashmir and Palestine.[76]

In February 1948, Imām Yahya was assassinated and succeeded by his son, Ahmad, who was a fierce enemy of al-Hakimi and the Free Yemen Movement. Lawless claims that, in 1950, the new Imām found copies of *Al-Salam* placed mysteriously in his bedroom in his palace accompanied by a note pinned to his pillow simply saying, '*alayhi al-salām* ('upon him be peace'), a posthumous Islamic prayer recited over the deceased.[77] Imām Ahmad was convinced that al-Hakimi was supported and sponsored by the British Government and he rapidly set about funding a pro-Imāmate movement within the British Yemeni communities. In an effort to undermine the growing popularity of the Free Yemen Movement, Imām Ahmad struck a blow at the heart of the 'Alawī *ṭarīqah*, when he liberally funded a rival pro-Imāmate movement in the UK. In Cardiff, this pro-Imāmate movement was ironically led by another ʿAlawī *ṭarīqah* shaykh, Hassan Ismail. The Shaykh had previously been al-Hakimi's deputy for many years but both became bitter rivals in the late 1940s and early 1950s resulting in a few reported disturbances between opposing factions across the British Yemeni communities. However, the overall outcome was that the majority of British Yemenis were eventually won over to the pro-Imamate movement led by Shaykh Hassan Ismail. This move had perhaps less to do with the realpolitik of the Yemen and more to do with the transnational tribal loyalties and allegiances ever-present within the global diaspora. With most of their families and tribesmen still living in the Yemen and under the direct rule of the Imām, it would not make good political sense to offer any hostile opposition to the Imām that might result in remittances not reaching dependants and also possible reprisals against relatives back home.

4.3 *Prince Hussein, the son of the Zaydī Imām, Yaḥya, taken in the Yemen, circa 1930s.*

In May 1952, al-Hakimi closed down his *Al-Salam* publication and announced he was returning to Yemen where he intended to publish the periodical from the British Protectorate of Aden.

However, once there, the British authorities refused to permit him a licence to print the magazine. This decision was probably as a result of their unwillingness to offend the ruling Imām of North Yemen. Further, when al-Hakimi arrived in Aden in January 1953, where he was welcomed by thousands of Free Yemen Movement supporters and activists, he was arrested just a few days later and charged with smuggling arms and ammunition into Aden. The Cardiff police had apparently informed the British port officials in Aden of the alleged smuggled cargo and as a result the Shaykh was sentenced to a year's imprisonment. There is little doubt that the arms had been planted in the Shaykh's luggage, but whether that was done by the British authorities or by supporters of the Imām is difficult to substantiate. However, after a hearing at the court of appeal, al-Hakimi was released in October 1953. Thereafter, he was elected President of the Yemen Union, an Aden-based democratic political party that sought both political reunification and an end to the Imāmate. Unfortunately, within the same year, the Shaykh fell seriously ill and was eventually admitted to hospital with a kidney infection in August 1954. When I met with al-Hakimi's elderly grandsons in Sana'a in 2005, they both confirmed that they believed the Shaykh had been poisoned by an agent of the Imām whilst in hospital in 1954. No official confirmation of this claim has ever been issued but, whatever the cause, the life of a man who might perhaps have gone on to become the first president of an independent South Yemen after the withdrawal of the British in 1967 was cut short.

Al-Hakimi's Legacy

It could be argued both the purpose-built mosques that exist in the Butetown Yemeni community today remain as tributes, not to Shaykh Abdullah Ali al-Hakimi, but his pro-Zaydī Imāmate rival and one-time deputy of the 'Alawī *ṭarīqah*, Shaykh Hassan Ismail. Furthermore, while there exists only a remnant of the great missionary work established by Shaykh 'Abdullah al-Hakimi across the British Yemeni communities and the particular legacy of al-Hakimi's Sufi *daʿwah* is sadly, slowly evaporating, it is a fact that Sufism within British Islam is experiencing a renaissance as a reaction to nihilistic, extremist and violent forms of Salafiyyah and Wahhābiyyah scriptural literalism. The history of Sufi expressions of Islam in Britain however cannot be written without the inclusion of the unique emergence and spread of the 'Alawī *ṭarīqah* amongst British Yemenis. The establishment of this particular branch of Sufism is result of the vision and undertaking of one man, Shaykh Abdullah Ali al-Hakimi. His extraordinary efforts not only transformed the British Yemeni community from a disparate and invisible group of transient docklands settlers into a fully-fledged religious community that was both organized and dynamic, locally and nationally, but they also resulted in the formation of a nascent and authentic manifestation of 'British Islam' that stretched from south Wales to north-east England. The introduction of the 'Alawī *ṭarīqah* to British Yemenis also precipitated a significant identity shift from race and ethnicity in a distinctly discriminate and excluding minority context to a religious identity that was both, geographically transcontinental, linking Arabia, Africa and Europe, and spiritually universal, developing a distinctly *ummatic* sense of British Yemeni 'Muslimness'.

4.4 – A young Shaykh Saeed Hassan Ismail and Mosque Trustees survey plans for the rebuilding of the Nur al-Islam Mosque, Cardiff, after it was bombed in a German air raid during the Second World War, circa 1942.

The institutions and centres established by al-Hakimi and his followers created a tangible rootedness and cultural anchoring of a specific religious expression within the British context as the indigenous wives of Yemeni settlers were transformed as Muslim converts from peripheral non-entities into empowered individuals who were proud of their new-found faith. Equally, the progeny of such 'mixed race' marriages became the heirs to a unique and distinct form of 'Muslimness' that inculcated a sense of cultural affirmation and religious authenticity. This inspired confidence within the British Yemeni community was openly manifest in very public processions organized across Britain, marking significant Islamic festivals and events. Al-Hakimi was not simply a religious missionary and spiritual reformer, he also propagated very particular political views that sought radical reforms to the Yemen that had suffered from centuries of oppressive dictatorship under Zaydī Imāmate-rule and more recent imperial and colonial division by both Ottoman and British imperial expansionism. Al-Hakimi's political activism was less successful than his religious proselytizing and, where spiritual transformation and religious belonging instilled a unity of being and believing, the politics of revolution instead fissured and fractured the recently established sense of unity. Further, whilst al-Hakimi's politics was eventually vindicated by the overthrow of the Imām and the ousting of the British, eventually leading to reunification in 1990, he could not transcend the reality of continued tribal bonds and allegiances that pervaded the diasporic, transnational facets of 'Yemeniness'.[78]

Ultimately, it could be argued that al-Hakimi's forlorn political endeavours seriously impacted on his religious efforts, effectively ensuring the decline of the 'Alawī *ṭarīqah*'s Sufi mission across the British Yemeni community. But al-Hakimi's mistimed revolutionary politics were not the only factor in the waning of Sufism amongst British Yemenis. Theological tensions began to emerge as a new wave of post-World War Two Yemeni migrants began to settle in the UK and brought with them their puritanical and scripturally literalist expressions of Islam, akin to the Salafiyyah and Wahhābiyyah reform movements, supported and propagated by Saudi

Arabian 'petrol-dollars'. This later migration of Yemeni settlers were extremely antithetical towards all forms of *taṣawwuf* (Sufism), which they interpreted as both religiously heterodox and culturally anachronistic, charging Sufism with not only compromising *tawḥīd* (the doctrine of the unicity of God), but also for the decline and malaise of the *ummah* and the subsequent colonization of Muslim lands by European imperialism.[79]

Ironically, the last decade has witnessed a resurgence of and growing interest in Sufism across Muslim communities in Britain and the west. This is partly due to a steadily declining influence of more puritanical and literal expressions of Islam as a post-9/11 and 7/7 reaction. As a result, new generations of British and western-born Muslims are rediscovering esoteric Islamic practices through the traditional *ṭurūq* (plural of *ṭarīqah*) of Sufism. In the process, there are a growing number of adherents to the ʿAlawī *ṭarīqah* in the UK. The renaissance of traditional Sufism within British Islam has witnessed an intellectual engagement that transcends the original charismatic and cultic aspects of the more popular manifestations of earlier Sufism as observed by Shaykh Abdullah Ali al-Hakimi and his community. These neo-classical forms of Sufism are more academically robust and, as a result, an indubitable theological discourse is emerging as a potent antithesis to the seemingly discredited and defunct 'jihadi' nihilism espoused by the scripturally literalistic puritans who had unfortunately gained a small but significant number of adherents amongst the previous generation of British Muslims.

POST-WORLD WAR TWO MIGRATION, THE *MUWALLADŪN* AND SHAYKH HASSAN ISMAIL

IN THE AFTERMATH of the Second World War, Britain was forced to take stock of the cost of its defeat of Germany in terms of the social, economic and political impacts on its post-war society and, as a consequence, its ever-dwindling imperial power over its colonial dominions. Whilst victory for Britain meant freedom for Europe and Russia from the tyranny of facism under Hitler's Nazi yoke, the sheer human cost of the war, both in military and civilian terms, was counted in the tens of millions. This cavernous loss in Europe's population created a genuine and significant shortfall in the number of men available to help rebuild Britain and Europe's industrial economies. Former imperial powers like Belgium, Britain, France and Holland, had little option but to reach out to their now declining empires across Africa, Asia, Arabia and the Far East to fill the desperate labour shortage. This particular late twentieth-century migration process – single-male, transient economic migration of UK Commonwealth and colonial subjects – is the catalyst that has reshaped our ideas about 'being and belonging' in contemporary twenty-first century Britain and Europe.

For many migration observers and commentators, this phenomenon is where Muslim migration to the West begins but, in reality, the focus on this particular migration event conveniently overlooks the history of an earlier and continuous colonial migration stretching back for well over two centuries. However, what is specific and perhaps more significant about post-World War Two migration are the sociological and political factors that underpin it. In the British context, the arrival of what misleadingly appeared to be relatively high numbers of Commonwealth and post-colonial subjects, particularly marked out by their ethnic and cultural differences, was responded to in highly emotive and discriminatory language that borrowed much from a previous imperialist and orientalist placing of the subjugated and colonized 'other'. In the knee-jerk racialized narratives that plotted this new migration of former subjects into the imperial metropole, the social, economic and political necessities precipitating it were conveniently forgotten. Halliday has commented on this period of migration as:

> Overall a great uprooting of peasants from less developed countries took place; in contrast to the myths of many in the importing countries this was a process carried out above all in response to the *demand* of these countries.[1]

Post-World War Two Migration

Added to the migrations of South Asian, African, Arab and Far Eastern single men into Britain's post-war labour force were substantial numbers of migrants from the Caribbean, Cyprus, Malta, Poland, Italy and Ireland. All of these transient workers were expected to undertake the dirtiest, hardest, most dangerous and lowest-paid jobs that the indigenous, white working-classes across Britain and Europe were increasingly less willing to take on. As a result, what emerged is what has been described by Halliday as 'a new lower stratum' of the working classes across industrialized Europe that was distinctly marked by three primary features: (i) its unskilled condition; (ii) its immigration status; and (iii) its racial, ethnic and cultural differences.[2] In many ways, Yemeni migration to Britain during the same period was similar, if not typical, of this post-war migration. Similar to the South Asian economic migrants from Pakistan, India and, later, Bangladesh, Yemeni migrants were drawn to the unskilled jobs in the industrial centres of Birmingham, Sheffield and Manchester. Yemenis also settled into the same depressed and run-down urban residences of late Victorian terraced houses that still line the landscapes of many post-industrial cities up and down Britain. However, just like the lascar Yemenis who preceded them a century earlier, this 'second wave' of Yemeni migrants to Britain experienced a very similar fate.[3]

The new Yemeni migrants became 'invisible' by virtue of their comparatively fewer numbers compared with their South Asian counterparts in much the same way that the earlier Yemenis were woven into the overall descriptive of 'oriental lascars'. As if to reinforce the idea of lascar sameness, the colonial British governed the Aden Protectorate from the India Office until 1937, effectively annexing the Protectorate of Aden, established in 1839, to the geopolitics of colonial India and its people for almost 100 years. Like the lascars before them, Yemenis now became part of the generic 'Black' and 'Asian' migrant workers. Many research respondents described how they have been continuously racially abused as either a 'nigger' or a 'Paki' by white co-workers, resentful neighbours or local thugs. Employment choices for 'second wave' Yemeni migrants also appear to have been particularly limited to heavy industrial engineering or steel working. This could largely be accounted for by the smaller numbers of migrants and the subsequently limited options for employment through the process of 'chain migration'. Chain migration is described by Muhammad Anwar as:

> The movement in which prospective migrants learn of opportunities, are provided with transportation and have initial accommodation and employment arranged by means of primary social relations with previous migrants.[4]

Anwar's definition of was originally used to describe the particular migration patterns and processes identified with Pakistani male migrants to Britain in the post-war period, but the phenomenon of 'chain migration' has been replicated, almost identically, by Yemeni male migrants to Britain. Further, with the lack of any male relatives in other industrial cities and towns such as Bradford, Leeds,

Glasgow, Leicester, Nottingham and London, there is a noticeable absence of settled Yemeni communities in these locales. However, in Birmingham and Sheffield, the 'fanning movement', originally observed by Pnina Werbner amongst Pakistani-Kashmiri settlers in South Manchester,[5] of Yemeni settlers from the industrial urban areas to more leafy suburbs of these major conurbations has witnessed the relatively new phenomenon of 'satellite' communities in Sandwell (Birmingham) and Rotherham (Sheffield), with both communities established around the late 1970s and having a small population of no more than a thousand. Added to the above settlement and community formation developments is the associated notion of attachment and belonging to Britain in a longer-term context.

Halliday has focused on this particular feature of Yemeni settlement asserting that their detachment from any idea of being either permanently settled or geo-culturally fixed to the UK is something that has uniquely 'separated them off from most other immigrants for a very long time ... they were "sojourners": they did not consider that they had come to Britain to settle.'[6] There is some credence to Halliday's theory relating to a small minority of Yemenis in Britain, but it certainly cannot be applied to the majority of settlers. What Halliday has identified is a particular 'mindset' that exists amongst a few single-male, Yemeni economic migrants to the UK. He describes this group as 'sojourners', having lived in Britain in some cases as long as 30 years as virtual bachelors, leaving their wives and children 'back home' in Yemen. As such, they are happy to continue living frugally, saving the majority of their wages or sending substantial remittances to their dependents. Their strong ties with their families and tribesmen in the home country meant that they generally developed fewer links with wider British society than their peers. The established pattern for most 'sojourner' Yemenis was similar to that of most Commonwealth and post-colonial migrant workers in the immediate post-war economic boom: to come to the UK for three to five years and then return to the Yemen for an extended stay for anytime up to 12 months before returning to the UK to repeat the process. The single-male, migrant worker phenomenon has previously been observed amongst the British Yemeni communities by Dahya and Halliday, and has also featured in other British Muslim communities observed in the studies of Jeffery, Anwar, Werbner and Joly.[7]

Although single-male, migrant workers are now practically non-existent in other British Muslim communities because of changes in migration and settlement patterns, they are still present in the Yemeni communities across the country and there appear to be three major reasons for their continued presence. Firstly, many first-generation migrants to Britain refused to bring their families to the UK and a small group of now elderly Yemeni males live within the communities as virtual 'bachelors'. As a result, many have been effectively exiled by their families back in the Yemen, most of whom no longer receive financial remittances from their fathers' meager state pension and many seem unwilling to allow a virtual stranger back into their lives. Consequently, these aged exiled Yemenis live lonely and solitary lives in a country they originally considered a temporary abode. When I visited the hamlet of Wādī al-Jassar, near Hajdah in northern Yemen, I passed on a photograph of an elderly 'bachelor' Yemeni living in Eccles, Greater Manchester, to his relatives in the hope that they might take pity on their father only to discover some years later that the sojourner's family had sent money from the Yemen to pay for the return of their father to their village where he now lives out the final years of his retirement. Secondly, a number of second-generation Yemenis, some of them British-born, have travelled to the Yemen to marry and then returned to Britain, leaving their new families in the Yemen. When I asked one respondent, 'Do you think that you will bring your wife and children here from the Yemen?,' he replied,

> Yeah, yeah, I, you see, I've always, erm, I've always delayed bringing them to the UK, and getting a visa [for his Yemeni-born wife]; and my son, he's got a British passport. I've always delayed bringing them to the UK simply because you know, I feel ... I just want to really check the situation [laughs nervously] basically, because I don't feel ... I want to really want them to be fitting in well. I know my family

> [mother and sisters] and everything is here but I always tell them, you know it's different. Maybe it's me I'm a bit too protective but I always think if she goes out on her own and someone you know makes any racist remarks or ... I won't be happy about that, I won't like for her too get hurt. So, she's studying English in the Yemen now, I don't know ... I think to prepare herself to come over.[8]

The justifications given by the respondent for leaving his family in the Yemeni village in which his father and his wife were born mirror those given by first-generation migrants who also left families in the Yemen. It would appear that fears of racism, assimilation and acculturation have been completely internalized by the respondent, a Salford-born British Yemeni. Thirdly, within the community there exists a phenomenon that could be described as 'third wave migration'. This new form of migration is a development from the first-generation 'lascar migration' to British port cities and the 'second wave migration' from the docklands to the industrial cities of Birmingham, Sheffield and Manchester, observed by Halliday. Accepting Halliday's 'first' and 'second wave' migration theory in the specific context of Yemeni settlement in Britain, 'third wave' migration extends this theory to encompass a relatively new migration phenomenon beyond Halliday's observed two-wave process. The phenomenon of 'third wave migration' occurs as a result of the migration of Yemen-born children of first-generation migrants who are British nationals. In most cases 'third wave migration' only occurs after the return to the Yemen of first-generation British nationals either through retirement or voluntary repatriation. Immigration applications are made through British consulates in the Yemen and, where successful, the Yemen-born offspring then migrate to the diaspora community of their former migrant fathers. Thus 'third wave migration' results in a transnational continuum between Yemen and Britain in which the two locales both represent 'home' for British Yemenis.

Discrimination and Racism

The decline of Britain's once vast empire and the migration and subsequent settlement of large numbers of post-colonial Muslim communities occurred almost simultaneously. In the tensions that surfaced as power shifted from ex-imperial 'masters' to former colonial subjects during the post-war struggles for independence and economic migration to Britain, an increased polarization between Britain's population and its former colonized nations developed. Compounding the post-colonial liberation experience was the sizeable existence of ex-colonials in the UK, particularly when the commonly-shared perception was that the ethnic migrant workers' presence in Britain was a temporary one.[9] As we have previously observed, British imperialism brought an influx of Yemeni Muslim settler-workers to the UK in two distinct waves. The first wave witnessed a small number of 'Adenese' colonial subjects in the mid- to late nineteenth and early twentieth centuries, as lascars and dockworkers across Britain's industrial port cities. The 'second wave' came after World War Two when the British government, prompted by leading industrialists, encouraged large numbers of predominantly South Asian Commonwealth subjects, which included a significant number of 'British Adenese', still a British Protectorate until 1967, during the country's post-war economic boom. The introduction of post-colonial 'others' into post-war Britain was used to ignite racist fears of being both 'dominated' and 'overrun' by the beliefs and customs of the newly-introduced racial and ethnic minorities.[10]

Given that the largest religious grouping amongst Britain's ethnic minorities, which includes Yemenis, is Muslim it has been easy to wrongly conclude that Islam represented the biggest supposed 'threat' to the 'British way of life'. The visible manifestation of this erroneous belief is today often expressed through what is now termed as 'Islamophobia'. This perceived threat led to a series of 'race riots' in the 1950s after tensions mounted in the face of mounting racial discrimination against the new migrant worker communities. The Yemeni communities of Cardiff, Liverpool and

South Shields, once again became the targets of racial hatred. In the aftermath of the riots, political responses also became polarized, whilst the then ruling Labour government condemned the riots and opposed racial discrimination and immigration controls, the Conservatives manipulated the issue as an election manifesto 'rally cry' which eventually saw a newly-elected Conservative government introduce a Bill in 1959 to control Commonwealth immigration to Britain which became, the Commonwealth Immigration Act, 1962. This single act of legislation appeared to confirm the opinion that ethnic minorities were 'invading' the UK. It is certainly true that the 18-month period between the introduction of the Bill and it becoming law witnessed a 'beat the ban' rush of dependents migrating to Britain to join their male relatives. As a result, the Commonwealth Immigration Act became an act of law that, somewhat ironically, is singularly responsible for the significant Muslim migration, settlement and community formation in contemporary Britain.

The impacts of the post-war economic migration of colonial, Commonwealth and post-colonial males into the factories and foundries of British industry not only transformed the country's flagging economy in the immediate aftermath of the costly allied victory over Germany, but the 'blood, sweat and tears' of immigrant labourers lifted the UK's national economy to that of one of the richest in the world. In the process, this particular migration phenomenon also inextricably transformed the ethnic, religious and cultural landscapes of modern Britain. The various migration patterns of sizeable minority communities to Britain in the latter half of the twentieth century have forced a rethinking of what and who is 'British'. And, whilst politically being British has no relation to being either 'white' or 'black', historically the idea of 'Britishness', as an identity of both exclusiveness and belonging, has always been associated with race and ethnicity. Hence, the reality is that *being* British has been synonymous with being English ('white') and Christian (Protestant) and is, therefore, racially and religiously exclusive.[11] For over 60 years, academics in the social sciences have conducted a constant series of research studies that seek, in their own particular ways, to observe and explain the effects and impacts of settling migrant communities in Britain. The cumulative consequences are usually measured not only against those communities migrating, but also upon those communities to whom migration has occurred. The sheer volume of these various migration studies is clear evidence that the host society has become consumed, if not obsessed, with immigration and its unsettling impacts on an imagined and idealized 'British way of life'.

From this huge body of existing and continuously expanding field of studies, it is possible to plot both the migration, settlement and community formation narratives of particular minority communities, such as the British Yemenis, and the shifting descriptions, typologies and representations of the 'minority other' from indigenous British perspectives. K. L. Little's, *Negroes in Britain*, published in 1947, presents itself as a study of 'racial relations in English society' in the immediate post-war period. The fact that the 'Negro' and 'Moslem' communities observed were based in Cardiff, Wales, is a detail lost in Little's anthropological study, which erroneously refers to 'English' society and not, 'British' or even 'Welsh'. This misplacing of the settler, Anglo-Saxon English over the indigenous Welsh is in itself revealing of the dominant cultural and ethnic hierarchies present within mid-twentieth-century Britain. However, Little's published work gives us a fascinating insight into how the Yemeni community in Cardiff's Butetown area was seen in the 1940s. The researcher tells us that, in 1938, Cardiff had a population of 228,000 compared to that of only 1000 in 1801 and only 10,000 in 1838, a year before Britain established its Protectorate in Aden.[12] Little describes Cardiff's weather as being conducive to the 'coloured' sailors because of its 'mild climate all the year round' and, therefore, a possible reason for the seamen choosing it as their home and a part of the UK to which they keep returning regardless of which other port in Britain they are discharged.[13] But whether the imagined suitability of Cardiff's climate actually had any bearing on the physical condition of 'coloured' people or not, the reality was that Cardiff was at the time Britain's main centre of the maritime 'Tramp trade', which meant that, regardless of a sailor's race or ethnicity, by residing at the port, available resident seamen would be given preferential employment. The 'Tramp trade' also secured a longer voyage than that of a liner but was a less permanent form of employment.[14] Little's research also noted that the Arab boarding-house keepers had developed a custom of 'buying' jobs for their lodgers stating:

> Individual boarding house keepers kept closely in touch with the second engineers of steamers, who were on the lookout for many men as firemen and stokers. A job could be secured by means of a 'backhander' of two pounds to the 'second', supplied by the man requiring it.[15]

However, as noted previously, the boarding-house keepers were regulated by a series of ever-increasing regulations regarding their lodgers and Little stated that they were required to provide at least 30 cubic feet of air space for every person in their dormitories and that they could not at any time accommodate a larger number of lodgers than that authorized for each boarding house by the local authorities. Little listed 17 Arab-owned seamen's lodging houses in Cardiff in his survey undertaken in 1946, with a total capacity of 186 beds. This figure far outnumbered that of any other non-European seamen's lodging houses in the city for the same period. He further states that the Arab boarding houses had 'a very high reputation for general cleanliness' but commenting on the area in which they were located, he remarks, 'so plentiful are the dark skins in comparison with light in Loudon Square and its satellite streets that a stranger entering the district for the first time might well imagine himself in some oriental town.'[16] His reference to the Cardiff's 'Live Register – Coloured Alien Seamen' attests the overwhelming majority of 'alien' seamen whose Arab (Yemeni) presence in the city had slowly dwindled from 993 in 1934 to 209 by 1938, giving a degree of empirical evidence to support the theory that British Yemeni populations in the UK were severely reduced during the interwar period largely because of decreasing employment opportunities that resulted in a significant number of migrations back to the Yemen. Little's publication makes no secret of the squalor and dilapidation of the Butetown area after the war. He notes that both the *Western Mail* and *South Wales Echo* (8 July 1935) quoted a report by a joint committee of the British Social Hygiene Council and the British Council for the Welfare of Mercantile Marine as saying:

> Cardiff has before a social problem that cannot yet be solved. Hundreds of Arabs and other coloured seamen have settled in the city. ... They construct their own places of worship in ramshackle sheds behind their lodging houses, and they mate with the type of women who are willing to accept them because there are none of their own kind to be had. ... Morality and cleanliness are as much matters of geography as they are dependent on circumstances. The coloured men that have come to dwell in our cities are being made to adopt a standard of civilisation they cannot be expected to understand. They are not imbued with the moral codes similar to our own, and they have not assimilated our ways of life. They come into intimate contact with white women, principally those who unfortunately are of loose moral character, with the result that a half-caste population is being brought into the world.[17]

The above quote typifies the way in which colonial and Commonwealth migrants to Britain were both morally and civilizationally 'placed' within the colonial social hierarchy of imperial Britain. The residue of such embedded racial and discriminatory representations of the subjugated and colonized ethnic and racial 'other' have permeated successive generations of British society and still exist, to a much lesser degree, in current times.

Regarding the impacts of the effective 'colour bar' on Britain's post-war ethnic communities like the Yemenis, Little comments:

> in most of the larger ports [in Britain] the colour bar has operated fairly generally, and the coloured populations have been relegated to the slums, or more dilapidated quarters of the town; there has been the same difficulty in finding work for the juveniles, and shore work for the men.[18]

Little sees a distinction between the Cardiff lascar community and those of London and Liverpool and the amount of racism and discrimination the individual communities faced by stating that in both other cities immediately after the First World War 'there were severe race riots ... and subsequent discrimination against the coloured seamen was not infrequent.' He concludes that the Cardiff lascar community had suffered a greater amount of prejudice and racism because of the 'concentration of coloured families' in one small area of the town, which had led to the creation of a 'special focus of prejudice' that was only occasionally abated by rather 'sporadic attempts at amelioration'.[19] He makes reference to a contemporaneous study of the Cardiff lascar community conducted by Philip Massey in 1940, who had previously observed the distinct lack of employment and relative squalor of Butetown, stating, 'These [coloured] men have practically no hope of alternative employment; their labour was used by the local shipowners when it was needed.' Massey further observes regarding the lascar community that:

> Many of the shops are closed, others appear to be on the point of doing so, most are devoted to the sale of cigarettes and the cheapest of meals. An air of misery hangs over the whole long streets; dreariness far beyond that of the mining districts.[20]

Although Little tried to establish the actual population size of Cardiff's immediate post-war lascar community, it was quite difficult to ascertain. Citing the 1942 'Live Register' of all seamen unable to prove their British nationality, Little says that 'Arabs' accounted for 30% of the total figure with Somalis making up 20%, Africans 2%, West Indians 6%, and 'Malays, Indians, Portuguese and 'doubtful', making up the remaining 32%. However, these cursory figures could in no way be used as an accurate measure for the actual population of the Yemeni community of Cardiff at the time. When Little explored the figures for the official return of the 'Coloured Alien Seamen' taken in the year immediately preceding the Shipping (Assistance) Act, 1935, when most non-white sailors were registered under the Aliens Order, 1925, he extrapolated that 40% of the seamen of Butetown were Arabs (majority Yemeni). A clearer figure may further be gleaned from the local police estimate of around 3000 in 1938 and, added to this figure, Little estimates that around 370 'half-caste' children, the progeny of Yemeni British marriages needs to be factored in. In conclusion, Little says:

> on this broad basis, and taking into account the white wives, other dependents, and more transient inhabitants, a total in the neighbourhood of 6000 might be postulated for all the population [including Yemenis and other minority groups] covered by this study.[21]

All of the above figures would appear to indicate that Cardiff had the largest post-war Yemeni population in Britain. This fact would perhaps explain why Shaykh Abdullah Ali al-Hakimi eventually left South Shields for Cardiff. It is certainly possible that the Shaykh had realized that Cardiff's larger Yemeni community needed his guidance in order to organize and oversee its religious and social life. Little's publication not only compares the conditions of Cardiff's 'Negro' and 'Moslem' communities, but it also explores the growing population of 'Negroid', 'Anglo-Negroid' and 'half-caste' children born from the resulting 'mixed race' marriages between settling lascars and indigenous Welsh-British wives. Little's focus on this particular social phenomenon presents itself as, at best, an obsession and, at worst, as a fetish on the spectacle of 'mixed race' children:

> In the present case the average Anglo-Negroid child was medium-headed, medium-faced and medium-nosed, with black frizzy hair, and unexposed skin yellowish-white, becoming yellowish-brown on the face and the back of the hands; his size and stature was approximately the same as that of the average 'white' child with whom he was compared.[22]

Little is quick to make a clear racial distinction between the 'Anglo-Negroids' and the progeny of the Yemeni and British parents, noting:

> The Anglo-Arab cross, as seen in a small number of subjects, appeared to be rather shorter in stature and lighter in weight than the white child. Difference in skin colour is scarcely appreciable, despite certain shallowness on the part of the Arab and a lack of ruddy complexion often found in the 'English' [*sic*] child. The faces of the former are also narrower.[23]

Little's imposed anthropological notions, value judgements, ideas of physical beauty and relative racial intelligence suggests an apparent 'scientific' pretext for racism through imposed stereotyping that alludes to racist evolutionary theories that employ both phrenology (skull reading) and physiognomy (reading facial features), which reinforce ideas of racial superiority and help to maintain, justify and perpetuate discrimination, racism and ethnic 'purity'.[24] However, despite the racist connotations of Little's study, it offers us an almost unique glimpse into the population size and social conditions of Cardiff's Yemeni community in the middle of the twentieth century. It also provides us with a stark demonstration of how discrimination and racism plagued post-war British society.

The *Muwalladūn*

The earlier studies undertaken on the British Yemeni communities, particularly those of Little, Collins, Dahya and Lawless, refer to Yemeni migrants intermarrying with local women and resulting in what they generally describe as 'half-caste' children. This racial interpretation and 'placing' of second-generation Yemeni-origin children does not consider the *muwallad* definition from the Yemeni perspective, which is not a racist or derogatory term. Yemeni cultural identity in the context of the British Yemeni communities appears to be largely constructed upon ideas and notions of tribal belonging and, for most Yemenis I talked to, their tribe represents their primary cultural identity. Within the concept of tribal identity, the idea of belonging to a 'place' or a 'people' has a fixed or located centre, namely the tribal village or region and a common ancestor – *min jadd wāḥid* ('from one forefather'). Wherever a bondsman travels and regardless of how far, tribal belonging offers a specific and fixed 'place' where identity and all of its human products, artefacts, customs and traditions originate. One remains a member of the tribe by the bonds of blood and *'urf* (tribal customs) passed on from generation to generation. A respondent told me emphatically:

> This is your identity you can't ignore it. You belong to your tribe; your generation is your tribe. For thousands of years we have so many kings and so many systems, they have gone, but the tribes are still there.[25]

Notions of cultural identity based on tribal blood ties within diaspora Yemeni communities appear to transform when cross-cultural or 'mixed race' marriages occur. The offspring from mixed marriages have a unique status that is signified by the use of the term *muwallad*. Pedro Chalmeta's article offers an interesting etymological definition of the word *muwallad*, stating that it belongs to the vocabulary of stockbreeding and it refers to the 'crossing (*tawlid*) of two different animal breeds, thus a hybrid, of mixed blood.'[26] But where does this hybrid identity of the *muwalladūn* place them within the notions of 'Yemeniness'? Adnan Saif, a prominent member of the Birmingham Yemeni community, explained that:

> In mixed marriages it's a strange [situation] ... we have a lot of young people whose mums are English, Irish or Moroccan, and ... there are those who see it [Yemeni identity] as an interesting and novel thing and they really are, you know, they like to be associated with it but don't necessarily understand its [tribal] implications.[27]

Evidence shows that many early Yemeni Muslim settlers to Manchester and other British cities married local women. Conversely, the majority of South Asian Muslim migrants did not, preferring instead to remain single or to bring their wives from their country of origin. Studies on diaspora Yemeni communities suggest that cross-cultural marriages have been a common occurrence wherever Yemeni migrants have settled. Ulrike Freitag's study of Ḥaḍramī Yemeni migrations to India and the Far East observes that some emigrants who intermarried with their host societies integrated so completely that within two generations their descendants could no longer be considered as part of the diaspora Yemeni community.[28] This process of indigenization and assimilation is also present amongst a small number of second-generation *muwallad* children within the British Yemeni communities. A respondent described their seemingly forced assimilation into the wider indigenous society in quite dramatic terms:

> I'll tell you most of them had Arabic names but because their fathers had left, their mothers changed their names. Er, because I mean, I had friends who were mixed race and they told me that my name used to be 'blah, blah, blah, but my mum changed it to Tony Stephens and David Stephens.' But his sister kept her [Arabic] name, Sadia Stephens. But, she took her mother's name Stephens. But, apparently they were called Ahmed or Hussain Ahmad. And, also like some of them, who were like called Norman, probably were called Numan. So, you know, they tried to change them a bit.[29]

5.1 – British Yemeni muwalladah, *Attegar al-Hubabi, daughter of Saeed and Josephine, and her Yemeni husband, Muhammad Kasseum, circa 1940s. Note the sea-connected anchor broach on Attegar's lapel.*

Whilst a complete assimilation of some children from intermarriages is a phenomenon in most diaspora Yemeni communities, Freitag has also noted that other intermarriages appear to have been more successful in producing what she describes as 'a fairly stable community of *muwalladūn* ('mixed race' Ḥaḍramīs), which was regularly refuelled by new arrivals.'[30] Yemenis in Britain generally refer to the children of mixed marriages as *muwalladūn* (singular, *muwallad*). When I asked a respondent whether his Madagascar-born Yemeni wife was a *muwalladah* (female form of *muwallad*), he replied, '*Muwallad*? Call her? Yeah! They [are] born outside the Yemen. You could have Yemeni father and mother but if you born outside the Yemen you are *muwallad*.'[31] But when I then inquired whether he also considered his British-born son to be a *muwallad*, he said:

> He's Yemeni! [laughs] He go back home and marry. He's in the university now. My first wife was from here but no women she look after him [a Yemeni migrant] when he going old and now second wife is from the Yemen [*sic*].[32]

The respondent's reply seemed to also confirm a patriarchal bias in the determination of who is or is not a *muwallad*. However, genealogical links to the tribe are exclusively patriarchal and, therefore, as a result so are ideas about 'Yemeniness'. And, whilst my respondent's reply seemed almost contradictory, a Yemeni born in the diaspora from both Yemeni parents would be less likely to be considered a *muwallad* than a child born to a Yemeni father and an indigenous mother. Further, in the case of the particular respondent, admitting his son to his second Yemeni *muwalladah* wife might be tantamount to denying a bloodline or tribal belonging to his diaspora-born son. The respondent also appeared to have learnt from what he perceived to be the error of his ways in marrying a local non-Muslim English woman, a marriage that had resulted in two *muwallad* children and then divorce. I asked him if he thought that it was right that Yemenis should marry English wives to which he replied:

> No, no, no! You see if I myself I know she's a good Muslim and I marry her that's very nice. But, if I go to work and she's going out. I go to work and she going to the pub, what is the life? So, we are did mistake but *Allāh ya'rif, Allāh yafhama* [Allāh knows, Allāh understands]. We did wrong but we don't know, we don't know! We married, it's *ḥalāl* [permissible] but she no pray with me. When I tell my children, 'Islam that way, Islam belong to that way' and I'm going to bed she say, 'don't believe him!' My wife she tell them, 'don't believe him!' [laughs] Really, she told them that, so said you know that's enough, *khalāṣ* [finished]! Some of the kids [from mixed marriages] they gone [from the community and Islam], they gone, even they go to Yemen but later they gone. What can we say, we want our children to become good and peaceful ... *alḥamdulillāh* [praise be to God]![33]

The term *muwallad* was used historically and more broadly to describe the children of the indigenous Muslims and converts to Islam in early medieval Spain under Muslim rule (711–1492 CE). The *muwalladūn* were also known as *al-sālimūn* ('the submitters') and *al-musālimūn* ('the submitted') and they formed a large and important group amongst the Muslims of the Iberian Peninsula under Umayyad and Moorish rule.[34] Reinhart Dozy has commented on the Arab domination of Muslim-ruled Spain saying that, 'the most discontented class were the Renegades – called by the Arabs *muwalladūn*, "the adopted",' but Dozy's interpretation of the word *muwallad* conflicts with the body of linguistic and historical definitions.[35] He further claims that the *muwalladūn* were 'secret Christians' who were disgruntled because Arab domination had excluded them from lucrative posts and government offices because their sincerity to Islam was doubted. The author also claims that this apparent form of discrimination and racism by the Arab population precipitated the 'revolt of the Renegades', also referred to by Thomas Arnold and Manazir Ahsan. Ahsan claims that as the Muslim demography of Spain shifted from Arab ascendancy to indigenous Spanish Muslim rule, a 'nationalist sentiment' began to surface in which 'conflict and rivalry not only between the Arabs and Spanish Muslims, but also among the various Arab tribes inevitably arose.'[36] Ahsan's research confirms Arnold's earlier work, which details the intra-Muslim ethnic factionalism that was so intense in early Muslim Spain. By the late eighth and early ninth centuries CE, the *muwalladūn* were attempting to shake off Arab Muslim hegemony and form what Arnold describes as a 'national party of Spanish Muslims'.[37]

Ahsan has also referred to some of the incidents of *muwalladūn* rebellions in Muslim Spain as power shifted from the migrating Arab invaders to their indigenous progeny and converts to Islam.[38] Sayed Amir Ali has mentioned that marriages between Arabs and Berbers and then later between North African Muslims and Spanish converts and Christians, especially in the northern provinces, were quite common and that offspring from such unions were called *muwalladūn*. Ali defines the term as 'born in the Arab race' and attributes the Spanish word *mullato* and the French word *mulatre* as corruptions of the Arabic word *muwallad*.[39] Ali also agrees with Dozy's interpretation of Arab racism, stating that the pure-bred Arabs looked down on the *muwalladūn*. Arnold translates the word *muwallad* in the context of Muslim Spain as 'a term denoting those not of Arab blood',[40] a definition very similar to that applied by the Yemenis in Eccles and the diaspora. Linda Boxberger's study has noted that 'the *muwalladin* [*sic*] tended to assimilate to the local culture, to the consternation of their fathers.'[41] Boxberger, like Ahsan and Arnold, also records the cultural divisions between migrant Arabs and their *muwallad* descendants stating:

> The Hadhramis of the East Indies responded to the social tensions resulting from the increasing alienation of the *muwalladin* from the language and culture of their fathers by forming associations that attempted to implement new educational institutions to serve their community. [42]

This phenomenon has also been observed by Freitag who states that Yemeni offspring in Indonesia formed a federation of *muwallad* organizations known as *Indonesisch-Arabisch Verbond*, in order to further their integration and advancement into Indonesian society. She records that another organization established in 1935 and presumed to have been led by Yemeni *muwalladūn* founded an anti-usury association, the *anti-wockereijvereeniging*.[43]

Similarly in Britain, the Yemeni Community Association (YCA), based in Sandwell, West Bromwich, is headed by Salem Ahmad, a *muwallad* of Yemeni and British parentage. As with other Yemeni diaspora community organizations, the YCA shares similar concerns and objectives to those associations observed by Freitag and Boxberger. The 'mission statement' of the YCA declares that their aim is:

> To respond to the wishes and needs of the Yemeni community and other families in the Sandwell area, by providing cultural orientation, educational development and skills training for children and adults through the provision of accessible community services and activities run by the YCA.[44]

Boxberger also notes that emigrants would usually marry 'an indigenous woman or a woman from mixed blood from the Ḥaḍrami expatriate community' and that 'they considered children born in the *mahjar* [place of emigration] as Ḥaḍramī.'[45] This attitude is mirrored by the respondent from the Eccles Yemeni community who considers his British-born son to be 'Yemeni' rather than a *muwallad*. The research undertaken by Boxberger has also observed that Yemeni settlers would usually try to send their sons back to the homeland to learn the language and customs and to marry there.[46] It would appear that the Arab acculturation of *muwalladūn* was a primary concern of both Northern and Southern emigrant Yemenis and the practice of sending children back to the Yemen still exists and is widely practised within British Yemeni communities. A female research respondent from Eccles described how she was eventually received into her father's tribe whilst on her first visit to the Yemen:

> Until my father came to stay with us and they realized he was a *qābilī* [tribesman] and then the treatment changed

> overnight. Oh, then they were welcoming, they were really nice, I'd get a loaf ... the treatment changed overnight because they knew that ... I think they saw me as *muwalladah* ... I think they got ... and when they saw my dad I got the seal of approval, oh yeah![47]

Mohammad Abdul-Wali, the famous Ethiopian-born Yemeni author, was a *muwallad* whose father came from the North Yemen and mother from Ethiopia. In 1940, at the tender age of 14, he was sent to the Yemen to marry his cousin and this was his first stark encounter with the country. He later briefly became Director-General of Aviation of North Yemen but, after political quarrels with the government, he was imprisoned for some time before fleeing to Aden in South Yemen, where he was killed in 1973 in a plane crash. He produced a number of works of fiction with many stories relating to the Yemeni diaspora, often recounting his own early experiences in Ethiopia.[48] Whilst the word *muwallad* appears to be a term of exclusion, denoting those 'not completely of Arab or Yemeni blood', the application of this definition is strictly limited to ideas about cultural identity through matriarchal bloodlines and patriachial tribal bonds. Being a *muwallad,* however, is not a factor that restricts or inhibits religious identity or 'Muslimness' or national identities, such as 'Britishness' or 'Yemeniness'. For example, Shaykh Said Hassan Ismail, the late *imām* of the South Wales Islamic Centre, Cardiff, was himself a *muwallad*. The Shaykh has described himself in terms of his own self-identity, saying, 'I am a British-born Yemeni Muslim, the product of a mixed marriage.'[49] The developed hybrid sense of self-identity articulated by Shaykh Said Ismail has also been expressed by a number of *muwalladūn* research respondents from the Eccles Yemeni community, who have described their particular notions of their 'mixed race' identity:

> My mum is half-Arab and my dad is full-Arab and my mum's other half is English, but because we were brought up with my mum and her boyfriend I had a sort of like mixed English identity and didn't learn about the Arab side ... I sort of said well I'm half-Arab and half-English so I can

> come here and be Arab and then when I go home I can be English. [50]

> 'Salwa's' mum ... she was half-Yemeni, half-English. She was born and brought up in Liverpool. But, you know, very westernized, very English ... I've noticed that all the ones [*muwalladūn*] who are not fully Arabic, have got a different way of thinking as they've grown older. Because the way they've been brought up, if they were told off, their dad, you know, would say, 'Hey, we don't do that', but the mum, she can override it, you know.[51]

> To be honest with you, apart from 'Khadijah', you know our friend, apart from her, most of the other ones [*muwalladūn*] that you know had English mums and Arab dads. Their dads weren't there ... a lot of them weren't there because you know they'd disappear again, and you know you'd see them come home every five years apart from the odd one or two, and then you wouldn't see them again for God knows how long. So, they were with their mums all the time, so you know, they were brought up with their mums and their mum's family – if their mum's family accepted it [the mixed marriage].[52]

The employment of the 'half-caste' definition used by previous observers reflects their interpretations of diffusion and assimilation of the Yemeni community in Britain. Researchers who used such racial definitions have even alluded to the perception that 'mixed race' marriages reinforced fears of an emerging 'mongrel race'. But, in reality, the *muwalladūn* represent the socially integrated development of the Yemeni community and their ethnic and cultural identities in the diaspora. The Anglo-Arab experiences of the Yemeni communities in Britain, particularly those of the *muwalladūn*, represent both the transformations and the consistencies of the Yemeni migration, settlement and community formation processes. Whilst a minority of *muwalladūn* are assimilated and indigenized, the majority are able to tap into their 'Yemeniness' through a number of means: the family, the community, satellite television, visits to the Yemen and marriage to a partner from 'back home'. By engaging in the social institutions and activities of their communities, the *muwalladūn*, through the process of socialization, can move from the periphery to the centre of Yemeni community and its socially-constructed sense of 'Yemeniness' in the diaspora.

Little's earlier research into the interracial, Yemeni-British marriages and the subsequent 'mixed race' progeny alludes to the experience of the *muwalladūn* children and their many convert mothers, describing a significant number of indigenous wives and 'mixed race' children as having been 'islamized'[*sic*], although he asserts that this is manifest in many ways and differing degrees.[53] In identifying the 'mixed race' progeny of British-Yemeni marriages, Collins makes an important observation on where and how a significant number of the *muwalladūn* place themselves both within the British Yemeni community and the wider British society into which they belong:

> There is also a religious fringe represented by various types. There are some while claiming Moslem [*sic*] affiliations at the same time neglect their ritual obligations. Others do not conform to Moslem mores and are severely criticised by the community. And some members of the second generation by kinship and residential connections are designated Moslems by whites, although they do not adhere to Moslem teachings. [54]

Collins concludes that this particular 'religious fringe' contingent of the community is 'comprised mainly of British-born Moslems [*sic*] and some young immigrants, who tend to be guided by the norms and values of British society', suggesting that assimilation is an inevitable consequence of habitation for Muslims in the UK.[55] For many *muwalladūn*, their sense of Britishness was usually fostered as a result of the long absences of their Yemeni fathers at sea, leaving them under the sole influence of their local British mothers who were often unable to imbue a sense of Muslim identity in their children due to their own lack of knowledge of basic Islamic teachings. For these British-born Muslims, the use of

English as their 'mother tongue' facilitated assimilation into British society. Collins refers to a particular *muwallad* man who took his mother's maiden name rather than his father's surname in order to remove the handicap he might face if identified as being an Arab.[56]

Integration and Community Formation

In describing the geography of the late 1940s Butetown Yemeni community, Little observes that the boarding houses along Bute Street and several streets leading off it 'cater mainly for Arabs and Somalis, whose presence is another sub-congregation of the population' to that of the married seamen and their largely 'mixed race' families.[57] Little identifies a 'Moslem mosque' located on Sophia Street, which, he says, 'is an ordinary house whose rooms have been converted for religious purposes'. He informs us that the front portion is used for prayer and behind it is a 'cleansing room containing wash bowls and shower baths' where shoes are removed and clothing is changed.[58] Another room, which Little describes as being constructed rather like a 'pen', is used as a small *madrasah,* 'where young Moslem [*sic*] boys are given instruction in the Koran [Qur'ān], repeating the verses after their Somali teacher'.[59] He confirms that the community had previously 'possess[ed] its own mosque but it was destroyed by a bomb during the war' and that a temporary mosque and 'Moslem school' was established at Sophia Street, all of which were 'carried on under the auspices of a resident sheikh and a small staff of assistants'.[60] Little notes of Shaykh Abdullah Ali al-Hakimi that '[he] always wears Arab dress and is accompanied on his perambulations round the district by a small attendant, [he] acts also as an unofficial banker for his "parishioners".'[61]

The money deposited by the Yemenis, which we are told amounted to many hundreds of pounds, used to be kept in a safe in the Peel Street mosque. However, when the mosque was bombed the safe and its contents were destroyed. During the war many Yemenis were eager to volunteer for ARP (Air Raid Patrol) duties within their communities in addition to the large numbers of Yemeni volunteer sailors in the war effort and the conscription of their British-born children into the British army. Little's research noted that the Yemeni Muslim community, as compared with other faith communities, were particularly religious, stating: 'the adherents of this creed [Muslims] not only carry out the ritual and religious obligations with vastly more fervour and enthusiasm than the rest of the [Butetown] community, but are correspondingly surer both of themselves and their own way of life.'[62] This statement offers clear evidence, if any were needed, that the religious initiatives and spiritual reforms introduced by Shaykh al-Hakimi had completely transformed the Yemeni communities' sense of self-worth and religious identity. Little's published research on minority 'Negro' (Black) and 'Moslem' (Yemeni) communities in 1940s Cardiff is a valuable study of how Yemenis in Britain, as colonial and Commonwealth migrants, were viewed in post-war Britain and how the particularities of social exclusion and racial discrimination were manifest in British society in that period. Ten years later, a similar study was conducted by Sydney Collins entitled, *Coloured Minorities in Britain*, published in 1957. This book was based on Collins' ethnographic research undertaken on the 'Negro', 'Moslem' and 'Chinese' communities in South Shields.

What is perhaps most immediately noticeable with this work is just how little the situation had changed regarding how ethnic minorities were seen and observed in the decade between Little's earlier study and that of Collins'. In the introduction to his monograph, Collins notes that:

> Race relations seem to worsen in times of unemployment as during the economic depression of the nineteen thirties, and are aggravated by large influxes of immigrants, as recent racial incidents in London, Birmingham, Liverpool and elsewhere show.[63]

Clearly, Collins' work was rooted in the subsequent racial tensions that surfaced as a result of the 'race riots' that erupted across the industrial cities of Britain in the early 1950s and, like Little before him, Collins sought to find answers to the problems of racial difference by engaging in fieldwork observations among the Black, Chinese and Yemeni communities of South Shields. By exploring the social and economic conditions of particular minority communities and why their presence creates so much racial hostility, Collins provides us with an incredibly detailed 'snapshot' of the South Shields Yemeni community in 1950s Britain. His study was initially conducted between 1949 and 1951 but, the author made several later visits before finally publishing his findings. Collins' research identified that the 'Tyneside Moslem [*sic*] community has been separated not of much of its own choosing, but as a result of the policy of the municipal housing authorities; while in the Welsh town [Cardiff], Moslems like negroes [*sic*], have been separated mainly through racial discrimination of a less formal kind.'[64] The particular housing scheme Collins refers to was begun in the 1920s when the old buildings in the Holborn area of the South Shields docklands was cleared away and replaced with newer dwelling houses and factories. In the space of a century, the population of South Shields increased from 2800 in 1851, to 190,000 in 1950.[65] Collins estimated that the Muslim population of the town was placed at 850 in 1948, a figure which included the 'British wives and children of Moslems [*sic*]'.[66]

However, Collins suggested the figure at the time of his publication was more likely to be around a thousand. Of this total Muslim population figure, he asserts that more than 50% of the male Muslim population 'are Arabs [Yemenis]', and that the Pakistanis were the most recent arrivals to the town.[67] The resettlement of the Yemeni community from the redeveloped Holborn docklands area to the municipal housing complex was sold by the Town Council to a private housing Trust 'on the condition that the houses would be rented to Moslems [*sic*],'[68] which effectively perpetuated a Muslim 'enclave' within the town. And, whilst Collins alludes to the desire of the community to be housed within close proximity of each other, the local authority's policy was in effect responsible for the continued segregation of the Yemeni community in post-war South Shields. This policy was continued until the early 1980s.[69] The researcher tells us that the reaction to the separation of Muslims from the white community was varied but, 'The white wives [of Yemenis] and their children reacted unfavourably. "Look how they have put us to ourselves", a house wife remarked.'[70] Towards the front of the council housing complex, a row of houses was rented to white families only, presumably because it was commonly and erroneously considered that indigenous white tenants would take much better care of the upkeep and appearance of their homes, which opened directly on to a main thoroughfare. On 8 November 1937, reporting just after the completion of the housing project, the *South Shields Gazette* wrote:

> Whites have claimed the front street. They claim priority in choice, because they have lived there first and do not want to pass through the Arab section. Sixteen [white tenants] have signed a petition to this effect. The Arab replied, 'We don't want any trouble. Let the people who have lived at the front street stay there a long time. We want to live *peacefully* [author's italics].[71]

This overwhelming attitude towards the Town Council's housing policy preference of the white residents over the Yemeni minority is yet further evidence of the effective 'colour bar' that blighted Britain's post-war society. Identifying the embedded racism and discrimination the Yemeni community experienced, Collins illustrates the blatant stereotypical attitudes directed at them by citing a council discussion regarding the proposed housing complex subsequently erected which was published in of the *South Shields Gazette*:

> Alderman C [the author anonymized the cited councillors] referred to the proposed flats (for Moslems [*sic*]) as a devil's hole, a monstrosity and a potential cesspool of slumdon. He suggested that instead, separate houses should be built; a life in flats is bad for any people.[72]

> Councillor H was opposed to the building of flats. Too many coloured [*sic*] people should not be encouraged to live here. Councillor L supported the remarks by saying that the town should see that they do not get too many of these people.[73]

> Unless the council provides them (the Moslems [*sic*]) with specific accommodation, there is a danger of the [Yemeni] Arabs penetrating, as they have already done, in isolated cases into good-class residential areas. Members of the council are opposed to the alternative of allowing them to migrate along with displaced white slum dwellers to the new Housing Estate. Public opinion is inclined to believe that they should be kept together.[74]

Whilst describing a typical Yemeni home in South Shields, Collins noted that a number of Yemeni families displayed photographs of Shaykh Abdullah Ali al-Hakimi and 'another of the Chief Imam in Morocco',[75] possibly alluding to Shaykh Aḥmad Muṣṭafā al-'Alawī, the founder of the *ṭarīqah*.

Collins' study also confirms the continued presence of 'Arab-only' boarding houses, an important feature of the late nineteenth- and early twentieth-century docklands Yemeni communities, still actively operating in late 1950s Britain. He noted regarding the boarding houses that 'the transient or newly arriving immigrant finds accommodation at short notice. The boarders are assisted in various ways by the proprietor, who is called the master. He protects the seamen's belongings, and is entrusted with the keeping of money during the men's absences at sea.'[76] Referring to the many 'mixed raced' marriages between Yemeni settlers and their white indigenous wives, Collins appears to suggest both reluctance and reliance, in terms of their efforts to speak English and integrate into wider British society, commenting, 'The Arab has difficulty with the English language, and consequently is reticent, or shows much dependence on his wife for purposes of communication.'[77] However, dependency on their British wives to communicate with wider society was not always a negative or debilitating factor for Yemeni settlers. One boarding house 'master' from South Shields sent his wife to Scandinavia and other northern European ports to negotiate contracts with shipping companies for the supply of Yemeni crews.[78] He makes another rather strange claim by stating that 'a large number of Arabs on Tyneside are Yemenites and therefore aliens, and some of those who were born in the Colony or Protectorate of Aden do not possess birth certificates or other papers of British identity.'[79] Collins' claim is clearly an erroneous assumption, albeit a pervasive one of the period. The overwhelming perception of Yemenis in post-war Britain was both framed and understood by imperialism and colonial subjugation, which placed lascar settlers as perennial 'aliens' and 'others', firmly fixed outside the exclusive ideas of 'being and belonging' to Britain.

5.2 – Chewing qāt *in the* maqṣūrah *of the* masjid *in Wādī al-Jassar, Yemen, original home of the Kholaidi tribesmen who have settled in Eccles, Greater Manchester.*

This social reality was perhaps most clearly demonstrated during the riots immediately after the First World War when some 600 Yemeni lascars were forcefully deported from Britain in order to pacify white, indigenous sailors who claimed the lascars were taking their jobs. For the Yemeni colonial British subjects, their status as British citizens was effectively revoked by the deportations.[80] Even as late as the 1950s deportation was still imposed on the British Yemeni community and Collins notes:

> Being aliens, two contingents were deported from Tyneside after racial disturbances in the port, and on previous occasions [Yemenis] were deprived of employment on British boats, because preference was being given to [white] British subjects.[81]

In the same context, Collins noted that Arab cafés and boarding houses were frequently raided by police in search of illegal drugs and gambling groups, an activity that further alienated and increased the reticence of Yemenis to integrate actively into wider British society. Ironically, at the individual level, most settler Yemenis had successfully integrated through the process of marriage to white, indigenous wives. Collins refers to a local Welfare Officer from Tyneside, who had spent over 15 years working with the Yemeni community, who suggested the reason why many British girls become so attracted to Yemeni settlers was because of 'the latter's generosity to their women'. He also cites a local police officer as saying that his impression was that 'the [Yemeni] men are faithful husbands to their wives and children', adding that a white seaman had also remarked that he had frequently observed that when a 'coloured' [*sic*] seaman entered a port, he tried to find a shop to purchase a present for his family.[82] However, despite the relatively loving and generous nature of Yemeni males, Collins also informs us that a Welfare Officer said, 'if a white women is seen with a coloured [*sic*] child ... she is usually thought to be in an improper sort of sex life.'[83] Conversely, Collins' study of a number of British-Yemeni 'mixed-raced' marriages, testifies that home life was usually modified by customs and habits introduced by the husband, 'especially those values affecting religion, food and leisure'.[84] He observed that five daily prayers (obligatory *ṣalāh*) was either offered in the *zāwiyah* or at home and that Ramadan (the Islamic fasting month) was faithfully observed by most families who enjoyed locally-produced *ḥalāl* meat and many traditional Yemeni dishes, prepared by the British wives. In addition to prayers and fasting, children were also given religious instruction on how to recite the Qur'ān and the doctrines of Islamic faith. He further noted that:

> A more formal attempt at teaching Moslem [*sic*] children was undertaken by one of the sheikhs, who organised evening classes in the zoaia [*zāwiyah*] for this purpose, and three boys were sent to school in Aden for special training in Moslem [*sic*] religion and culture. [85]

'Muslimness' and the *Zawāyā*

Collins refers to the *muwallad* children as 'Anglo-Asiatic' and notes that despite the best efforts of their parents and community to educate them into Islamic beliefs and practices, a number of the 'mixed-race' children 'are attending dances, and some have taken to an occasional drink of alcoholic beverages, although this is prohibited [*ḥarām*] by their religion.'[86] Whilst a degree of cultural assimilation was observed amongst the *muwalladūn* of Collins' study, there can be little doubt that Shaykh al-Hakimi's efforts, through the establishment of a number of *zawāyā* across the British Yemeni communities, offered a strong sense of religious identity and cultural belonging for the overwhelming majority of Yemenis, their convert British wives and their *muwallad* progeny. In fact, Collins stated that the most remarkable feature of the Yemeni Muslim presence in Britain was 'the dominant integrating role of its religion' and specifically, the place and importance of the *zāwiyah* upon community life. He says emphatically that the *zāwiyah* is 'the central institution in the community, and its rôle may be compared with that of the Synagogue in the American Jewish community of Louis Wirth's [*The*] *Ghetto* [1946].'[87] Noting the establishment of the *ṭarīqah*'s Mutual Aid Society, Collins observed the charity operated with a particular 'religious basis [that] functions as an auxiliary of the zoaia [*zāwiyah*]' and that through the *zāwiyah* 'Moslems [*sic*] came into touch with current events effecting their lives, which makes it one of the most effective media of approach to the whole community.'[88]

During the period of Collins' initial visits and research into the Yemeni community, he notes that, 'a religious leader called a sheikh, or Imām [al-Hakimi] resides in Cardiff and is represented by a local assistant.'[89] The researcher astutely identified what he described as 'important integrative factors', uniquely present within the British Yemeni communities: (i) the basic religious beliefs and rituals observed by all immigrants who form the core of the religious institution – the *ṭarīqah*; (ii) the loyal response of the Muslim community to the leadership of the 'highly esteemed' Shaykh,

Abdullah Ali al-Hakimi, who organized the *ṭarīqah* from the 1930s to the early 1950s; and (iii) the incorporation, through marriage of the white, British convert wives and the children of these marriages, who were all included, trained and educated into the Islamic way of life.[90] In identifying these three essential facets of the British Yemeni community, Collins has succinctly analysed Shaykh al-Hakimi's phenomenal success in introducing his Islamic *da'wah* (literally, 'invitation', but understood as religious proselytizing), via the 'Alawī *ṭarīqah* to the British Yemeni community in the first half of the twentieth century. Through Collins' published study, we are able to ascertain that, as with the Cardiff Yemeni community of the 1950s, the South Shields community also established two *zawāyā* which appears to reflect the tensions that existed between the initiates who became embroiled in the differences that erupted between Shaykh al-Hakimi and his one-time confident, Shaykh Hassan Ismail over the politics of Zaydī Imāmate rule in North Yemen.

Collins tells us 'the community has two zoaias [*zawāyā*] one of which is a room set aside in a boarding house and large enough to accommodate fifty worshippers'. The other *zāwiyah*, he informs us, 'was purchased by the Moslem [*sic*] community' and was formerly *The Hilda Arms* public house, a project initiated by Shaykh al-Hakimi, which we are told 'consists of rooms set apart for religious purposes, as well as living quarters for the shaykh.'[91] The upkeep of the second *zāwiyah* was maintained from voluntary contributions made by the community and by rent collected from the tenants. Collins also notes that this *zāwiyah* contained an anteroom where the men could change their outer garments and working clothes and don a *fawṭah* (sarong) and *shawāl* (headdress) in preparation for congregational prayer, a phenomenon I have also witnessed during my fieldwork amongst the Yemeni community in Eccles, Greater Manchester, some 50 years later. Although Shaykh al-Hakimi had actually departed from the UK and subsequently died in Aden in 1954, Collins noted that the imam of the larger, second *zāwiyah* in South Shields 'is under the supervision of the sheikh in Cardiff [presumably by 1954, Shaykh Hassan Ismail], who visits Tyneside periodically.'[92]

According to Collins the duties of the imam were, 'leading the daily *rakahs* [*sic*] or prayers and the annual celebrations, officiating at funerals and weddings, visiting the sick and taking care of the zoaia [*zāwiyah*].'[93] Collins appears to have genuinely confused the 'Alawī *ṭarīqah* with the heterodox Alawite sect, stating, 'Extreme Alawis are said to believe that Ali was an incarnation of God Himself', he further claims that 'The Allawains, also known as Alawis, in the strict sense are a sub-sect of the Shia derived from the supporters of Ali, the husband of Fatimah, daughter of Mohammed [*sic*].'[94] Unfortunately, while Collins' footnoted reference to the Allawains or Alawis is correct, they are entirely different in genealogy and theology to the 'Alawī *ṭarīqah* of North Africa.[95] However, it is interesting to note that critics of the *ṭarīqah* amongst other Yemenis were on the grounds that they were 'more a political than religious group'.[96] This particular criticism would have certainly been valid later when Shaykh al-Hakimi's Free Yemen Movement was responsible for the eventual split with Shaykh Hassan Ismail and his majority Shamīrī tribesmen as the pro- Zaydī Imāmate adherents within the *ṭarīqah* – an episode curiously absent from Collins' published research.

5.3 – Shaykh Hassan Ismail officiated over the marriage of Sadia al-Hubabi and Muhammad Abdul Aziz ('George') and poses with the extended al-Hubabi family outside their large house in Liverpool, circa 1940s.

Shaykh al-Hakimi, although not mentioned by name in Collins' work, is accredited with a number of groundbreaking initiatives, such as successfully persuading the local municipal council to set aside a section of the local cemetery for the exclusive use of Muslim burials and proposing the building of a purpose-built mosque in South Shields, a project into which community members donated generously. The project was later abandoned as the scheme was considered too expensive for such a small population and was moved to Cardiff instead.[97] Collins also says that the Shaykh initiated separate rooms for men and women in the *zāwiyah* for prayers 'and as classrooms for the religious instruction of women and children' confirming, like Little's research before him, that:

> The attitude of the sheikh towards women with regards to the Moslem [*sic*] religion was a deviation from the normal pattern to which the immigrants were accustomed. Consequently, they reacted unfavourably to his departure, opposing the practice of women having a room in the zoaia [*zāwiyah*] for their religious meetings.[98]

Collins notes that eventually the classes for women and children were discontinued, the reason given was the lack of sufficient time for both classes but, Collins concludes that, 'a more likely explanation, however, would seem to be the removal of sheikh Ahmed [Abdullah Ali al-Hakimi] to Cardiff.[99] Al-Hakimi's legacy upon the British Yemeni communities created a uniting influence through religious reform and spiritual progression that transcended, if only temporarily, all cultural and sectarian divides of tribal allegiances and religious sectarianism. His educational programmes addressed the high illiteracy amongst the Yemenis. Collins' study remarks that, 'only a few Tyneside Moslems [*sic*] are able to read the Koran [Qur'ān], nevertheless, the immigrant can repeat in Arabic and from memory the prayers and verses in the ritual.'[100] Elderly members of the community often refused poor- or old-age relief from welfare charities or state organizations but instead received financial assistance from al-Hakimi's Allawaian Society and Collins states that when the Society ceased to function, after al-Hakimi's fateful return to Yemen, these aid contributions continued on a voluntary basis. Further, during the economic depression of the 1930s, several Yemeni boarding house 'masters' gave substantial loans to a number of unemployed lascars. When war was then declared, many lascars died at sea before being able to repay their debts, resulting in a few 'masters' suffering great financial loss.[101]

The Succession of Shaykh Hassan Ismail

The turning point in al-Hakimi's leadership of the British Yemeni community began soon after the Second World War, when his anti-Zaydī Imāmate stand was openly challenged by an opposing group of Shamīrī-clan Yemenis led by his own deputy imām, Shaykh Hassan Ismail. The main issue over which disagreement arose was the conflict between religious and political interests. Whilst the majority of British Yemenis were happy with the religious and spiritual reforms introduced by al-Hakimi, with the exception of his progressive educational initiatives for British convert wives and their children, they were far less reticent over his opposition to the ruling Imām in North Yemen.[102] Al-Hakimi had considerable prestige not only within his own community but also in the wider society and to some extent across parts of the Arab-Islamic region. In order to progress his political cause he employed three particular methods: (i) conferences to openly debate and pass resolutions on the political situation in North Yemen and across the Islamicate East; (ii) the use of his printing press, situated at the back of the Peel Street, Nur ul-Islam Mosque, to produce his newsletter, *Al-Salam*, and publish anti-Imamate literature such as, *Da'wat al-Aḥrār* (*Call to Freedom*); and (iii) his frequent visits to Aden and beyond as a means of strengthening his political links.[103] Al-Hakimi's political activities were not openly opposed so long as they did not clash with the interests of the British Yemeni community. However, when a number of Yemeni deportations from Britain occurred during the 'race riots' over labour disputes during the 1920s and 1930s, an increasing number of British Yemenis saw this not only as an extreme measure, but perhaps somewhat erroneously as Britain involving itself in Middle Eastern politics. The British government and its Protectorate at Aden were on friendly terms with the North Yemen, Zaydī Imāmate government and the majority of British Yemenis who were North Yemeni Shamīrī tribesmen considered that the anti-Imāmate attitude of Shaykh al-Hakimi was detrimental to the overall Yemeni community in the UK. As a result, and encouraged by Shaykh Hassan Ismail, they began to redefine the role of the Shaykh as being exclusively religious and, therefore, antithetical to particular political activities. This meant the death knell for al-Hakimi's leadership of the British Yemeni community as he was already too deeply involved and wholeheartedly committed to the overthrow of the Zaydī Imām.

5.4 – Shaykh Hassan Ismail attends an official farewell dinner as chief guest of the Mayor of Cardiff with his adopted son, Saeed Hassan Ismail, at his side in 1954.

Ultimately, after many attempts at reconciliation, Shaykh al-Hakimi was forced to give up his position and subsequently left the country for Aden in 1952. After al-Hakimi's withdrawal, the leadership of the 'Alawī *ṭarīqah* and effectively of the British Yemeni community was assumed by Shaykh Hassan Ismail. Although Ismail tried hard to consolidate the activities and organization of the *ṭarīqah* through the local *zawāyā* across the British Yemeni communities already established by al-Hakimi, his religious conservatism meant that the educational reforms aimed at British Muslim convert wives and their *muwalladūn* children initiated by al-Hakimi eventually waned. Shaykh Hassan Ismail had originally travelled to Britain in 1929 and was eventually appointed *imām* of Nur ul-Islam mosque on Peel Street, Cardiff. The miraculous event of the German bombing of the mosque when Shaykh Ismail was leading congregational prayers at the time and none of the worshippers were killed, added to the Shaykh's perceived 'spiritual prowess' among the British Yemeni community. Further, his adoption of war-orphaned British Yemeni children and his gentle and generous approach towards youngsters generally – he is fondly remembered for his kind gifts and toys given to children who completed their religious instruction and Qur'ānic examinations – meant that he was affectionately known as *aba* ('father') within his community. Despite Shaykh Ismail's best efforts in trying to unite the British Yemeni community, both the 'Alawī *ṭarīqah* and the community was effectively split into two camps, for and against the Imām. This deep-rooted rift continued to blight the community until the eventual reunification of North and South Yemen in 1991. Some time after Shaykh al-Hakimi left Britain in 1953, Shaykh Hassan Ismail was eventually recognized as the religious leader of over 20,000 Muslims in Britain. The British government was keen to be seen to reward the British Muslim community for its loyalty, particularly during the Second World War and, in acknowledging the efforts of the community, Shaykh Ismail was offered a knighthood. After receiving the official notification and invitation to the investiture, the Shaykh enquired as to the exact ceremonial procedures. He then respectfully declined the honour, saying that he could 'kneel nor bow before no-one except Allāh'.[104] On 10 January 1956, after almost 30 years of service to the British Yemeni community, Shaykh Ismail decided to perform his *ḥajj* (religious pilgrimage to Makkah) and then return to the Yemen. He was the invited by the Lord Mayor, Alderman Frank Chapman, to the City Hall, Cardiff, as the guest of honour at the Lord Mayor's banquet. The Shaykh's departure was covered by the *Daily Herald* in a feature entitled, 'Sheik [*sic*] off to Mecca, weeps as he says farewell':

> Dozens of Moslems [*sic*] were in tears as they lined up at Cardiff Railway Station yesterday to bid farewell to Sheik Hassen Ishmail [*sic*]. For 27 years he has been leader of Islamia Allaouia, the biggest Moslem religious society in Britain. He is now rejoining his wife and young son in his native Yemen and making pilgrimage to Mecca ... As he stood yesterday at the window of the Southampton-bound train with his suitcase labelled for Aden, the 55-year-old sheik told his followers: 'If Allah wills, I will come back. Cardiff has become my home. As I leave here I am crying for my love of Cardiff.' His followers were weeping too, as they lined up to kiss their leader ceremoniously on the shoulders. To the 250 Moslem children who live in Cardiff's dockland the sheik was 'Ubba' (father) – the man who brought them clothes and toys when they passed their scripture exams. Forty children were amongst those who wished him farewell. They led him to the station repeating a chant which simply meant 'God speed.' The Sheik leaves many friends outside his own community. On behalf of the City, the Lord Mayor, Alderman Frank Chapman, invited him to the City Hall to say goodbye. The new Sheik is Hassen Ishmail's 25-year-old adopted son, Said Hassen, a war orphan.[105]

Shaykh Hassan Ismail's decision to return to his family in his native Yemen meant that once again the leadership of the 'Alawī *ṭarīqah* and the British Yemeni community passed from one religious scholar to another. For Shaykh Hassan Ismail, there was only one suitable contender, Shaykh Said Hassan Ismail, the man whom he had adopted as a young war orphan and had spiritually trained at his own feet, thereafter sending him abroad to study as a traditional *imām*.

SHAYKH SAID HASSAN ISMAIL AND 'SECOND WAVE MIGRATION'

Shaykh Said Hassan Ismail

One of South Shields' proudest and most prestigious sons is the late Shaykh Said Hassan Ismail, successor *imām* and adopted son of Shaykh Hassan Ismail. Shaykh Said was born in South Shields in 1930 to a Yemeni sailor and an English Muslim convert mother of Italian extraction. At the age of nine, Shaykh Said's father was killed at sea as he was serving as a stoker on board the *SS Stanhope*, when his ship was attacked by an enemy aircraft in the Bristol Channel and sunk while shipping vital supplies to British troops.[1] Like many Yemeni sailors from British ports, the shaykh's father gave his life in the *jihād* of defending his adopted country.[2] After hearing about the young orphaned boy's plight, Shaykh Hassan Ismail came across Said while visiting South Shields on a trip from Cardiff. The Shaykh approached the young boy's mother and requested to take him back to Cardiff so that he might be taught the rudiments of the Islamic faith. After initially declining the Shaykh's offer, Said's mother eventually conceded and, in 1940, the young Said arrived in Cardiff. Shaykh Said later said, 'I was brought up in an atmosphere of praying and fasting, these things. And that is how I am today.'[3] Recollecting his childhood, Shaykh Said has said that he could not remember any instances of ethnic tension or religious discrimination during his formative years in Cardiff and that Muslims would celebrate Christmas, and the Welsh children would join in Muslim festivals, such as Eid al-Fiṭr at the end of Ramadan. The Yemeni community were happy, he said, because they were a 'minority within a minority'.[4]

He remained in Cardiff until the age of 16 when he was then taken by his adopted father to Yemen to receive his formal religious training and education, which he duly completed in 1950. The Shaykh claimed that this period spent in Yemen was vital in being able to accomplish many of his later duties, preaching and teaching in the mosque and acting as arbiter in local disputes. During his time in Yemen, the Shaykh recalls the unforgettable experience of meeting the Zaydī Imām, Ahmad whom he described as 'heavily built with great piercing eyes, holding court on cushions and carpets, surrounded by sacks of correspondence'.[5] After his time in the Yemen, Shaykh Said returned to Cardiff to assist his foster-father in serving the religious and spiritual needs of the Yemeni community. In 1956, when Shaykh Hassan decided to return permanently to Yemen directly after a planned trip for *ḥajj*, Shaykh Said took the mantle of a community *imām*. Patricia Aithie's published obituary of Shaykh Said noted:

> He was aware of the sensitivities of being from a mixed race background, wryly observing that he was often 'either too white, or too black'. British since birth, he recalled the irony of being asked, during a visit to Aden, to leave the beach at Gold Mohur 'because he was not British.' Although he declined the offer of dual nationality, he was at heart both British and Yemeni, subject to his impish proviso that 'if Yemen ever starts playing Rugby, I will have problems!' The physical fitness which Sheikh Sa'id enjoyed as a younger man and a one time boxer did not last all his life, for he was later troubled by a kidney condition which in his last years compelled him to spend several days a week on dialysis.[6]

He continued faithfully with this duty until his death in 2011 at the age of 81 and although towards the end of his life he was unable to perform his full duties as *imām*, he remained the figurehead of his community and is one of Britain's longest-serving *imāms*. Throughout the Shaykh's tenure as *imām*, the problems of Yemen played themselves out within the Cardiff Yemeni community. Shaykh Said once admitted that the Cardiff Yemenis knew more about what was happening 'on the other side of Ta'izz, than they did of Cardiff'. Welsh Yemenis were sometimes divided in their political allegiances. There were those who followed Shaykh Hassan Ismail, Shaykh Said's adoptive father, who, as a Shamīrī tribesman, supported the former Zaydī Imām, and those who followed Shaykh Abdullah Ali al-Hakimi, proponent of the Free Yemen Movement and harshly critical of the Imām and his feudal regime. Shaykh Said, however, took the view that whatever was happening in Yemen was a problem for the people there, and that 'we have to look after ourselves here in Britain.' His astute and gentle diplomacy prevailed.[7] Shaykh Said also travelled widely in the Arab world to raise money to build the new South Wales Islamic Mosque and Community Centre in Alice Street, Cardiff, completed in the early 1980s, and a project which he counted as one of the great achievements of his life.[8] The Shaykh had very forthright ideas about the role and status of an *imām* and for the majority of his working life he combined his night-shift factory work as a metalwork welder with his religious duties as an *imām* by day. He referred to his approach thus:

> I've been an Imam here since I was 25 and I have never received a penny from anybody. I have always worked. We haven't got the capability of paying anybody £200 a week or whatever ... They cannot criticise me if I am not here. I can say, 'You're not paying me.' But I am always here.[9]

It was in a spirit of devotion and self-sacrifice with which he loyally served his community for well over five decades. His length of service as a British *imām* is beaten only by Shaykh Muhammad Qassim al-'Alawī (1909–99), who served the Yemeni community at the *zāwiyah* in Birmingham from 1940 until his death in 1999. Cardiff currently hosts 12 mosques but during Shaykh Said's period as Imām at the South Wales Islamic Centre, he was the only *imām* in the city who was legally authorized to act as Registrar of Births, Deaths and Marriages, in addition to his duty as chaplain to civic leader, Paddy Kitson, the erstwhile Chair of South Glamorgan County Council. As a result of his high profile in civic life, Shaykh Said is affectionately remembered by both Muslims and non-Muslims alike as the person who 'conducted their marriages, buried their dead, taught their children how to read the Qur'ān, healed their disputes and acted as an advocate and guide.'[10] Numerous children will remember the Shaykh for his warm-hearted welcomes during the many school visits he facilitated at the Alice Street Mosque for schools and visitors from all sectors of south Wales society. All visitors were greeted by the smiling Shaykh, usually dressed in his traditional *jalabiyyah* and accompanied by his broad Geordie-Welsh accent and pleasant, informal style. Referring to the visiting school children he said, 'I have games and fun with them. I make them laugh. And you know, I try to tell them what we do, in a different way than I would tell a grown-up.'[11]

In his later years, Shaykh Said came to prominence as recognition of his role as one of Britain's longest-serving *imāms* grew. He was emphatic in stating his love for his adopted Wales and for Britain as a place in which British Yemenis and Muslims in general should strive to mix and associate with wider society, away from the exclusivist identity politics of dress, language and culture, commenting:

> Some people say you must always wear a beard, and you must always wear a turban. Why? I'm still a Muslim although I wear a collar and tie. It is best to have a beard but if you don't have one it's not making you any less Muslim. I've seen Muslims with big beards who cheat and tell lies. [12]

Shaykh Said's focus on the need to acculturate and indigenize Muslims within the wider context of British society and civic life did not entail a wish to compromise the essence of Islamic beliefs and teachings, but, rather, he sought to ground the faith and its adherents in a new socio-political and geo-cultural setting. To this end, he was keen to see the establishment of British-born and trained *imāms* who would be more than adequately equipped to serve the spiritual and social needs of their communities: 'Indigenous people who live here, were born here and who will look after our mosques in the future. We really need them.'[13] Speaking regarding the use of the English language as a primary medium for teaching and learning in Britain's mosques and Islamic centres, he said:

> Some of them [Muslim scholars] say it can't be done in any other language, only Arabic. But what is the use? I mean if people don't know what you are saying, you're missing the point. If you are speaking to me in Chinese, well I might as well go home![14]

In Rachael Morton's *One Island Many Faiths* (2000), a brief cameo of the Shaykh is featured including a wonderful photograph of him captured while conducting a *dars* (traditional Islamic studies class) in the mosque and accompanied by the following statement:

> I am a British born Yemeni Muslim the product of a mixed marriage. Recently, I lost my wife of 40 years which caused my great grief and sorrow. However, being a Muslim eased my suffering because death is an experience that every living creature has to face – as the Holy Qur'an states: 'Every one shall taste of death ... and when the term comes, neither can they delay nor can they advance it one hour.' Islam has relieved me of the burden of death and has taught me to accept it. Believing in Almighty God and preparing myself to meet Him when my term ends on this earth is at the heart of my faith. Any Muslim who spends his life obeying his Creator and shunning all evil can only relish death.[15]

On hearing of the passing of Shaykh Said, the former First Minister of the Welsh Assembly, Rhodri Morgan, said, 'His wise council at times of a crisis made him a truly significant figure in the shaping of modern Wales.'[16]

The sad demise of Shaykh Said Hassan Ismail in 2011 marked the end of an era for British Yemenis, halting the direct line in the legacy of Shaykh Abdullah Ali al-Hakimi's 'Alawī *silsilah* in British Sufism. And, although there has been a recent revival of the street parades originally organized by Shaykh al-Hakimi and continued by Shaykh Hassan Ismail and Shaykh Said Hassan, their reinstitution by the 'Alawī *ṭarīqah* in honour of the passing of Shaykh Said actually serves as a demarcation between two distinct experiences in the organic growth of the community from its perceived, long-term 'invisibility' towards an increasing sense of communal self-confidence, community development and capacity building. In this specific context, the 'quietist' position collectively assumed by the majority of British Yemenis for generations and the growing idea of being and belonging culturally to Britain by the maturing consensus of British-born progeny, had two profound and distinct affects on the British Yemeni community. Firstly, the continued relative 'invisibility' of British Yemenis had meant that their presence in the UK remained virtually unnoticed by the wider population and, as a result, the unique aspects of their religious and cultural traditions were subsumed into broader and more generic ideas of the Muslim other within British society.[17] Just as the particular 'Arabness' of Yemeni sailors was 'invisible' in the colonial lascar presence within the industrial docklands of mid to late nineteenth-century imperial Britain, only coming to the fore as a result of their exclusion from maritime employment and sailors' rest homes and seamen's missions, in the same way, the post-war post-colonial Yemeni economic migrants were perceived in wider terms of their 'Blackness', 'Asianess' and 'colouredness' keeping them 'invisible' for decades in the latter half of the twentieth century. Secondly, as a generational shift occurred across the British Yemeni communities at the turn of the twenty-first century, the emerging, maturing British-born progeny were beginning to seriously question the 'myth of return' narrative perpetuated by preceding generations of sojourner Yemenis in Britain.[18] Searle asserts that Yemeni migrants in particular, 'doggedly held on to their myth – or what turned out to be a non-myth for three-quarters of the emigrant population – of return.'[19] This generational shift marked the cultural arrival, yet continued presence, of Britain's oldest Muslim community in the UK, serving as a wake-up call for a particular generation in terms of their sense of belonging, as Britons with their own distinctive religion, culture and traditions. In a very real sense, the idea of 'Britishness' in the specific British Yemeni context was visibly marked by a number of particular events and characters outlined in this publication. Searle notes that this generational shift is largely due to the fact that the younger generations of Yemenis had experienced state education in the UK.[20] The emergence of powerful and influential role models in the British Yemeni historical narrative provide much-needed cultural anchorage to developing claims of 'Britishness' in the minority community context. As a result of the newly negotiated identity constructions around what it means to be both Yemeni and British, the new generation of growing British Yemenis began to turn their attentions towards building and developing their various communities, already firmly established across a number of cities in Britain. The cumulative effects have ultimately been a wider growing awareness and facilitation of British Yemeni communities in the UK.

By 1965, Badr Ud-Din Dahya estimated that the migrant Yemeni Arab population of the United Kingdom was around 12,000.[21] He further claimed that the Arab migration to Britain began with the First World War, when Yemenis worked as stokers on British merchant vessels. Ally, referred to earlier, says that during the Second World War many Yemenis were also employed in the munitions and chemical factories in Manchester.[22] Muhammad Akram Khan further records that by the early 1940s the established Yemeni communities of Cardiff and South Shields were slowly 'settling in Manchester and Liverpool',[23] trickling from their traditional docklands settlements to other industrial cities in Britain. Humayun Ansari has described the early docklands communities as 'close-knit and relatively self-contained' but usually divided internally becoming 'urban villages' and 'interacting with the broader society surrounding them in a selective fashion'.[24] In terms of the settlement and formation of the Yemeni community in Manchester, it is a fact that the docks brought many Yemeni sailors to the area either directly from the British Protectorate of Aden or, from one of the already established Yemeni communities in Britain.

6.1 – Fadil Muhsin Sharker, a 'second wave' Yemeni migrant to Britain at work in a Sheffield steel works, circa 1970s.

Halliday notes that the Yemenis who came to Britain in the twentieth century were erroneously referred to as 'Adenis'.[25] In reality, of the Yemenis coming to Britain before 1967 through the British Protectorate of Aden, only a very small number would actually have been of Aden origin, with most coming from the rural northern highlands around Ta'izz or the southern hinterlands of Tihāmah. Dahya's study, conducted between 1950 and 1960, observed Yemeni male migrant settlement to Birmingham as a post-World War Two phenomenon. He asserts that of the estimated 12,000 Yemenis settled in the UK during the period that 10,000 actually came from Imāmate-ruled North Yemen, with the remaining 2000 coming from the British Protectorate of Aden. His study acknowledges that the traditional allegiances to tribal belonging (*qabā'il*) were extremely important to Yemenis, not just within the social context of their place of origin, the highlands around Ta'izz, but also within the social order of diapora migrant workers in Britain's industrial centres.[26] He noted that the population of the Yemen is divided into three main religious sects: (i) the Zaydīs, although a numerical minority, at the time of his initial research, the most dominant sect who ruled large parts of Yemen until their overthrow in 1962; (ii) the Shāfi'īs, the majority sect who belong to the Sunni majority tradition of Islam and inhabit the southern highlands and coastal hinterlands; and (iii) the western Ismāʿīlīs who are to be distinguished from the eastern (Nizārī) Ismāʿīlīs.[27] He rightly states that, culturally, Yemeni society is then further divided into broader categories of the *sayyid* (*al-sādah*) and the *qabā'il* (tribes), the *sayyid* claiming ancestry directly to the Prophet Muhammad through the bloodline of ʿAlī ibn Abī Ṭālib, the Prophet's cousin and son-in-law and Fāṭimah, the Prophet's daughter and ʿAlī's wife. Whilst Dahya correctly identifies the important social groupings of both *al-sādah* and the *qabā'il*, he neglects to include the *mashā'ikh* (religious scholars or, *imāms*), who also constitute a social group who command a degree of respect in terms of social hierarchy that places them between the *qabā'il* and *al-sādah*.

THE *SAYYIDS*, *MASHĀ'IKH* AND *QABĀ'IL*

In the Yemen, the social group of the *mashā'ikh* is extended to include both traditional scholars of religion and the families and descendants of renowned scholars who may be male or female. The families are usually associated as keepers of the tomb of a particular religious scholar and/or a shaykh of a Sufi *ṭarīqah*. The *mashā'ikh* also incorporates the tribal leader, to which the historical definition originally applies, as one who advocates and presides over tribal disputes and being acquainted with the *ʿurf* (tribal custom).[28] Linda Boxberger's study of Ḥaḍramī Yemenis has meticulously mapped out identity subgroups within the social hierarchy of traditional Yemeni society. Whilst the group categories she identifies have been somewhat attenuated, due to social reform during the influence of the socialist and Marxist government eras, she asserts that the historical processes of socialization within a particular cultural context are, 'imbued with meanings that have been routinised and reproduced in time and space'.[29] And, although Boxberger prefers to consider the social system as a 'matrix or web' rather than a hierarchy, she has identified the *sayyid* as the most prestigious of all identity groups in the hierarchical ordering of Yemeni society. The *sayyid* are closely followed by the shaykhs and she observes, although the *sayyid* claim superior position, the shaykhs maintained their status as religious specialists.[30] In fact, during the social reforms of the twentieth century, Boxberger notes that the *mashā'ikh* were involved on both sides of the debate, with some advocating Islamic modernist reforms whilst others took a conservative stance insisting on the preservation of particular cultural and religious traditions. However, the hierarchical relationship between different identity groups, particularly both the *sayyid*s and the *mashā'ikh* and that of the *qabā'il, musākinūn* and *ḥaḍar* ('tribesmen', 'settled tribes' and 'townspeople') is reciprocal. The Prophet's descendants and religious scholars both enjoy a privileged and prestigious position in Yemeni society, which appears to be religiously vicarious, a sort of piety by proxy, invested in the higher social strata by those of other identity groups. This is because, as Boxberger observes, 'neither men nor women of this group participated in religious education beyond learning the fundamentals of belief and practice.'[31] Acquiring elementary religious knowledge is often considered less important than learning the skills and knowledge of a particular craft or trade which, until very recently, was traditionally learnt on the job. However, each tribe is historically linked to a particular *sādah* or shaykh who they respect and refer to as a religious authority. To compensate for their lack of formal religious education and as a show of piety, prosperous men and women of the settled tribes often bequeathed large sums of money to *awqāf* (endowment charities) or Qur'ān schools.[32] Clearly, historically and culturally, there is an authority invested in the religious scholars that appears to have been reparticularized in the British Yemeni community context and was manifest in the loyalty and allegiance offered to Shaykh Abdullah Ali al-Hakimi and the introduction to the community of the 'Alawī *ṭarīqah*, a Sufi sect unknown at that time in the Yemen, but adopted wholesale by the overwhelming majority of Yemenis in the interwar period in the UK. In this specific case, the hierarchical relationship with the *mashā'ikh* and the prestige and social status afforded to religious scholars in Yemeni society ensured that the unchallenged religious authority remains with the *imām* as an implicit and imbued cultural practice even, it appears, in the diaspora.

6.2 – Shaykh Muhammad Qassim al-Alawi, who before his death in 1999 was Britain's longest-serving imām, *makes his supplications* (du'ā') *outside the* zāwiyah *he established at Balsall Heath, Birmingham, in the 1940s.*

Dahya, like Lawless, Dresch and Halliday after him, identified the important role of the *qabā'il* in traditional Yemeni village life as a primary facet of religio-cultural social order, commenting:

> Each tribe has its own customs, traditions and myths of origin and descent; it has its own tribal or customary law (*'urf*) and courts in addition to *sharī'a* (religious law) of the School [*madhhab*] to which its members belong.[33]

The tribal attachment and affinity described in Dahya's study is important in locating and explaining a specific form of migration both in the Yemeni context and the wider phenomenon of post-colonial and Commonwealth single-male economic migration to Britain after the Second World War. This particular form of migration was later termed 'chain migration',[34] but Dahya described the process thus:

> The migrant comes to Britain partly with the help of his father and the latter's kinsmen and partly with the help of a sponsor in Britain who may be an agnatic [related by descent or common male ancestry], an affine [promise or someone on oath], a cognate [blood relative] or a neighbour's son.[35]

The embedded social ties and reciprocal responsibilities ensured a subtantial supply of manual labour for the foundries and factories of British industry. Camilla Fawzi El-Solh has described the 1960s as an important turning point in the history of Arab migration to Britain, both in terms of the increasing diversity and numbers of national and 'class' origins migrating from the Middle East. She comments, 'The post war economic boom and the ensuing labour shortages led to Britain's active recruitment of migrant labour.'[36] The Yemeni workers studied in Dahya's writings were almost exclusively employed as labourers and unskilled workers, with a few employed in semi-skilled grinders and polishers jobs. Dahya claims that the Yemenis were employed in not more than 30 places in total and that a migrant normally obtained a job through his family and tribal connections, noting that 'it is common for groups of kinsmen and villagers to work for one employer.'[37]

Dahya also traced the 'inward migration' of Yemenis from the pre-World War Two port settlements, which occurred because 'as seamen they had lost considerable time waiting to "sign on" on vessels at various seaports and so decided to switch over to employment in industry ashore.'[38] The economic 'push and pull' factors referred to by Halliday that forced further migration from the Yemen in the latter part of the twentieth century has been explained by El-Solh in the distinct context of 'chain migration' through which, she asserts, the demand for labour encouraged more Yemenis to join their 'kith and kin' in Britain: 'Eventually this led to the emergence of additional Yemeni and Somali communities in manufacturing centres such as Sheffield.'[39] 'Many of these earlier migrants,' Dayha states, 'settled down, married locally and formed communities at places like Liverpool, Manchester, South Shields, Hull, Cardiff and London.'[40] He estimated that there were around 1200 Yemenis in Birmingham at the time of his research and that only 400 or so were actually 'Adenese', whilst the remaining 800 were from [north] 'Yemen', with about 5% of the community comprising of *sayyids*. The overwhelming majority originated from Shāfi'ī peasant villages and their ages ranged between 23 and 45 years old, with the majority under the age of 30. He claims that most of the older men in their forties 'had previously worked as seamen and include some of those who were among the first to move to the city'.[41] Dahya further claims that the apparent introversion that most Yemenis are said to manifest, and described by Halliday as 'invisibility', is largely due to the fact that 'their villages of origin are isolated because of physical barriers and rudimentary forms of communication.'[42] He located between 80 to 85 houses owned by Yemenis and scattered across a two-mile area of the city. The houses often acted as official boarding houses or as 'group shares' comprised of tribesmen and relatives. Ten of the houses were owned by *sayyids* and whilst *sayyids* would work side-by-side with *qabā'il*, sometimes even working in subordinate positions, it is rare for *sayyids* and *qabā'il* to reside in the same house:

> A *Seyyid* [*sic*] house usually has a group consisting of a *Seyyid*, his affine (who may be a *qaba'il*) and the latter's kinsmen, in addition to other groups comprising members of lineages from the same village as the *Seyyids*.[43]

The Making of the Urban Village

The acquisition of houses for Yemeni settlers was usually facilitated through informal loans collected from a number of Yemeni migrants and entrusted to a single Yemeni to purchase a house. This process was then repeated to enable others to become home owners. Dahya cites a particular example where a Yemeni landlord, who had been in the UK since 1954, was given £800 as a deposit to buy a 'fairly large house'. He notes that no documents were signed and no interest charged on the loan in accordance with Islam's prohibition of *ribā* (interest) but, however, 'When the house was ready for occupation, the whole village group moved in.'[44] For those still living as single males, either collectively in a shared house or a boarding house, the domestic needs of the migrants seems to have been a well-ordered affair with mealtimes being communal events and household needs attended to in a voluntary but structured way. To this end, Dahya observed that 'a member of the household group is made responsible for collecting rent and grocery bills from his group and he deals directly with the landlord, the grocer and the butcher.'[45] Not only did the shared houses and boarding houses preserve and maintain *qabā'ilī* relations, but they were spaces where Yemenis could relax and converse in their Arabic *lahjah* (dialect), wear their traditional dress – *fawṭah, jalabiyyah* and *shawāl* – and eat their traditional dishes: *asīd, salṭah* and *bint al-saḥan*. They could also extend their traditional hospitality to guests and visitors, offer their obligatory daily worship – *ṣalāh, sawm* and *qirā'at al-Qur'ān* – and commemorate religious festivals and festivities, such as Eid al-Aḍḥā, Eid al-Fiṭr and *mawlid*.[46]

Dahya asserts that this microcosmic cultural and religious environment exposed many Yemenis to aspects of cultural, religious and ritual observances that they may not have had access to as peasants arduously toiling the land in their remote villages in the Yemen. 'Thus,' he comments, 'in a strange land many migrants are learning about their religious beliefs and traditions for the first time in their lives.'[47] His research suggests that for Yemeni migrants, religion has become an important cultural signifier that imbues existential meaning into all their menial daily activities and mundane tasks – as a protection against *shayṭān* (Satan) leading them astray from their religion and culture in a non-Muslim country. He considered that for the Yemeni settlers he observed, their religion appeared to have 'embraced the whole of life and nothing can be considered apart from religion; it enters all aspects of their lives and not just one element besides.'[48] Capturing the experience of the lodging and boarding house phenomenon that had existed for well over a century among the British Yemeni community, Dayha remarks:

> When we look at the Yemeni migrant household, we find that an individual interacts with his fellows in a wide number of contexts. He shares with them his roles as a Kinsman, fellow villager, tenant, co-worker, as a member of the congregation and of the domestic sub-group.[49]

Halliday confirms Dahya's original findings regarding the habitation of Yemeni settlers in the larger communities of immigrants in some of Britain's bigger cities by the 1960s and 1970s.[50] He makes specific reference to the Balsall Heath and Small Heath areas of Birmingham, the Attercliffe and Burngrove areas of Sheffield,

Eastwood in Rotherham and Eccles in Greater Manchester. By the 1970s, it appears that most Yemeni settlers in the inner city areas across the UK were living in late Victorian, red-brick terraced houses. This reality is contrasted with the continued seaport communities of Cardiff (Butetown) and South Shields (Laygate), where the city councils replaced the run-down early Victorian dwellings with new council house schemes specifically designed with the local Yemeni residents in mind.[51] Intrinsically linked to the developing industrial communities were the Arab cafés, which provided the same service and function as they had previously in the original seaport communities – as *de facto* community centres. As recreational and social institutions, the cafés were places in which Yemenis could congregate in a culturally familiar and religiously conducive environment. Halliday notes that 'in these cafés there was Yemeni music on the jukebox, Yemeni food and bread: dishes such as *asīd* (stewed lamb) and *ḥilbah* (a kind of sweet dough) [*sic*].'[52]

However, whilst Halliday describes the amenities of the cafés with a degree of accuracy, *asīd* is actually a sweet dough meal and *ḥilbah* is fenegreek. The settlement clusters of the Yemenis into the inner city areas of Britain reflected a broader tribal identification and national belonging. In Birmingham, most North Yemenis tended to reside in Balsall Heath, and immigrants from the British Protectorate, becoming South Yemen after independence in 1967, settled in Small Heath. These settlement patterns were more to do with the habitation of single kinsmen in a particular area which then precipitated other kinsmen and their families moving to the same place than any hostilities between the then North and South Yemen.[53] Halliday's study discovered that 'in one street [in Balsall Heath] there were eight Yemeni houses, all inhabited by the people from the Ta'izz area, and, a rare occurrence, even the shop on the corner was run by a Ta'izzi.'[54] By the 1970s, there was a degree of consolidation amongst the newly-settled inner city Yemeni communities and most experienced relative economic stability as a direct result of Britain's industrial and manufacturing boom of the 1960s. Halliday noted that 'after the initial years of hardship and confusion, most Yemenis had by the mid-1970s achieved a settled if difficult level of existence.'[55] However, by far the most important observation of Halliday's study is the distinct absence of any visible presence of Yemeni migrant women amongst the settling British Yemeni communities until the late 1970s. The given reason for this reality was firstly, the distinctive character of Yemeni migration to Britain which, although stretching back to the mid-1800s, was always considered, at least by the Yemenis themselves, to be on a temporary basis.[56] Secondly, for the early lascars in nineteenth-century imperial Britain, their life was a shifting and constantly transient existence, with many sailors without families or responsibilities back in the Yemen. Hence, a large number of Yemeni lascars married either Welsh or English wives.

6.3 – Josephine Hassan al-Hubabi with her daughters, Attegar and Sadia, during one of their many visits to the Yemen in the 1950s.

With the 'second wave' migration experienced towards the end of the interwar period of the twentieth century when settled Yemenis moved from their traditional maritime employment, away from the British ports into the inland industrial cities with their families, they were joined at the outbreak of the Second World War by single-male economic migrants directly from the Yemen. Practically until the 1980s, Halliday asserts:

> There was, and is [at the time of his research], little migration of peasant women from North and South Yemen to other countries, whether other countries in the Arab world and beyond.[57]

In addition to the dictating socio-economic 'push and pull' factors which sanctioned the flow of labour migration to Britain after World War Two, Halliday maintained that there were also 'very strong pressures' within the village communities in the Yemen for the women not to migrate. He states that this was because dependent relatives believed that once the women and children joined their husbands and fathers in the UK, they would loose the much-needed benefit of the remittances sent by single-male workers. In addition to this, in British-ruled South Yemen, it was government policy to prevent female dependents and their children from migrating to Britain and abroad in an effort to stop a reduction in the flow of foreign currency into the country and loosen ties between the migrant and the home community until the early 1980s, almost 20 years after independence from British colonial rule.[58] As a result, the developed temporary character of Yemeni migration created an imposing precondition on migrants framed by a strong economic dependence that both formally and informally prohibited workers from bringing their wives and families to Britain.[59]

The Diaspora and Yemen

In the modern period, the Yemen has been a poor country and, according to UN statistics, it is considered to be one of the least developed countries in the world. It has relied heavily on the remittances from Yemenis working abroad, so much so, according to Dresch, that emigrant money transferred back home often saved the government from financial collapse.[60] In the 1980s, the *per capita* income of the combined former Yemens was still below $300 per annum.[61] The North Yemeni economy, after the ravages of the oppressive Zaydī Imāmate rule, became heavily reliant on the remittances of emigrant workers.[62] Previously, at the start of the Second

World War, three factors had further boosted migrations from the Yemen: (i) the development of the port of Aden as a major British military and naval base and oil refinery; (ii) the rising demand for an increased labour force, not just in Britain, but throughout Europe and the US; and (iii) the desperate and deteriorating economic conditions amongst the northern Shāfiʿīs at the hands of the Zaydī Imām, particularly in the wake of a failed leadership coup in 1948.[63] As a result of the British Merchant Navy policy of employing crews from the same tribal groupings, often numbering up to 16 on some ships, Yemeni rural tribesmen became global travellers and pioneers of early Yemeni communities throughout numerous American, European and British port cities.[64] For Halliday, Yemeni migration to Britain reflects two larger trends of both Arab migrations in general and the large-scale modern migration to Britain.[65] He asserts that:

> All labour migration, like inflation, is a mixture of 'push' and 'pull' factors, of both supply and demand; and beyond that the absolute fact of poverty it is possible to identify certain specific 'push' and 'pull' elements.[66]

The process of emigration from the northern highlands in recent times has had a devastating effect on the traditional rural village society. Agriculture has declined, except for the increased production of *qāt*, which is particularly cultivated on the lands of emigrant tribesmen.[67] Migration divides families, and simply due to economic pressures single-male migrants live miserable and melancholic lives separated from their wives and children in forced economic exile for years. The theme of exile has been frequently explored by many Yemeni poets and writers including the *muwallad* author, Mohammad Abdul-Wali, who has explored issues relating to the Yemeni diaspora in his translated novella, *They Die Strangers*.[68] The firstborn sons of rural village communities tended not to migrate and instead the second or third sons, who perhaps in more buoyant economic times may have inherited land, left the village in search of a better future for themselves and their dependants.[69]

In Paul Dresch's fieldwork study undertaken in the early 1980s on male employment in Bayt Ḥusayn, a northern Yemeni village, he discovered that out of a total of 147 males employed in various professions from agricultural to military service, 27 of them were emigrants. This represented 18% of the male workforce of Bayt Ḥusayn. Dresch explains further that this figure is actually lower in comparison to some more northerly tribal areas.[70] Halliday raises an important question in relation to the real and long-term benefits to the Yemen of the inward flow of capital from migrant workers, asking, 'how far [do] the remittances enable their country to redress the imbalance between itself and the countries which absorb its labour?'[71] The reality is that those villages largely dependant on emigrant economic support suffer even greater deprivation when remittances decline or cease due to the employment circumstances of their relatives abroad. From an estimated number of 1.235 million globally-dispersed Yemeni emigrant workers in 1975, it was calculated that each sent home roughly $1 a day.[72] Both the northern and southern regions of the Yemen have experienced emigration for centuries and merchants from the Ḥaḍramawt have established communities across the Indian Ocean and the Hijaz region of modern Saudi Arabia. Recent migrations, from the mid-nineteenth century onwards, have witnessed a two-wave migration pattern; the first wave witnessed large numbers of emigrants from the North, travelling through Aden on ships to work in America, Europe and Britain. The second has resulted because of the oil boom elsewhere in the Arabian Peninsula, which has seen almost one million Yemenis working throughout Saudi Arabia and the Gulf states.[73]

While Halliday notes that by the 1970s there were second- and third-generation *muwalladūn* children of Yemeni-Welsh or Yemeni-English heritage across the docklands communities, the post-World War Two migrants did not really bring their families from the Yemen until the 1980s.[74] For the few Yemeni women who had found their way to Britain before this period, whether by joining their seafaring husbands in Cardiff or South Shields or migrating to the industrial sprawls of urban Britain with their husbands after the war, their lives were less integrated into the wider society than their male spouses who could at least interact at work or socialize in the Arab cafés or burgeoning mosques. For traditional Yemeni women, even the weekly household shopping was conducted by the males and so life in Britain was quite often lonely and somewhat isolated. Halliday's study undertaken in the 1980s found that the situation for many Yemeni women, in general was bleak and restrictive with very few outlets for women and girls to either socialize or engage in community and educational activities that appeared to be available to Yemeni men and boys. He concluded, rather pessimistically 'in the community's spontaneous interaction with British society and its initial organizational activities women did not apparently find any means of escaping – from the double restrictions of Yemeni society and of an entrapped condition within the alien, industrial, Britain.'[75] But adjusting to new sociocultural conditions from a traditionally religious and conservative patriarchal society in the villages of North Yemen to a modern, liberal and secular democratic society of industrial post-war Britain would require a large degree of skilful cultural reorientation on the part of the Yemeni settlers. El-Solh also claims that the increasingly restrictive immigration rules by the late 1960s and early 1970s encouraged many Arab migrants to bring their families over to Britain 'thus transforming what was originally intended as a temporary migration into a long-term settlement'.[76]

6.4 – Officials and trustees of the mosque pose with the Yemeni Ambassador to the UK during an official visit to the Nur al-Islam Mosque, circa 1970s.

For the male emigrants who decided not to bring their wives and families to the UK from the new post-Imāmate North Yemen, their financial difficulties stemmed from the fact that despite having wives and children back in Yemen, who relied solely on the remittances from their emigrant husbands and fathers, they were taxed in the UK as single males. And, although they could apply for tax rebates on all dependant children under the age of 16, the UK tax authorities often demanded forms of proof such as marriage and birth certificates and affidavits from Yemen government officials, all of which either did not exist or were extremely difficult to produce.[77] Added to the protracted and sometimes very complicated legal battles in an effort to try to reclaim years of overpaid taxes was the problem of nationality and migrant status. For most Yemenis, their passage to Britain was legally facilitated by colonial passports issued in Aden, which included Yemenis who were technically British subjects, as citizens of Aden and the Protectorates, but also included North Yemenis who were allowed to travel to South Yemen for work. When the British were forced to withdraw from Aden in 1967, South Yemen did not join the Commonwealth, unlike the majority of former British colonial countries. For Yemenis who had travelled and settled in the UK through the Aden Protectorate, they faced some difficulty when their passports expired after 1967. Their dilemma was that if they opted for British nationality, they might well face difficulties when returning to Yemen. Equally, if they declined British nationality and instead opted for Yemeni nationality, they could equally face problems getting back into Britain for work.[78]

The various options open to Yemenis caught in the nationality status trap were British nationality, North or South Yemen nationality, or 'alien' status. With each option carrying its own particular consequences, common to all of them was the reality that emigrant settlers were exposed to varying degrees of bribery and corruption, or what is euphemistically referred to in Yemen as *ḥaqq al-qahwah* ('the right of coffee'). This situation occurred because Yemeni migrant workers in the UK and other places of economic emigration – the US, Middle East and Far East – were often seen by their compatriots as economically 'flush' and, therefore, as a result of their particular vulnerable migrant status were in a position of need (official document, *tawẓīf*, legal certificates, affidavits etc.) and able to pay for those needs through *ḥaqq al-qahwah*. Consequently, in the same way that the early Yemeni lascars needed to grease the palms of the *muqaddam* and *muwassiṭ* in order to ensure both passage from Aden and then later continued employment on merchant ships from British ports, post-Second World War migrants to Britain were still exposed to *ḥaqq al-qahwah* a century later.

6.5 – The last of the lascars. Retired Yemeni sailor, Abdul Rahman, and perpetual sojourner, poses for a portrait in Britain's last 'Arab only' boarding house in South Shields, circa 2005.

Halliday frames the issue of corruption faced by many Yemeni settlers in the UK into a wider social and cultural context:

> The issue of 'corruption' is a difficult one, both in definition and in the manner of best dealing with it. The basic cause was the same as that of Yemeni emigration generally: the poverty of the country and the extreme need of the people for work. On the other side, there are those in both Yemen and Britain who are willing to use their power to grant Yemenis access to work so as to line their own pockets.[79]

However, by the end of the 1970s, it appears that within both developing North and South Yemen states that the practices associated with *ḥaqq al-qahwah* were largely on the decline. It could be that the culture of corruption and bribery, associated with Yemeni migration experiences, were directly affected by the sharp decline in Britain's manufacturing industry as a result of rapid economic depression. The impact of the recession saw an immediate reduction in the value of the remittances sent to the Yemen as a direct result in the fall of the value of the pound. In real terms, this meant that migrant remittances to the Yemen from UK workers were actually reduced by two-thirds in value from what they had been in 1970.[80] Added to this was the difficulty faced by many returnee migrants to the UK after their extended visits to Yemen. An increasing number also experienced problems in finding employment with companies they had previously worked for due to many firms going bankrupt or large numbers of redundancies and staff being 'laid-off' as a result of the tightening recession.

Political Activism and Community Development

By 1975, increasing Yemeni political activism in the UK was reflected in the establishment of the Yemeni Workers Union (YWU), which at its peak had a membership of 1900 from across the British Yemeni communities. The stated aim of the union was to 'forge a link between workers here and the workers' movement and the revolutionary socialist movement in the homeland.'[81] But despite the aim of strengthening international socialist links between Yemeni workers and the Arab nationalist movement, two factors witnessed an almost immediate demise of the British Yemeni mobilization. The first was the growing economic recession across the engineering industry in the UK that ultimately increased unemployment among British Yemenis, forcing many to seek more lucrative jobs in the Gulf or back in the developing Yemen. As a part of this particular emigration, a number of key figures and organizers in the YWU also left the UK for greener pastures.[82] The second factor was the increasing instability between the two Yemens which had seriously deteriorated by the late 1970s to the brink of all-out war in June 1978, when the former president of South Yemen, Salim

Rubiyya Ali was killed. The hostilities not only impacted on the unity of British Yemenis but also the success of the YWU as the UK community became embroiled in the protracted North–South Yemen divide.

With the eventual demise of the YWU by the early 1980s, most of the former local branches simply morphed from workers' union branches into Yemeni community associations and organizations.[83] Further, the transformation from political to community organizations meant that, while funding from local and central governments had not been available, the newly reformed organizations, as community groups, could apply for funding to support their events and activities.[84] As the political divisions between North and South Yemen began to heal after decades of confrontation eventually culminating in the reunification of 1991, British Yemenis began to realize that tribal loyalties and factional politics particular to the Yemen were somewhat misplaced, if not highly disabling in the UK. Thinking and moving as a single community both in Yemen and Britain meant that diaspora Yemenis could finally work towards developing their seriously underfunded communities.

In the UK, this also meant seeking compensation for employment injustices and injuries suffered by Yemeni workers after years of labouring in heavy industries such as steel manufacturing. In Sheffield, for example, Yemeni community organizations working with the Sheffield Occupational Health Project found that 90% of 800 Yemeni workers surveyed had developed a serious hearing loss,[85] due to the excessive noise in the factories and foundries where they worked, significant enough for them to be entitled to industrial compensation.[86] Further, another 30% were found to be suffering from asthma and dermatitis as a direct result of the dirt and dust constantly present in the atmosphere of the steelworks. Others had experienced broken limbs, amputations and serious injuries, all occurrences within the workplace and often due to a distinct lack of protective clothing and safety procedures. Searle's research is littered with the personal narratives of former Yemeni steelworkers and their struggle to receive compensation for their industrial injuries.[87] As a result of the injustices and discrimination the majority of Yemenis experienced, as recorded in his research study, Searle concludes:

> The empirical data presented ... shows that the economic crises in the steel industry and the resultant tight monetarist policies, the racialised political climate during the early Thatcher era, and the persistent feeling of cultural estrangement that was felt by the emigrants, all converged to strike the Yemeni steelworkers and former steelworkers in a unique way during the recession.[88]

The sudden visible presence of large numbers of unemployed black and ethnic minority men were exploited by right-wing political parties and politicians such as the National Front and Enoch Powell, who capitalized on the economic recession, typically linking it with immigration and employment. With the increasing economic downturn came a sudden and dramatic shift in the fortunes of minority communities in Britain and where once communities like the Yemenis were seen as loyal, trustworthy and hard-working employees who were often preferred over their white counterparts, as the encroaching depression set in, they were instead transformed into 'spongers' and 'scroungers' who were draining the welfare state through their dependence on state benefits and reduced council housing rents.[89] This gross misrepresentation, perpetrated by the far right, provided a convenient and oversimplified scapegoat for Britain's post-war industrial decline. Whilst the rise in racial tensions in the 1970s did not particularly develop a distinctly anti-Arab sentiment, which emerged in the late 1990s through the phenomenon of Islamophobia, the homogenization of race and ethnicity conversely witnessed British Yemenis once again becoming an 'invisible' community in the wider context of racial discrimination and social exclusion experienced by black and ethnic minorities in 1980s Britain. Describing the historical placing of Yemenis in the developing racial tensions of modern Britain, Halliday has concisely defined their experiences thus:

> [They] encountered hostility because they were seen as members of a broader immigrant community: just as the

> Yemenis in Cardiff in 1919 were attacked because they were seen as 'black men', so Yemenis in the 1970s were seen as 'coloured' or 'Pakistanis' of a generic kind.[90]

As the research by Little, Collins, Halliday, Lawless and Searle on British Yemeni communities have observed, racism and discrimination have been consistent features of Yemeni community formation and settlement experiences in Britain.[91] However, resistance to such social injustices has also been a persistent feature of British Yemeni history. In the mid-1970s, Yemeni communities rallied support to protest and demonstrate against National Front events and gatherings in industrial cities and towns like Bradford and Rotherham.[92] This unified and organized response against racial hatred, which was neither directly aimed nor specifically targeted at the Yemeni community, forced Yemenis to consider that the attacks on the wider black and ethnic communities was also an attack on them despite the general feeling amongst Yemenis that their presence in Britain was an impermanent one.

The 'Prince' Naseem Factor

A distinct and developed sense of 'British-Yemeniness' did not really begin to emerge until around the same time as the appearance of the influential Sheffield-born, British Yemeni boxer, 'Prince' Naseem Hamid in the early 1990s, whose phenomenal sporting success helped to bring the Yemen and the British Yemeni community to the fore of the wider British public's consciousness. Hamid was born to Yemeni parents in Sheffield in 1973.[93] He started boxing as a flyweight in 1992 and soon rocketed through the rankings as his unorthodox boxing style brought many fans through his antics and showmanship as well as many critics and detractors. After signing under the management of boxing promoter Frank Warren, Hamid became the number one featherweight contender and defeated the defending Welsh champion, Steve Robinson, in 1995.[94] From then on, Hamid went on to win a series of world titles after convincingly beating a host of world-class challengers. His final bout took place in London's Docklands, on 18 May 2002, against the European champion, Manuel Calvo. However, despite wining the fight comfortably with a unanimous decision, Naseem underperformed badly and was booed and derided by watching fans for his lack of effort in the fight. After the contest, Hamid vowed to return to the ring but no clear commitment has ever been given.[95] The boxer subsequently stated that he left boxing due to his increasing family commitments from which training had kept him away for months at a time. He also suffered chronic hand problems forcing him to have tendinitis injections before every fight.[96] In the boxing profession, Hamid is largely seen as an unfulfilled legend who had the potential to become one of the world's greatest-ever boxers. In 1996, at the height of his fame, he released a hip-hop song with the group *Khaliphz* entitled 'Walk like a Champion', which reached number 23 in the UK's singles chart.[97]

His influence on British Yemenis is almost immeasurable and he is partly responsible for placing Yemenis on the UK's cultural register. Hamid's philanthropic endeavours have supported a number of development projects in the Yemen, including the construction of a substantial mosque in the capital, Sana'a. The emergence of 'Prince' Naseem as a British boxing sensation imbued a great sense of pride and belonging in the Yemeni community and whilst he was seen largely as a positive role model for many British Yemenis, as his boxing career ended, and after a series of later, quite public, misdemeaners away from his profession, his once huge popularity slowly waned. A number of British-born Yemeni respondents described how the original rise and public favour of 'Prince' Naseem Hamid, had instilled a sense of pride, self-awareness and being of their distinct cultural identity:

> 'Prince' Naseem came on the scene, speaking Arabic and saying in the ring, 'Allāhu Akbar' ['God is Great'], it was, 'I'm from the Yemen, you know "Prince" Naseem?' And that made it like alright and cool.[98]

> I know it sounds silly, things like 'Prince' Naseem, put Yemen on the map [*sic*]. Then, 'I'm a Yemeni', 'Where's

> that?' 'Y'know, "Prince" Naseem's country.' That made us feel good because nobody ever knew us and what we were and what we were like.[99]

Indeed, the importance of such high-profile and positive role models is a determining factor in creating 'bridges' between minority subgroups and their inclusion and sense of 'place' within mainstream British culture and society. The meteoric rise of 'Prince' Naseem as a British (Yemeni) national sporting hero and cultural icon appeared at the time to represent all that is good, wholesome and healthy about being Yemeni, Muslim and British for young British Yemenis:

> Well, I always struggled when I was younger because until 'Prince' Naseem came on the scene, because, I was always classed as a Pakistani, and due to that I became quite racist, because I knew I wasn't Pakistani, I knew I was English and Arab and I didn't want to be associated with Pakistanis and I was very sort of like degrading towards them [*sic*].[100]

> When I started to know about ['Prince'] Naseem being Yemeni when I got a little bit older I wanted to read anything you know that had him in and I started to watch programmes on going to Yemen and things like this and sort of like started to think, 'well, I am a Yemeni, what is this Yemen' and things like that.[101]

For many young British-born Yemenis, it seems that Naseem Hamid appeared to qualify them as a minority in their own right, where previously they had been lost in the monolithic 'other' representation, often seen as 'Asians' or 'Pakistanis'. 'Prince' Naseem's impact and influence on the Yemeni youth has similarities to that of the British-born, Pakistani-origin boxer Amir Khan or the Pakistani cricketer, Imran Khan, whose affect on the identity of young British Pakistanis, as a sporting hero and pious Muslim role model has been briefly explored in Pnina Werbner's study.[102] For other British-born Yemenis, the boxer began to represent a tangible and real manifestation of the 'imagined Yemen' and 'Yemeniness' that had been merely inherited from parents or simply adopted as a communal identity:

> But then when 'Prince' Naseem sort of like came onto the scene I felt I started to feel proud to be an Arab, because I knew I was Yemeni then, and I noticed that I actually looked like him, so I actually trained. This is when I became more aware of myself.[103]

> I was an Arab because of ['Prince'] Naseem, but actually the Muslim community I was always classed as Pakistani and when I met Arabs they were shocked that I was an Arab, they'd look at me and say, 'Yeah, you're Arab', you know, 'Yeah, I am an Arab' and 'Why don't you speak Arabic?'[104]

The transformative influence of 'Prince' Naseem Hamid had a measurable bearing of the developing 'British' identity of the British-born progeny of Yemeni settlers in the UK. At the same time, a generational shift in the identity politics of who represents the British Yemeni communities was also occurring. In this process of new identity construction, the traditional concepts and values of parents, their ideas and expressions of Yemeni and Muslim identity, may lose their significance in the experiences of acculturation, social interactivity and day-to-day life in Britain of second- and third-generation Yemeni children. A female respondent expressed her experience of acculturation thus:

> I don't know, I just find my values ... there's a lot of values, I mean, most of the values I have are both Islamic and the values I have been brought up with in [British state] school and so they don't conflict.[105]

This paradigm shift is present among the generations of Yemenis largely because the young are interacting in a completely different way within wider society than did their migrant parents. And, in contrast to their parents, British-born Yemenis have to negotiate multiple identity choices as a result of their differing social circumstances.

Here, identity constructions are formed to facilitate both contrasting identities, often 'bridging' the inherited traditional world of their parents and their own experiences as contributing social actors. The resultant hybrid or hyphenated identities reflect the multiplicity of their identity experiences as British Arabs, British Yemenis and British Muslims. In these multi-identity formations, the young need be conflicted in being 'Yemeni', 'Muslim' or 'British'; rather, they can exist under the wider umbrella of British identity that includes varied forms of being British.[106] Further, because religion and religious communities are among the oldest forms of transnational movements that are not bounded by to the nation-state, the emergence of a British Muslim identity conforms to both 'local' and 'global' paradigms. In this new hybrid identity construction, British-born respondents are able to tailor the cultural and religious facets of 'who they are' in order to accommodate their own social realities. In other words, the universality of Islam as a religion with its own way of life and belief system, and its localized assemblages of organized social structures and institutions that are geo-culturally specific, accommodate a fusion of facets of British (cultural) and Islamic (religious) identities – 'British Muslimness'.[107]

Whilst the Yemeni community of Britain, compared with other Muslim communities in the UK and the West, has experienced a certain degree of cultural displacement as a result of migration and settlement processes, these experiences have been counterbalanced by the establishment of religious and cultural practices and institutions that both maintain traditional aspects of communal identity and facilitate new expressions of self-identity. Simultaneously, the new forms of identity manifest among second and third generations often display a distinct facet of acculturated 'Britishness'. These hybrid identities still exhibit a degree of cultural distinctiveness but are specifically located within the emerging cosmopolitan spaces of the urban metropole. Noha Nasser argues it is becoming increasingly difficult to comprehend the emergence of multicultural locales in British cities without any recourse to an understanding of the colonial legacy that has precipitated the processes of decolonization and migration.[108] In the specific context of the Yemeni community, this study indicates that a regional or local identity is more pronounced and assimilated than any notions of 'belonging' to a British national identity. The evolution of regional and localized hybrid identities displayed by minority Muslim communities in Britain has also been observed by Nadeem Malik in his study of how Muslim communities identify themselves both locally, as British Muslims, and globally, as members of the universal family of Islam. Malik raises many questions concerning the connection between legal recognition of British Muslims, as a social minority, and the concept of citizenship, what he calls the 'citizen link'. He concludes that as British Muslim communities slowly became noticed, and, despite the experiences of oppression and prejudice, 'They did not seek to dominate the host community politically or militarily, they simply wanted to live in a different place according to their own customs, values and beliefs.' [109] Malik has questioned where the boundaries of citizenship and belonging lie by challenging the rationale of the assimilationist argument against the reality of a historical background of strongly-bonded regional British identities, in addition to new British identities as part of a post-colonial phenomenon.[110] But the regional identities of new Britons are less contested than their inclusion into a British national identity, as Barry Carr's study of the acculturation of Yemenis and Bangladeshis into notions of a north-eastern 'Geordie' identity shows. Carr observes that once the children of the Arab and South Asian communities opened their mouths to speak, they made their bid for regional identity.[111] However, whilst a local identity may be easier to negotiate than a national one, Carr also admits that as the traditions and values of a region are eroded, racism may become a more dominant force, excluding 'new settlers' and their children from developing regional 'Geordie', 'Mancunian', 'Brummie' or, 'Cockney' identities.[112]

7

BECOMING VISIBLE: THE EMERGENCE OF BRITISH YEMENIS

IN MANY WAYS, the organized Yemeni responses to the right-wing racist attacks on immigrant communities in the 1970s mirrored the earlier reactions to the employment injustices and racial discrimination that Yemeni, Somali and South Asian lascars had experienced in the British maritime industry at the turn of the twentieth century. In this case, Yemenis actively joined and formed seamen's unions to protect and secure sailors' employment rights in the face of blatant discrimination they experienced across the British port cities.[1] Against the backdrop of mounting economic recession and increasing racial hatred in 1970s Britain was the increasing and genuine need of Yemeni settlers to bring their wives and families to join them in the UK, despite severe difficulties and restrictions. As previously mentioned, both North and South Yemen governments were historically reluctant to allow women and children to leave the Yemen because they feared that the mass emigration of dependants would stem the flow of huge amounts of financial remittances pouring into both countries from Yemeni male migrants in the diaspora. Searle asserts that 'the economic considerations were so great that the South Yemen government restricted the migration of women until 1980.'[2]

In North Yemen, restrictions on dependants' emigrations were somewhat relaxed after the overthrow of the Zaydī Imāmate regime in 1962 but, as Barbara C. Aswad's research on Yemeni settlement in southeast Dearborn, Michigan, shows, Yemeni government restrictions on women migrations had been a significant contributor to the predominantly male composition of the Yemeni American community until the 1980s.[3] Obstacles were also encountered from the British immigration authorities in the form of restrictive legislation, including the 1969 Immigration Appeals Act, which required dependants to be in possession of an entry certificate in order to be able to gain access to the UK.[4] The acquisition of this document was fraught with difficulties and challenges as the certificate was only issued from the British Embassy or High Commission from the country of residence, and issued by the Entry Certificate Officer, which meant both a lengthy waiting and processing period and the possibility of bribery and corruption by petty employers through *al-ḥaqq al-qahwah*. Searle's research on the Yemeni community in Sheffield focused on the personal narratives of Yemeni settler experiences of life and work in the inner-city districts and steelwork plants of an industrial British city. His study captures the combined affects of racism and discrimination the settlers faced at work and home, from the police and immigration officials and at the hands of the indigenous community, in which he notes:

> The relationships between the [Yemeni] emigrants and the host population appeared to deteriorate as time progressed into the 1960s and 1970s. In the areas where they encountered national and local officialdom and bureaucracy, the Yemenis who attempted to secure the immigration of their families ... faced long and arduous battles against increasingly strict and unsympathetic police and immigration officials. [5]

Ansari has stated that the presence of the migrants' wives, despite overriding difficulties in bringing them to the UK, strengthened family ties both here in Britain and back in the country of origin, reinforced a sense of cultural identity and established a heightened awareness and observance of religious practices.[6]

What is clear is that the formation of family units, particularly for

British Muslim communities, including Yemenis, both improved economic circumstances by removing or greatly reducing remittances and providing a powerful resistance against the perceived corrupting and corroding influences of British culture.[7] Ansari agrees with Halliday's assertion that the emigrant wives experienced a large degree of cultural displacement, social exclusion and individual isolation as a result of their initial migration to Britain. This social phenomenon is confirmed by a number of research studies on the psychological and emotional impacts on emigrant women to Britain across a number of minority settled communities in the UK.[8] However, despite these initial difficulties in adjusting to a new life in Britain, the majority of settler wives soon adapted and reoriented themselves to their new social environment and cultural conditions.

Acculturating British Yemeniness

Acculturation into British life by Yemeni wives and children settling into the developing industrial communities of Sheffield, Birmingham and Manchester in the 1970s and 1980s can be contrasted with the assimilated Yemeni communities that were established in the port cities of South Shields, Cardiff and Liverpool as early as the mid-nineteenth century. In 1985, Zubayda Umar wrote an article for the *Afkar* magazine entitled 'Yemen to South Shields', which focused on the role of Jāmiʿ al-Azhār (al-Azhar Mosque), which was erected with financial help from the Saudi Arabian government in 1972.[9] The initial project was established by Dr Khalid Sheldrake of the Western Islamic Association in 1935, who had represented the Yemeni lascars during their struggles with ship owners and port authorities for employment rights in the interwar period, and had noted that the existing *zāwiyah* was simply too small to cater for an expanding community.[10]

The al-Azhar Mosque is perhaps most famous for hosting the Islamic wedding of the world-renowned boxing legend, Muhammad Ali, to the actress Veronica Porsche in 1977. Umar wrote that the mosque committee were also planning to establish a school for their children and students flats to accommodate the growing number of Muslim students who came to South Shields to study.[11] While stating that the aim of the school and the student accommodation was to 'limit the effects of culture shock and assist them in the performance of their duties as Muslims', Umar was also keen to mention that the South Shields community was 'by no means a minority community which finds itself isolated and alien within a larger English society.'[12] Instead, she asserts that the community was both long-established and 'integrated with the native population while retaining its own religion and identity.'[13] The comparative success of the South Shields Yemeni community to integrate into its wider indigenous population was elevated as a model for other racially diverse and multicultural British cities and towns. To this end the article informs us that, 'policemen involved in community relations travel south to give lectures and advice to other forces and organisations.'[14] However, as Umar's article and others on the South Shields community reveal, this idyllic integration model was only a relatively recent development and in the process the community had experienced a high degree of hardship and suffering through racism and discrimination in its long settlement history. The article makes a particular reference to Shaykh Abdulla Salem, at the time one of the oldest and most respected members of the community. Shaykh Abdulla came to South Shields from Aden in 1928 after both his father and grandfather had previously visited Britain while serving on British merchant ships. The Shaykh's grandfather came to the town as early as 1906 along with other Yemeni compatriots. After his initial arrival by ship, Shaykh Abdulla then had to wait for six years before he could find work on another ship and in the interim period he spent his time working in many of the 'Arab-only' boarding houses located in the Holborn district of the town. Despite the economic depression of the inter-war period, many Yemenis still made their way to Britain, usually financially supported by family relatives and tribal kinsmen who covered the average cost of £12 for a passage from Aden to Britain.

By the mid-1930s the Yemeni community in South Shields numbered around 4500 and the rapid overcrowding forced the local council to build new houses in the nearby Laygate area of the town to accommodate the lascars and their families, as previously documented in the extended studies of both Little and Collins.[15] In 1937, the South Shields town council leased a burial plot to the local Muslim community on a 50-year renewal and today the plot bears witness to the huge sacrifices made by the local Yemeni community on British vessels, both in war time and at peace. Explaining the dwindling population of the community during the 1980s and making a vague reference to the increasing numbers of British Yemenis who sought work in the oil industry in the Middle East, Umar states that:

> while others go abroad looking for more lucrative work, or travel south to Birmingham or Cardiff to join the Yemeni communities there, just as more of the men bringing their families over from the Yemen tend to take them to one of the southern cities rather than the economically depressed north east.[16]

Searle has also recorded the significant drop in the Yemeni population of Sheffield and Birmingham during the recession of the late 1970s and early 1980s, stating, 'the mass exodus of Yemenis ensued from the declining industries of South Yorkshire and the West Midlands, back to the oil producing states of the Arabian Peninsula. In Sheffield the community shrank by three-quarters.'[17] Umar put the Yemeni population in South Shields around 3000 at the time of writing her article, observing that that the community was neither dying nor loosing its identity but, rather, it was transforming as its members were becoming more sedentary and as a result they were more concerned with issues of development and inclusion in which, 'meetings are held to discuss the future and plan the proposed schools and student flats as well as the curriculum of the mosque's own *madrasah* held on Saturdays and Sundays....'[18] As if to offer reassurance against becoming an isolated and insular community, Umar writes:

> They want it [the school curriculum] to remain within the framework of the local authorities' educational programme

> and do not want to segregate their children by implementing a stringent religious or language curriculum within the school at the expense of other subjects.[19]

The claim is that such inclusive and integrated policies adopted by the community have ensured the treasured 'racial harmony' between the Yemeni community and the wider South Shields indigenous population which Umar says had protected the town from the racial violence that had erupted in other English cities and towns during the early 1980s. She points out that, '[u]nlike Bradford, there is no sign of native opposition to the establishment of a school by the Yemeni community and indeed the authorities are cooperating with the community in this and similar projects.'[20]

7.1 – A 'Geordie' Yemeni complete with accent on a visit to the homeland village of Hajdah, near Ta'izz, in 2004.

Referring to the patterns of marriage and the various degrees of integration as a result, the article maps out the varied ways in which the South Shields Yemeni community chooses its marriage partners, witnessing many community members marrying Yemenis from within the local community or relatives and friends from other British cities, others marrying abroad with a number of Yemenis traditionally marrying wives from Morocco to the Gulf 'over the last four generations'. Others were marrying unrelated members of other Muslim communities from abroad, while a minority married native English spouces who had converted to Islam.[21] Umar also notes that the Yemeni community had extremely cordial relations with other Muslim subgroups: Somalis, Pakistanis, Bangladeshis and Malaysians who were also settled in the town. In all, Umar's feature presents a very positive picture of successful integration of the Yemeni community into the wider population of South Shields and she emphasizes:

> Relations with the local authorities are obviously very good and the Community Relations Council in the north-east cites South Shields as an excellent example of how racial harmony can be achieved between the immigrant and local population.'[22]

Umar concludes her article by posing the rhetorical question, 'What about the apparent drift of members of the community to pastures new and green, abroad and in the south?' To which she answers, that the mosque and school projects are revitalizing the community and helping to retain younger members in the town, stating, 'the problems of development are financial rather social or cultural'. This population retention, she claims, is because the attachment to the town has been established over a number of generations in which many community members are South Shields born-and-bred. As a result, Umar concludes that the community would continue to flourish in the area.

'Anglo-Arabs' and 'English Muslims'

William Dalrymple's delightful vignette of the South Shields community in the late 1980s begins by reminding us that it was the Venerable Bede, a Christian monk and early medieval historian, who in the eighth century resided just two miles up the river Tyne in Jarrow, and was one of the first writers from Britain to mention Muslims or the Prophet Muhammad. Although Bede's vague references to Islam only serve to reveal that he understood very little about the new faith and saw Muslims simply as idolaters, 'hargens' and 'saracens' well over a thousand years on and just a short trek away from the isle of Lindisfarne, that ancient bastion of Christianity, one cannot help but wonder how Bede would have reacted to the distinct presence of 'Geordie Muslims' in South Shields today. Dalrymple traces the settlement of the original Yemeni lascars to the seaport through the establishment of their boarding houses in the Holborn area of the town and the difficulties of employment and racism suffered by the lascars in the early twentieth century.[23] He focuses on the fraught community relations as a result of the 1919 Mill Dam riots and informs us, 'The Yemenis continued to uphold the laws of their religion, but they also began to intermarry and take on Geordie accents and Geordie habits.'[24] In his endeavour to portray the Yemenis as fully integrated members of the wider South Shields community, he writes, 'by the time of the ship-building recession of the late-sixties and seventies they had become virtually indistinguishable from any other South Shields Geordies.'[25] In the context of the publication of Salman Rushdie's *The Satanic Verses* (1988), Dalrymple's portrait presents the community positively: 'The successful integration of the large Muslim minority in South Shields is certainly an optimistic omen at a time when relations between the wider British Muslim community and its host country are at an all-time low.'[26] He also sees the mass movement of the community from the late Victorian slums of the Holborn area of the town to the municipal houses and flats built by the town council just after the war on Ocean Road, Laygate, as a positive contribution towards social integration.

With the Yemenis now relocated in rows of conventional terraced houses and 'neat council flats', he notes that, 'The buildings are utterly English. It is only inside the largest of the boarding houses that things are a little exotic.'[27] His description of life inside one of Britain's last remaining lascar boarding houses provides us with a fascinating, if not unique, glimpse of the lascar experience in which a sitting room full of elderly Yemeni sailors sit around a coal burning fire, playing cards and dominoes and reminiscing about life on the ocean waves. Dalrymple informs us:

> The men in the boarding house were bachelors, although one or two of the older ones had wives back in Yemen', and one former sailor retorted, 'It's too cold for Arab children

> here.' While others assured the writer that they regularly returned to Yemen to visit their wives and children; 'We're all seafaring men here' said one old man, a little theatrically. 'We could never settle down in one place in a house of our own.' The seadogs paused from their dominoes to nod sagely.[28]

The article claims that of the 1000 Yemeni male adults living in the town, at the time of writing, fewer than 100 had full-time jobs and most of these were in factories. The old sailors, Dalrymple tells us, spent their days 'pottering around the job centres and shipping agencies looking for work'.[29]

The piece also captures the aging generation of local women who became the devout Muslim wives of the Arab sailors, many of whom had converted to Islam well before the Second World War. Others, like Mrs Sylvia Hussein, were the progeny of 'mixed race' marriages who, as a result, appeared no different from their indigenous counterparts but, were extremely well versed in the Arabic language and the teachings of the Qur'ān and *aḥādīth*.

> Mrs Abdulla converted to Islam before the Second World War. Her road to Damascus was on the bus between the town centre and Laygate when she sat next to an old Arab who was reading the Koran [*sic*]. He invited her to Koran lessons and a year later she had submitted to Islam; her mother was 'very understanding'. Only much later had she married a Yemeni husband.[30]

Dalrymple also observed that the Muslim women were both assertive and quite outspoken, 'one thing was quite clear ... [the women had not] ... allowed the Islamic ideal of the shy downward-looking female to loosen a Geordie wife's traditional grip on her husband.'[31] Issues of integration, assimilation and dissipation are also key themes briefly explored in the article and, similarly to Umar's article before it, Dalrymple's work explores the degrees of social interactivity experienced by successive generations of British Yemenis in South Shields, leading the writer to conclude, 'Perceptibly, the

South Shields Yemenis are becoming more Anglicised every year. They are becoming English Muslims.'[32] The evidence for his claim was that the habit of sending young males and females back to the Yemen for marriage 'has now but all died out'.

Furthermore, he also cites the distinct and surprisingly liberal responses to the publication of Rushdie's book: local Yemenis wrote to their MP to record their abhorrence of Ayatollah Khomeini's 'death fatwa' on Rushdie and refused to join local Bangladeshi and Pakistani Muslims on a protest march to London against the publication of the book. Dalrymple quotes Abdulla Hasan as saying, 'You can protest in a civilised way by boycotting Penguin Books [Rushdie's publishers]. But acting like a bigot and sentencing someone to death: that only makes matters worse.'[33] After experiencing the generous Yemeni hospitality at a Ramadan *ifṭār* meal held in the al-Azhar Mosque, he ends his article by commenting, 'As Mrs Hussein and other South Shields Yemenis demonstrate, integration and assimilation take time, but Englishness and Islam are not incompatible.'[34]

Is Chewing *Qāt* Consuming Yemen?

Perhaps one distinctly Yemeni tradition brought to the UK by northern emigrant tribesmen, and unlike any similar British habits such as alcohol or tobacco consumption, is the chewing of *qāt*.[35] Dalrymple presented the partaking of *qāt* as a luxury that Yemenis in Britain could only afford when people were in employment or by clubbing together to enjoy communally:

> It looks a little like dill, green and feathery. The Yemenis like to chew the leaves then leave them tucked in the pouch of their left cheek. It sends them into a state of befuddled bliss, takes away the appetite and makes it impossible to sleep. The Yemeni women, who it seems, are not invited to the qat-chewing sessions, disapprove of it.[36]

This somewhat unusual custom observed by Dalrymple was first referred to in a British context by R. B. Serjeant in the 1940s.[37]

Qāt is a leaf chewed mainly by northern Yemeni tribesmen, the effects of which according to Serjeant both 'stimulate and bemuse, but leaves the eater sleepless and depressed. It is not a dangerous practice and is universal in the Yemen.'[38] Despite efforts to curtail its consumption by the British colonial government in the Aden Protectorate, the practice still continued to a lesser degree. In the 1940s, Serjeant noted that, in the UK, 'Within the last year or two a Yemeni discovered that a common English garden shrub possesses similar properties, so they can now obtain as much as they wish, costly though it is in the Yemen.'[39] However, this indigenous plant never really replaced the *qāt*-leaf which has now become increasingly available as links between the Yemen and British Yemeni communities have intensified, where previously, Serjeant noted, 'it was brought to England in powdered form, but the difficulties in obtaining it have inspired this new discovery.'[40]

The majority of northern Yemenis are obsessed with chewing *qāt*, which is actually a mildly narcotic leaf known botanically as *catha edulis*, whose stimulant effects are similar to that of nicotine or caffeine. Hugh Scott wrote a scathing attack on the obsession with the production and consumption of *qāt* describing it as 'a baneful little tree' and blaming it for the decline of Yemen's once thriving agricultural coffee industry.[41] Sir Bernard Reilly, former Chairman of the Commission of Enquiry in connection with the ban of the import of *qāt* into British Aden (c.1950s), described *qāt* as 'a product of some social importance' but also as a shrub which yields 'a habit forming drug to which most Yemenis and a great deal of Adenese [as then colonial subjects] are addicted and which is exported to neighbouring territories.'[42] Harold Ingrams said that *qāt* was grown principally in the Yemen hills and exported to other parts of the country. He also thought that, 'it must be a very acquired taste, for I have tried a leaf or two and thought it was filthy', but at the same time alluding to alleged stimulating effects of the plant he admitted, 'what tales fishermen and golfers would tell if they took *qat*!'[43] In the Yemen, *qāt* sessions tend to consume most of the afternoon and throughout northern villages and cities men sitting in shaded circles, lazily munching on small green leaves literally brings industry and commerce to a standstill. But some might argue that working in the blazing heat of the midday sun is itself a largely unproductive endeavour. In many rural areas, local incomes and economies are almost totally dependent on the production of *qāt*, a plant that has no value beyond the Yemen and East Africa.

Brian Whitaker claims *qāt* is five times more profitable than other crop and, unlike others, it produces an all-year-round income.[44] Further, John Vidal says that *qāt* nets a cash-crop profit of about $60 million per annum in Ethiopia alone.[45] Whilst the implications of *qāt* production on the economy of the Yemen are disturbing to some analysts, Dresch sees the *qāt*-chewing sessions as a positive contribution to the preservation and maintenance of traditional Yemeni society. He claims that the *māqil*, or 'conversation gatherings' facilitated by chewing *qāt* are places where crops are discussed, disputes mediated, poems recited and exchanged and even the political problems of the country are debated.[46] So institutionalized are the afternoon *qāt* sessions that, even during the protracted civil war and tribal hostilities of the late twentieth century, *qāt* trade agreements and shipments conducted between warring factions remained virtually unhindered.[47] But there are strong arguments against the cultivation of a plant with a limited economic value, particularly when the Yemeni economy is one of the most underdeveloped in the Middle-East. *Qāt* chewing is largely confined to the northern highlands and it is virtually unknown in the Ḥaḍramawt and south Yemen regions. Further, during the British Protectorate of Aden, the colonial government restricted the usage of *qāt* to the weekend (Thursday afternoon to Friday evening in Muslim countries), a restriction which helped to make the plant unpopular in the south. Even after reunification when the ban was lifted, 'chewing' had become almost exclusively a 'northern' habit.[48] In addition, the majority of Yemeni *'ulamā'* believe *qāt* to be *makrūh* (literally, 'reprehensible' but, as an Islamic legal term, it means, 'disliked, but not forbidden'), prompting Whitaker to comment, 'one of the few things that radical Islamists and secular modernizers in Yemen agree upon is that qat is evil.'[49] Islamic scholars claim that the social 'evils' of *qāt*: the misuse of land cultivating it and the wasting of money and time consuming it, far outweigh the harmful physical effects caused to the body by the plant. However, despite religious objections and rulings, *qāt* remains a popular social habit amongst most Yemenis, even those in the diaspora. El-Solh claims that *qāt* consumption in the UK is a growing problem among British-born offspring,

> In the case of young Somalis [and some Yemenis], for example, this feeling of entrapment [by social exclusion] has encouraged the regular chewing of *gat*, a debilitating escape which has inadvertently perpetuated their social isolation from the world outside their immediate community.[50]

Halliday claims that Ethiopian *qāt* (pronounced there as *khāt*) has been readily available in the UK since 1978. He traces the *qāt* supply to a Yemeni named 'Haj Salih' who came to Sheffield in 1956 and later moved to Stepney in London to open an Arab café. Stepney was at that time home to four Arab boarding houses and in addition to supplying the small community with traditional Yemeni dishes, 'Haj Salih' began to import *qāt* from Ethiopia.[51] He also refers to the surrounding controversies associated with the social and physical effects of *qāt* on Yemeni and East African societies. In Britain, the consumption of *qāt* amongst the settled Yemeni communities had come under the same religious scrutiny by Muslim activists influenced by the religious reform party, Al-Iṣlāḥ, an Islamist group that found prominence during the reunification of the Yemeni in 1991.[52] In Sheffield, a community project, the Yemeni Community Association, was urged by a group of Yemeni women to assert its influence by discouraging the consumption by older Yemeni men. British supplies of the plant became more available by the 1980s and it was flown in on a twice-weekly basis to Heathrow from Ethiopia where it was then distributed amongst the Yemeni, Somali, Ethiopian and Kenyan communities throughout the UK. Today, *qāt* is now delivered daily from Kenya and twice-weekly directly from the Yemen. The East African *qāt* is preferred by the Somali settlers in Britain and is of a higher 'quality' than Yemeni *qāt* which has a courser stem and is quite bitter by comparison.[53] However, the Yemenis have a preference for 'home grown' produce and the plant, which sells for around £5 a bundle, is usually sold by local Yemeni and Somali grocers in small bunches often wrapped in banana leaves.

The media fascination with the UK presence of *qāt* appears to resurface with increasing frequency. Halliday's study details sensational newspaper articles demanding a ban of the 'killer drug available for sale in Britain' (*The Observer*, 18/10/1987)[54] and more recent articles include, 'chew on this' (*The Guardian*, 5/2/2004) and 'International Olympic Committee prohibits qat' (*Yemen Observer*, 21/8/2004). Journalists are 'shocked' that, despite being banned in the US, New Zealand and 'large parts' of Europe, it still remains widely available in Britain. Media coverage tends to focus on the physical effects of *qāt*, which have been compared to cocaine, marijuana and amphetamine, but the on-going debates by medical experts on the actual and real effects of the plant deem it to be far less harmful.[55] The claims that *qāt* is a 'classified drug' or an 'illegal narcotic' are spurious and the cathinone (an amphetamine-type substance) contained in the plant is minute – less than 36 parts per 100,000 when freshly cut. After cultivation, the cathinone quickly breaks down and within 10 days it is reduced to only one-hundredth of its original level. The amount of cathinone in 100 pounds weight of 10-day old *qāt* is the equivalent to 0.04 grammes of amphetamine.[56] It is little wonder that prosecutions for possession of *qāt* as an illegal substance in the US are difficult and instead acquittals are far more frequent. But exaggerated reports give detailed accounts of journalists' hair-raising experiential 'trips' under the influence of *qāt*.[57]

Other journalists claim that the leaf induces dreaminess, lucidity and a sudden surge of energy or that its effects are the equivalent to 'a couple of spliffs [marijuana cigarettes] and six double espressos',[58] a 'cocktail' that would seem to cancel out the accumulative effects of each other. The origins of these vivid accounts of 'tripping-out' on *qāt* appear to have their roots in Kevin Rushby's neo-orientalist travelogue in which he offers his own lucid accounts of *qāt*-induced experiences.[59] Whitaker's article quotes Rushby at some length as someone whose personal obsession with *qāt* evokes images of opium den-like darkened rooms, filled with mysterious oriental strangers strewn across the floor like boats cast from their moorings, lost at sea. Rushby's 'Oriental adventure' faithfully retraces the Aden–Zeila–Harar route traversed by the great Orientalist, Richard Burton, some 150 years previously. The author considers both Burton and the French poet, Rimbaud, who preceded Rushby in recreating Burton's journey through the Yemen, as the 'most noted Europeans of their age'.[60] Presumably, his admiration of these writers is as a result of the exotic representations of the orient both offered. Rushby's search for the Arab *kayf*, a presumed state of oriental contentment was identified and described by Burton as 'the savouring of animal existence; the passive enjoyment of the mere senses; the pleasant languor, the dreamy tranquillity, the airy castle-building'. Burton's classic Orientalist stereotype is dutifully cited *verbatim* in Rushby's contemporary work.[61] Rushby believes that chewing *qāt* might facilitate an esoteric journey into the 'Yemeni world', just as the exotic disguises facilitated his nineteenth-century literary mentors on their 'trips'. Like his predecessors, Rushby was also drawn to 'go native', adopting an Arab disguise to escape death in Ethiopia and so that he might wander undetected through 'untravelled and mysterious paths'. [62] Possibly inspired by Tennyson's popular poem, *The Lotos-Eaters*, he scripts his journey in the style of a romanticized travelogue laced with nineteenth-century Orientalist narrative constructions, complete with erotic fantasies about 'eastern' sexuality.[63] According to Rushby, it was through a developed fetish with oriental sexuality that allowed Burton to acquire 'prodigious knowledge of human sexuality with data on the preferred love-making habits of Somali women'.[64]

These repressed and transposed sexual desires 'acted out' by 'exotic others', albeit in the imagination of infatuated Europeans are best described by Rushby himself as, 'something like being caught spiking the curry, with curry powder'.[65] But the author's unreserved endorsement of Burton's explicit sexism and racism perhaps says more about Rushby than any supposed objectivity on Burton's part. Hence, it is somewhat disturbing to find that Rushby's neo-orientalist adventure forms the basis for much of the reports surrounding the consumption of *qāt*.[66] Ironically, as disturbing and 'decadent' as *qāt* chewing may seem to the outsider, the *qāt* economy has ensured that Yemeni agricultural economy has remained independent from the economic dependence of cash crops such as coffee, cotton, chocolate and sugar, whose market prices are fixed by powerful western consumers rather than developing world producers.

Chewing is popular among Yemeni males in Britain and 'chews' (a translation from the Arabic, *ghaṣṣan*, which literally means, 'choking') as they are locally termed, tend to happen informally, usually on weekends or special occasions like a wedding party or religious festivities.

> It tends to be a planned event, yes, erm, mainly *Eid* and things. It's mainly when a lot of people get together and you normally see a lot of Yemenis together, then someone will say, 'Hey, why don't we have a chew?' Everyone has to agree on it and we'll all just get some *gāt* and decide to have a chew and all just sit down together.[67]

The 'chews' in Britain are infrequent and on a much smaller scale than sessions in the Yemen which are a daily occurrence often involving scores of villagers and tribesmen. Most *qāt* sessions are preceded by a meal either at the host's home or taken before arrival at the *māqil* and are hosted in a special room called a *mafraj*.[68] The sessions I have attended in the UK usually started after midday or early evening and continued until late evening. In the Yemen, the sessions do not normally last as long during work days, although at weekends and holidays people are less pushed to return to the fields or attend their business. One British-born respondent recalled the *qāt* sessions that took place in his father's village near Laḥij during his visit to the Yemen to get married:

> Oh, it could go on all night, that was the thing, you know you'd go to someone's house and you'd get there you know

> round about say you went about three o'clock [in the afternoon] and dinner would all be over by four, four-thirty. They'd maybe start you know chewing and you might be there till twelve o'clock.[69]

Women do not normally chew and a female research respondent, whose migrant Yemeni father had never chewed in Britain, remembered her first visit to the Yemen and her astonishment at seeing the 'swollen cheeks' of Yemeni men:

> I remember when I first got there I was quite horrified [laughs]. Everyone had these lumps [of *qāt* in their mouths]. I was wondering to myself, and I was only about 17, 'everyone looks like they've got mumps.' I didn't know what was going on and then I realized, 'Why's everybody got this swollen thing?' And I was told what it was.[70]

During the *qāt* sessions I attended amongst the British Yemeni community the conversation was always engaging and people tended to discuss 'the best *qāt* I ever had', or generally recounted their experiences during visits 'back home' or news and stories from the Yemen related by their elders. Often *fiqh* was debated (inevitably and ironically, whether *qāt* was *ḥalāl* or *ḥarām*) and even Qur'ānic exegesis. The sessions were often held in the rented homes of single migrant worker Yemenis, or at a house where a family were not present so that they would not be disturbed by guests. A small number of Yemenis boycotted *qāt* sessions on religious grounds, as according to their understanding of Islamic law the consumption of the plant is the equivalent of smoking hashish or drinking alcohol. But most Yemenis do not subscribe to this religious view and instead believe that the plant has mythical medicinal qualities, although no evidence exists to substantiate this claim. However, it is interesting that *qāt* sessions seemed to subside during Ramadan and when I enquired if people still chew in the fasting month I was told:

> They do! One or two do, but it's hard because you've got your *suhūr* [pre-fast breakfast] and you've got your fasting

> and you tend to know who's chewed because they won't be there at *ẓuhr* [midday prayer] [laughs].[71]

The admission that *qāt* consumption is less desirable during the fasting month of Ramadan gives some credence to the opinions of more orthodox Muslim scholars who claim that chewing *qāt* is incompatible with religious adherence.

7.2 – A taste of the Yemen, the author chews qāt *with Kholaidi tribesmen in the* maqṣūrah *of the* masjid *in Wādī al-Jassar, Yemen in 2004.*

Some Yemenis often wear their traditional *fawṭah*, sometimes complete with a *shawāl* (traditional headscarf worn in a particular style). Bottles of water and cola are circulated and *qāt* connoisseurs keep a couple of bundles to chew leisurely. But not everyone at the *māqil* 'chews' and a few Yemenis attend simply for the company and conversation. One respondent showed me a video of a *qāt* session filmed at his 'home village' of Milah, near Radā', northern Yemen, sent to him by his relatives. After viewing the video, and then later attending *māqil*s in Yemen, I began to realize how important the *qāt* sessions were for many young males in the British Yemeni community and how they were careful to preserve this cultural tradition, making sure that all the *adab* (etiquette) and *akhlāq* (social mores) of the gatherings adhered faithfully to those sessions 'back home'. The conversations, dress codes, timings and usage of space for the sessions, complete with mattresses and cushions, all conformed to those I witnessed in the video and experienced in the Yemen. Chewing *qāt* is a distinctly Yemeni pastime and Yemeni *qāt* is also distinct from *qāt* plants found elsewhere. As a social and recreational event, the effects of 'chewing' are argued for and against on religious, social, economic and health grounds, but their impacts on the diapora community are far less damaging than they might appear to be in the Yemen. What is clear is that whilst *qāt* might be somewhat destructive to the economic development and modernization process of the Yemen, its consumption in the diaspora is an 'act' that bridges the 'time and space' factor between home and abroad. Consequently, by partaking in a *qāt* 'chew' Yemenis in Britain are metaphysically and quite literally consuming the Yemen.

While the consumption of *qāt* might be in important activity in preserving a unique and exclusive sense of Yemeniness among some British Yemenis, making inroads into the wider British society through the development of community institutions and associations is a growing concern across all the Yemeni communities in the UK. For example, the Yemeni community in Eccles, Greater Manchester, was comparatively the most underdeveloped and socially excluded of all the British Yemeni communities. In contrast, the Birmingham community under the auspices of the Yemeni-run Muath Welfare Trust manages a very successful inner city community centre, the Bordesley Centre, in the heart of the Yemeni community. The origins of the Birmingham Yemeni community date back to the late 1920s when lascars were forced by both legal restrictions and a decline in jobs from the dock areas into the industrial heartlands. Furthermore, when race riots of 1919, spread throughout the port cities of Britain forcing the deportation of over 600 Yemeni lascars, many sought other means of employment away from the racism experienced in the docklands.[72] The early Yemeni settlers in Birmingham influenced by the teachings of Shaykh al-Hakimi soon established a *zāwiyah* on Edward Road, Balsall Heath, and by the 1950s and 1960s, the community experienced a further migration of single males coming directly from the British Protectorate of Aden.

By the late 1970s, like the Yemeni community in Eccles, the emigrant workers to Birmingham were slowly joined by their families. At the same time, numbers of Yemenis came to Britain to undertake postgraduate studies and they were instrumental in initiating and organizing Arabic supplementary schools throughout the British Yemeni communities: 'They were well-connected back home in Yemen, so they managed to persuade the Yemeni authorities to provide some support to the school here.'[73] Unfortunately, by the late 1980s, economic decline and political tensions in the divided Yemen meant that it was not possible to maintain the level of economic support to communities in the diaspora.[74] Whilst the foreign student participation as teachers in supplementary schools was experienced throughout Britain, when Yemeni government funding waned, only communities with a greater population and a developed community infrastructure were able to sustain and build on the success of the schools. In Birmingham, the community moved from hiring classrooms in local schools and colleges to the acquisition of a centre in 1991.[75]

A Tale of Two Cities: Capacity Building

The Bordesley Centre is a fully-functioning community centre currently serving the Yemeni community and many other ethnic minorities within its local catchment area. It is an impressive, listed Victorian building with up to 10,000 users and visitors a week. Some of the services offered are youth and sporting activities through its sports complex, conference facilities, including three large function halls, and a day nursery catering for around 60 infants. Further, there is an Arabic elementary school at evenings and weekends, catering for 400 students aged from eight to 16 and community educational access courses designed to be culturally gender sensitive.[76] There are also daily and Friday prayer facilities, cultural and religious awareness programmes, Ramadan community fast-breaking events and supportive housing accommodation for the elderly.[77] The centre users come from both indigenous and ethnic minorities groups, of which about 75% are from the Yemeni community, and of the 70 full-time and part-time staff, around 50% are of Yemeni origin. It would appear that the partnership between the centre and the local authorities has nurtured the social inclusion and visibility of the Yemeni community in Birmingham.

Economically, the Bordesley Centre is almost self-sufficient and the former Executive Director, Adnan Saif, told me, 'about 80% of our revenue budget [is] generated internally, 20% is still done through fund-raising and I think that has been a negotiating strength with the local authorities.'[78] The centre has also recently secured funding from central government through the Agency for Regeneration Programmes totalling just over £5 million to refurbish their Grade 2-listed building.

A fair comparison between the developmental achievements of the Eccles and Birmingham Yemeni communities would have to consider the relative size of the two communities and the level of service provision and development funding provided by local authorities and central government. In Birmingham and the surrounding Black Country, the Yemeni community is estimated to be around 12–13,000 compared to a community of a thousand in Eccles. These figures, when added to the populations of Yemenis in Cardiff, Liverpool, Sheffield and South Shields seriously challenge Halliday's estimate of a total population of 15,000 in 1992. However, determining accurate population figures to support any claims for financial assistance towards community development of British Yemeni communities is fraught with statistical speculation based on the overall heterogeneous size of the British Arab population and the non-segmented dimensions of their 'ethnic' groupings.[79] In Eccles, the inability to determine an exact population size for the Yemeni community becomes an inhibiting factor when applying for community development funding through local agencies, particularly when the community appears to be invisible. During my contact with some local government departments while doing ethnographic research in Eccles, it became apparent that many Salford City Council officials did not know that the Yemeni community existed. Whilst Yemeni communities in other cities, including Liverpool, Birmingham, Sandwell, Sheffield, Rotherham, South Shields and Cardiff, have been able to develop through a number of local government supported projects, the Eccles community clearly did not fare so well in comparison until its acquisition of National Lottery Funding to develop the Yemeni Community Association in

2005 and its 'Yemeni Roots, Salford Lives' archive achieve project with the Ahmed Iqbal Ullah Educational Trust and the University of Salford in 2011.[80] Adnan Saif believes the problem of community development and social inclusion in Eccles was both structural and skills-shortage related. He informed me that, 'if you compare the community structure with the Pakistani community or the Indian community ... There are those [present in the communities] who came ready to explore and understand the system.'[81] During the late 1980s, the Yemeni communities throughout Britain mutually co-operated in a skills-sharing exercise to help develop and nurture religious and cultural identity through supplementary Arabic schools. Adnan Saif told me that, 'In Eccles, we went there say for about three years and we would send teachers every weekend sometimes from Birmingham, sometimes perhaps from Liverpool.'[82] As a result of this national self-help initiative other Yemeni communities were able to develop further. For example, 'in Sheffield they had a well-organized local structure; they had at least one or two prominent people who really looked after the community.' In addition, young people were encouraged to pursue university education and professional careers within local councils who could then lend their skills to the service and development of the community.[83]

As a traditional Arab community where tribal identity is a very important social structure in most Yemeni villages, migrants to Britain through the processes of 'chain migration' and family ties were able to maintain a strong sense of tribal identity even in the diaspora. The tribe, operating as an extended family and strongly bonded socio-political group, offers a strong support network and community structure.[84] In the Yemen, where central authority is relatively weak and the government's impact and influence extends little beyond the capital and main cities, within the rural regions and villages, Adnan Saif asserts that, 'the tribe, and the chief[s] of the tribes, still has a significant role to play'.[85] In the smaller British Yemeni communities where one particular tribal group has settled in the majority, a strong sense of tribal identity has been maintained. This appears to be the case in Eccles where most settlers belong to the al-Kholaid tribe. The tribe is located in the Maqbanah district in the Governorate of Taʿizz and includes the villages of Hays, al-Hugra, al-Qurayyah, al-Mahma, Wādī al-Dakhaylah, al-Turbah, al-Huqiaf, al-Mawj and Wādī Āl Jassār. The Kholaidis in Eccles emanate from Wādī al-Jassar, a hamlet a few kilometres north-west of the small town of Hajdah, near Taʿizz. Whilst a sense of community has been maintained in Eccles, through the preservation of traditional tribal identity, facilitated by the 'chain migration' process, in larger communities like Birmingham there are considerably less manifestations of tribal identity.[86] This is because the Birmingham community is greater in population and diversity, with people emanating from Sana'a, Taʿizz and Aden and their surrounding areas. Added to the imported tribal identities are the political factions and tensions of Yemeni transnational politics that can often further splinter the community and inhibit the process of mutual co-operation and development.

Preserving Tradition and Embracing Transformation

Much of Lawless's research on Yemeni settlement in South Shields at the turn of the twentieth century confirms the earlier observations of a less comprehensive study by Barry Carr, a chapter that focuses on the current issues relating to British Yemenis and regional identity.[87] Lawless's research, unlike Carr's, sees Yemeni and English intermarriages as an assimilation and diffusion of the Yemeni community, rather than an integration or organic evolution into wider British society. In contrast, Carr exemplifies the Yemeni community of South Shields as a model for racial tolerance and integration for the rest of Britain. He maintains that whilst South Shields may enjoy the luxury of excellent race relations, the early settlement history of the Yemeni community is in stark contrast to the present situation. Carr celebrates the transition of the Yemeni community from migrant Arab settlers into intermarried and culturally integrated 'Anglo-Arabs'. Nevertheless, the fact that Carr identifies the community as 'black' is perhaps a revealing insight into just how integrated they actually are, despite his claim that 'Black Geordies are "Geordies" first.'[88]

Conversely, Lawless does not interpret the development of the Yemeni community with the same positive enthusiasm as Carr, Umar or Dalrymple, that being the organic evolution of the ethnic, religious and cultural aspects of the community's identity into a more 'Anglo-Arab' experience. Instead, the conclusion to Lawless's study observes the disintegration of the Yemeni community through assimilation,[89] integration,[90] and acculturation[91] of the community. The increasing manifestations of the community's Muslim identity and the establishment of mosques and Muslim faith schools are interpreted by Lawless as anomalies, in contrast to the pervading trend of assimilation. The post-war years leading to the present, where the physical presence of the Yemeni community is less demographically concentrated and ethnically visible, represents for Lawless the demise or 'end of an era' for the Yemenis of South Shields. Conversely, Umar and Dalrymple believe, like Carr, that the dispersion of the community is as a result of both the decline of the shipping industry and the community becoming more English/British and less Arab. Referring to the social exclusion experienced by the Yemeni community Umar has said that, 'The problems of development are financial rather than social or cultural.'[92] However, despite Lawless' pessimistic vision for the future of the community, his work tracing the origins and early history of the Tyneside Yemenis provides an invaluable study of one of Britain's earliest Muslim communities.

7.3 – Yemeni Muslims enjoy iftār *at the Al-Azhar Mosque, South Shields during Ramadan, 2006.*

Fred Halliday's wider study on British Yemenis, unlike the historical and regional study undertaken by Lawless, examines the migration and settlement process of Yemenis at the national level and explores both historical and contemporary issues.[93] Again, Dalrymple's quaint portrait of the South Shields settlers, as successful and fully participating Anglo-Arabs contrasts with Halliday's study of exilic Yemeni communities dispersed throughout Britain. Dalrymple clearly sees a synthesis between Islam and the 'Britishness' of the Yemenis where Halliday instead refers to the strong cultural and psychological ties with their homeland, describing Britain for the perceived Yemeni exiles as 'the remotest village'.[94] His description illustrates that despite the migration, urbanization and industrialization of the Yemeni community in Britain, their world is still largely viewed through a traditionally rural and tribal Arab society. In many ways, this experience is not unique to Yemenis in Britain, and similarities may be present in other Arab or South Asian migrant communities. Certainly Halliday's observations of migration and settlement patterns mirror the findings of other studies undertaken on migrant communities to Britain. However, in his particular research, Halliday reveals a number of unique features related to the 'two-wave' Yemeni settlement explored in this study. What is clear from Halliday's research is that the politics of the Yemen are often transported into Britain and, as a result, often the conflicts and tensions concurrent in the Yemen surface amongst the British Yemeni community in microcosm. The growing politicization of the Yemeni community has been detailed by Halliday and he has traced the developments and origins of organizations and unions, in addition to linking them with the politics, historical changes and social transformations in the Yemen.[95] Halliday has also recorded the many racist attacks on the community. These particular events are also explored in the later study undertaken by Kevin Searle in his research on Yemenis in Sheffield. While Halliday is scathing of the racism and discrimination faced by Yemenis in Britain, he has also expressed his own personal perception of the Yemenis as 'other' when on one occasion whilst travelling with some Yemenis across Britain by coach he noted:

> One can only imagine what the few Birmingham residents then on the streets to get their morning milk and Sunday morning papers would have thought if they could have understood what these busloads of dark men were singing, attacking British imperialism and the perfidy of the Saudi ruling family.[96]

The fluctuating populations of the various local British Yemeni communities are often linked to the economic situation in Britain and, on rare occasions, to developing events in the Yemen. Liverpool was traditionally home to a small community of seafaring Yemenis but when the shipping industry declined in the 1930s, most of the community migrated to other cities and some even returned to Yemen. However, in the late 1960s, a small community of Yemeni shopkeepers and businessmen began to flourish as the city increased its post-war industrial migrant workforce. The result is that today's Liverpool enjoys a growing and revitalized Yemeni community, largely settled in the Toxteth area of the city, close to the Al-Rahma Mosque, Heatherly Street, and the Al-Ghazali Centre, Earle Road. In 1992, Halliday put the Yemeni population of Liverpool at 3500 and contrasted its growing number with that of decreasing numbers of other communities in British cities. Equally, he notes that when the Yemeni government relaxed its laws on allowing wives and children of migrant workers to leave the Yemen in the early 1980s, the migrant community in Liverpool and other British cities expanded further.[97] Although Halliday has observed that 'by the late 1980s there were fifth generation Yemenis living in Britain', and that on-going events in Yemen have helped British Yemenis to maintain very strong ties with their country of origin,[98] they have also contributed to the community's transnational identity and what he terms as their social 'incapsulation',[99] a passive segregation that is usually termed by social anthropologists as 'boundary maintenance'.[100]

Cultural traditions like the consumption of *qāt* and the continuance of arranged marriages with spouses from the Yemen seem to perpetuate the community's 'incapsulation' which is often perceived as their apparently rigid introversion or unwillingness to integrate. It is interesting to note that objections to 'arranged' marriages referred to in Halliday's work have now been replaced by objections to 'forced' marriages, moving the discussion away from the religious imperative to the cultural malpractice.[101] The terminology has rightly shifted from the association of 'forced' with the tradition and culture of mutually arranged marriage, quite acceptable and encouraged Islamically, to an attack on marriages where mutual consent is absent, which is expressly forbidden according to Islamic law.[102] It had been generally assumed that 'arranged' marriages were unpopular amongst British Muslims until the community could find a voice eventually to correct this false assumption of 'arranged' marriages being generally portrayed as 'forced' marriages.

Halliday, then, portrays British Yemenis as 'the invisible Arabs'[103] and concludes that they largely see themselves as sojourners, like the early post-colonial migrants from South Asia studied by Muhammad Anwar, who will ironically never return, rather than settlers who have come to terms with their shifting Arab and British identities.[104] His excellent sociological study of British Yemenis can leave one with the impression that, despite its long history, the community has failed to make any real or visible impact on wider British society. But this is because, despite its recent re-release, in 2010, under the new title, *Britain's First Muslims*, Halliday's original ethnographic research was completed in the latter half of the 1980s and, therefore, the shifting developments within the subsequent unfolding decades are absent.[105] Furthermore, whilst the original *Arabs in Exile* monograph presented us was a comprehensive social history of Yemeni community development in the twentieth century, the re-issue tells us nothing about British Yemenis over the last 30 years.

The change that has occurred has been a generational one in which post-Second World War migrant settlers have given way to their second-and third-generation British-born progeny. As a result, mirroring other Muslim communities in the UK, the paradigm shift has been from ethnicity to religiosity, an experience significantly accelerated by global events: the reunification of Yemen, the phenomenon of Islamophobia, the 9/11 and 7/7 terror attacks, the invasion of Iraq and Afghanistan, and the influence of the ever-changing events as a result of the so-called 'Arab spring' pro-democratic movements in the Middle East, including the Yemen. These important events and their cataclysmic affects, along with a detailed tracking of how British society has transformed within the last generation are all significant in the reshaping of British Yemeni narratives as events that could not possibly be envisaged by Halliday. However, what Halliday's research study does offer is a fascinating glimpse into how British Yemenis have gradually moved from the periphery of British society, as colonial lascars and 'invisible Arabs' towards their current position as Britain's first Muslims.

EPILOGUE

THE LATTER PART of the twentieth century has witnessed Arab migrations and settlement to Britain largely for educational and later for political reasons. Like their earlier Yemeni Arab counterparts, these large newly-settled diaspora Arab communities have had a significant part to play in changing the recent fortunes of their countries of origin through the democratization revolution sweeping across the Arab-Islamic regions. Madawi al-Rasheed has discussed both the invisibility and fractures present among Britain's Arab communities and she acknowledges a long and continued presence of Syrian and Moroccan cotton traders and Yemeni and Somali lascars across the industrial and port cities of Britain from as early as the mid-nineteenth century.[1] Al-Rasheed claims that beyond the 'push and pull' economic migration factors of Arabs to Britain and the west in the late twentieth century, unfavourable political conditions in the Middle East were also a major consideration for migration:

> The political instability which prevailed in the Arab world at that time manifested itself in a series of revolutions, coups, civil wars and partitions, none of which was particularly favourable to the creation of economic opportunities, development and long-term planning.[2]

Al-Rasheed's research engaged with official population figures from the 1981 Census relating to the number of Arabs in Britain and her enquiry sheds some light on the anomalies of the official statistics on British Arab communities, in which she observes that it is impossible to arrive at an estimate for the number of UK-born Arabs. This is because what she termed as 'second generation migrants' who are actually born in the UK, the progeny of Arab immigrants, do not appear in any official statistics as they are grouped under 'born in the UK'.[3] However, an interesting statistic according to the 1987 Labour Force Survey showed that Arabs constituted 3% of the ethnic minority population of the UK, which was estimated at a total of 2.5 million.[4] From this figure, al-Rasheed extrapolated that the UK Arab population was estimated to be around 75,000 in 1990.[5] However, by far the most intriguing figures came from a published article in the *Economist* on the Arab communities of Britain. According to their sources, 500,000 Arabs were residing in the UK in 1988.[6] The article claimed that the majority were migrant workers employed in menial work who intended to return to their countries of origin after forwarding substantial remittances to their dependants. While the article gave specific population figures for Egyptians (90–120,000), Iraqis (100,000), Moroccans (80,000), Palestinians (20,000) and Lebanese (20,000), it neither gave figures for Yemenis living in the UK nor did it reveal the source of its statistics, although al-Rasheed views them as quite credible, if not wholly accurate.[7] The perennial problem in terms of being able to identify and, therefore, visualize an 'invisible' community like the British Arabs is because, al-Rasheed tells us, 'it is difficult to break the category "Arabs" into its component parts as these are not listed individually in most government statistics.'[8]

The Arab communities are not socially and economically heterogeneous and they are divided along several lines: nationality, religious, economic and UK legal status. In fact, al-Rasheed divides them into four distinct categories: 'the wealthy Arab migrants, the professionals, the migrant workers and the refugees.'[9] But her categories of Arab settlers appears to be absent of any consideration of long-term Yemeni settlers and their progeny. She is, however, correct in asserting that as far as the UK policymakers are concerned Arab communities in Britain remain veiled. She continues by stating that this high degree of 'invisibility' is a significant indicator of a much larger problem associated with the Arab population of Britain, '[The] lack of visibility at this level means lack of recognition of the group's presence and an absence of commitment to its interests, grievances and problems.'[10] While al-Rasheed concedes that the complex diversity of the Arab communities could be a major contributor in explaining their continued lack of recognition, she notes that on British streets, and particularly in London, 'there are Arabs who are more visible than others'. Yet, she concludes, 'In general, the host society is more aware of the presence of wealthy migrants as a result of the media which are fascinated by the "exotic" and the "extravagant".'[11] This neo-Orientalist 'fetish' with the lavish spending of oil-rich Arab shaykhs appears to overshadow the majority of settled Arab communities in Britain and their particular concerns and issues of 'invisibility', racism, discrimination, Islamophobia and social exclusion.

Camilla Fawzi El-Solh remarks of British Arabs that, 'Be they economic migrants or political refugees, the presence of Arabs in Britain has tended to receive an almost incidental mention in published research on ethnic minorities, a trend more or less conspicuous to the late 1980s.' [12] El-Solh concludes that while studies on other ethnic minorities may be of limited relevance to marginalized Arab communities in Britain, they do not provide the specific insights needed to cover the central issues relating to the perpetual marginalization they face. 'Thus,' she states, 'in the first instance, a research agenda tailored to the needs of these Arab communities is needed to ensure that they may find their rightful place in British society.'[13] In fact, the increased focus on Arabs in the UK in the following decade was fuelled by negative stereotypes that pathologized Arabs as 'closet-Saddamists' as a result of the first Gulf war in 1991.[14] Conversely, it appeared that when Arabs are not being framed as a menacing and imminently dangerous presence their contrary depictions are 'images of affluence spiced with the exotic',[15] as 'petro-dollar' shaykhs who squander their millions away in London's casinos and nightclubs. These contradictory and erroneous representations have tended to undermine any serious consideration and engagement with British Arab communities. However, El-Solh points out that there is a growing realization amongst the broader spectrum of British Arabs, including the sizeable Yemeni community, that:

> The Arab presence in Britain is not a temporary displacement (however pervasive the myth of return) and thus ... the need to encourage more concerted efforts to ensure that the concerns of the settled Arab communities find a place on the British national agenda.[16]

Yet, establishing a credible population statistic for the number of Arabs present in the UK is, as El-Solh identifies, an on-going problem,

> For example, the annual Labour Force Survey [and the government Census] not only lumps Arabs into an undifferentiated category. Its estimate for the late 1980s of 73,000 Arabs does not tally with the 230,000 estimated by the Arab British Chamber of Commerce, or the 500,000 claimed by the *Economist* in the same period.[17]

After roughly computing the Home Office's statistics on granting work permits, asylum seeker status and permanent residences, El-Solh estimated that the Arab population of Britain by the end of the 1980s numbered around 250,000.[18]

It is widely agreed that there is a general lack of Census information on Arabs in the UK, which, as we have seen, has perpetuated a myth of invisibility and resulted in a distinct lack of provision at the local and national governmental levels, across a range of issues from health and education to employment and discrimination. Two recent, but limited, report studies into the situation of British Arabs currently exist. The first is by the London Greater Authority (LGA) who undertook a study of the numbers of Arabs as an ethnic identity present in the London boroughs in 2005. The study was based on the 2001 Census figures and only employed the countries that made up the Arab League, but it found that there were 55,884 males and 50,949 females making a total of 106,833 Arabs living in Greater London.[19] The second was conducted in 2009, when the Atlantic Forum organization surveyed 335 Arabs living in the UK in relation to identity, politics and community.[20] While both reports offer some understanding of the population figures and socio-political situation of some British Arabs, it is actually only the latest national Census that has yielded any significant understanding of the current British Arab communities.

After lobbying the government since 2004 for recognition of Arabs as part of the ethnic profiling widely used in all government and non-government documents, the National Association of British Arabs (NABA), successfully convinced the Office of National Statistics (ONS) that its representatives should be allowed, in 2005, to join the Diversity Group preparing for the 2011 Census. Recognizing that people often identify with a number of various categories, beyond a single 'tick box' approach: 'The ONS therefore revised the Census Form to allow maximum flexibility for all respondents.'[21] The NABA Report on the 2011 Census, *Arabs and Arab league Population of the UK* (May 2013), has produced an analysis of current available Census figures relating to Arabs in the UK. The Report combines a previous initial response with the current document which is yet to consider the, as yet, unpublished Census results from Scotland and Northern Ireland. NABA consulted with the ONS regarding traditional ways data is collected, the methodologies used and the different modes the newly introduced 'Arab' box of the Ethnic Origin category was ticked.

Furthermore, beyond the newly, agreed specified box for 'Arab', respondents were also able to 'write in' a more detailed, if not personalized, response:

> It is interesting to note from this section that very few of the Arab countries are actually represented in this section, indeed only Iraqi and Somali respondents appear to have filled in this section in addition to non-detailed 'North African'.[22]

This allowed a more specific identification regardless of the national identity, e.g. 'British' and also accommodated a 'national identity' which respondents saw as their original, i.e. 'British Yemeni', 'British Libyan' etc. In addition, by allowing respondents to answer the question 'Passports Held', this facilitated a declaration of primary and/or additional passports held.[23] In this context, it is important that respondents were made aware that the UK actually allows dual nationality. NABA also argued that the pre-existing 17 subcategories of ethnic groupings, which were broadly covered under five major headings, were considered to be inadequate for the proposed 2011 Census, given the range of migration to the UK:

> When the national identity question was introduced, there was some evidence to show that British-born people from ethnic minority groups were more likely to answer the ethnic group question if a national identity question was asked first, as it still allowed them to state that they were British.[24]

The 'written in' responses reveal a wide variation on how people viewed themselves, but the various descriptions do not reveal the specific figures given for each in the Census data. Therefore, whilst 'Yemeni/Yemini' is identified as 'Ethnic Group Code' number '460', there are no actual figures to indicate the current size of the current British Yemeni population.

However, the current available figures from the 2011 Census that show that the number of Arabs in England and Wales who 'chose to categorise themselves as ethnically Arab either by ticking the "Arab" box or writing in responses'[25] are as follows:

Arab	240,545
African Arab	3,393
White and Arab	10,058
Moroccan	6,651
North African	22,052
Other Middle Eastern	30,052
Somali	45,475
Somalilander	6,249
White and North African	2,294
Total	**366,769**

Table 8.1 – Breakdown of Arab categories taken from 'Ethnic Write-In Responses' (Information reproduced from Census 2011 Table CT0010EW)[26]

The total figure of 366,769 is absent of any indication of duplication – a respondent ticking both the 'Arab' box and another, e.g. 'Other Middle Eastern' or 'White and Arab', etc. NABA's report concludes that the total figure and the specific 'Arab' figure of 240,545 are both much lower than they had anticipated. However, after examining the numbers of respondents who identified themselves as being born in Arab countries as 404,207, they were surprised that this figure alone exceeds the stated total of 366,769. They insist that the anomaly can be explained, perhaps, by including people of other ethnic origins than Arab, being born in an Arab country. Further, extrapolating a definitive figure for the number of 'Mixed Arab[s]' (which would in the case of the British Yemeni communities include the *muwalladūn*) is also not possible from the current Census statistics. The figures for Scotland and Northern Ireland are also unavailable as the forms were absent of the 'Arab' box, but did include Arab League countries as a country of origin.

NABA's report raises some interesting questions regarding the current, and more inclusive, Census form, concluding:

> We would re-emphasise that the figures are therefore not definite ... the results show a limitation of response from many respondents, particularly in relation to the question of 'National Identity' and 'Passports Held'.[27]

They state that these limitations could be present because: (i) a misunderstanding of the availability and acceptability of identifying themselves in several different ways without contradiction; (ii) a reluctance to identify themselves too closely with their country of origin; and (iii) fear of admitting that they held more than one passport although this is legal in the UK.[28] Yet, beyond the difficulties of precise extrapolation and interpretation of the 2011 Census statistics for the UK's Arab population, NABA has confidently concluded the following:

1. Arabs represent 0.4% of the population of England and Wales.
2. 240,000 Census respondents identified themselves specifically as 'Arab' – this figure may or may not include those who have also put specific nationalities.
3. The numbers of people living in England and Wales who were born in Arab countries is 404,207 or, 0.5% of the total UK population – this figure does not include those born in England and Wales or outside the UK who consider themselves as Arabs.
4. Two London boroughs; Westminster (7.2%) and Kensington and Chelsea (4.1%) had the biggest proportion of people who identified as Arabs.
5. The seventh most commonly spoken language in England and Wales is Arabic with 159,000 (0.3%) of people speaking it.[29]

Finally, NABA state that the unknown variables still to be ascertained from the 2011 Census statistics in relation to the UK's Arab population are:

1. The status of the UK's Arab population, i.e. British nationals, permanent residence, asylum seekers etc.
2. The precise number of 'first generation' Arabs.
3. The educational qualifications of respondents.
4. The specific employment status (professional, managerial

etc.) of respondents.

5. The numbers of those respondents in employment.
6. The health status (good health, disabled etc.) of those responding.
7. A breakdown of the numbers of those from mixed marriages.[30]

Although NABA is still awaiting the relevant results from Scotland and Northern Ireland, they say they are satisfied that the figures obtained thus far 'represent a relatively clear picture of the Arab population of the UK'.[31]

In discussing the variations and fissures within the diverse Arab subgroups present in the UK – nationality, religion, socio-economic position, etc. – El-Solh also concedes that there is a degree of perceived collective Arab identity that has often emerged through a series of events such as Palestine, the first Gulf war and, later 9/11 and the subsequent invasion of Iraq. She states:

> For example, not surprisingly, such a collective consciousness was activated during the 1991 Gulf War, when Arabs of different national/socio-economic origins and political persuasions reacted in similar ways to what they perceived to be a double standard fuelling this war.[32]

This developed British Arab collective consciousness was also manifest at the outbreak of the second Gulf war, when the Bush administration in the US invaded first Afghanistan and then Iraq as part of its 'war on terror' strategy, which both stimulated and crystallized an assertive British Arab initiative as a major player in the 'Stop the War' campaign, vigorously supported by the Muslim Association of Britain (MAB). This anti-war organization was led by a number of second-generation 'Arab Islamists', including Anas Altikriti, Director of the Cordoba Foundation. MAB also attracted a high number of young British Yemenis into its ranks, particularly during the many demonstrations and marches that took place across a number of British cities. Equally, rapidly changing events currently sweeping across the Arab-Islamic Middle East in the so-called 'Arab spring' pro-democracy movements of Tunisia, Libya, Egypt, Syria, Bahrain and Yemen, are having a profound effect on the mobilization of young British-born Arabs. These diasporic Arab communities have been pivotal in keeping up political pressure and support to oust the many oppressive dictators: Bin Ali, Qadaffi, Saddam, Muburak, Assad and Ali Abdullah Salih, to name a few, who have consistently suppressed the masses and almost bled the wealth of their various countries dry. British Arabs have rallied support through continued fund-raising, demonstrations and awareness-raising events that have ensured that a degree of pressure is brought to bear on the various undemocratic regimes and dictators across the Middle East. In addition to manifesting their support of their fellow countrymen of origin, a number of British Arabs are also actively involved in representing the revolutionary movements in the western media. Britain hosts the biggest Libyan community outside of Libya, largely settled in Manchester, which also has an established historical presence of Syrians settled there along with large numbers of Yemenis and Iraqi Arabs and Kurds. As a result, the 'Arab Spring' has not just been witnessed in Tahrir Square or the streets of Benghazi and Damascus; it has also played out along Manchester's Oxford Road, Wilmslow Road and Albert Square. What is clear from this very diverse history of Arab communities in the city is that Manchester, like other major industrial cities of Britain, has for almost 200 years become the permanent home of a sizeable, yet relatively little-known Arab community.[33]

Halliday asserts that the Yemeni community in Britain is largely that of 'invisible Arabs' who live in 'incapsulated' communities forged out of internal networks of bonded tribal and family links, through the process of 'chain migration' and transnational identities. In short, he notes that the sojourner to settler experience has resulted in 'urban villages' of insular Yemeni communities throughout post-industrial British cities. His claim would certainly seem to reflect the migration and settlement experience of the community in Eccles, Greater Manchester, a community that has been the focus on my own ethnographic research conducted between

2000 and 2005.[34] But the apparent self-imposed segregation and lack of interaction with the wider society may in fact be due to a combination of external factors and limited skills and abilities within the Yemeni community. Adnan Saif notes of the British Yemeni community, 'You have got probably the oldest settled community here and yet in terms of development it is comparatively behind [those other minority communities].'[35] For example, a general ineptitude and understanding of English language and culture was a genuine problem for most first-generation Yemeni migrants to Britain. Translation and interaction was normally facilitated through the *muqaddam* or *muwassiṭ* on the ships and in the factories.[36] Dahya has previously argued that Yemeni resistance to the process of assimilation was as a result of fearing the consequences of competition and conflict with the indigenous population in three areas: jobs, housing and marriage to indigenous, white women. Earlier communities of Yemeni sailors experienced street battles, imprisonment and deportations during the race riots of the early twentieth century and, as a result, Dahya notes that 'the [Yemeni] migrants do not appear – in the eyes of the host society – as competitors and therefore avoid conflict situations',[37] it would seem that self-segregation was preferred as a means of avoiding any conflict through assimilation.[38] If Halliday's assertion is correct then it begs the question, is the Yemeni experience of segregation or 'incapusulation' in Britain normative for British Muslims or does their narrative represent a unique experience? The answer to this question lies in the exploration of whether the community is, as Halliday asserts, one of 'invisible Arabs'.

British Muslims are far from being a homogenous entity and their many diverse theological and ethnic subgroups present in the UK largely represent the Muslim world in microcosm. As such they are a matrix of national, ethnic, doctrinal and economic heterogeneity which collectively comprises the country's largest minority faith group.[39] Statistically, 60% of the British Muslim population is UK-born and aged 25 years and under. Further, around 40% of the total British Muslim population lives in the relatively prosperous south-eastern region and Greater London conurbations, with the remaining 60% placed within the urbanized and industrial heartlands of the Midlands and the North.[40] However, whilst statistics on the current social and demographic status of the British Muslim community provides an interesting overview of the collective community, there is some doubt concerning the 2001 Census population figure for British Muslims of 1.695 million. Muhammad Anwar disputes this official figure based on a number of factors relating to data collation and form filling inaccuracies by Muslim heads of households, he argues and estimates that there are 1.8 million Muslims in Britain.[41] The question on religious affiliation in the 2001 Census was only voluntary and, therefore, some Muslims may have wished to remain religiously anonymous, as Anwar explains:

> Given that the question on religious affiliation was voluntary, this information may be limited although there have been recommendations put forward and pressure groups have been lobbying for more information with regards to peoples religious affiliations ... Local councils and other service providers would need to know what proportion of local populations are Muslim.[42]

Iftikhar Malik has offered another explanation for the ambiguity concerning the exact figure for the British Muslim population as the hesitation on the part of first-generation settlers who, 'in some cases, were reluctant to register themselves for votes or in the Census.'[43] However, Anwar's predicted figure for 2001 has proved to be nearer the actual figure if we compare it to the 2011 Census figure for Muslims which is currently 2.7 million or, 5% of the total population of the UK.[44] The Census register anomolies identified by Malik are almost certainly a factor in the case of the Yemeni community in Eccles, where both the official Census figures of 1991 and 2001 show a population figure that is quite obviously well below the actual number of Yemenis living in Eccles. In the 1991 Census statistics the Yemenis of Eccles were, unlike Pakistani, Indian and Bangladeshi communities, unidentifiable because of the limited and non-segmented category of further ethnic groups as 'Other'. A fact previously referred to and confirmed by Salford

City Council, Ethnic Minority Monitoring Unit.[45]

The introduction of the religious affiliation question in the 2001 Census allows a cross-tabulation of both ethnic minority population statistics and religious affiliation population statistics which may help to establish a more accurate figure for the population of the Yemeni Muslim community in Eccles. However, any figures deduced by cross-tabulation still only provides an estimation, as there is no means of identifying either 'Yemenis' or 'British Yemenis' from the 2001 Census data. Madawi al-Rasheed has referred to this perplexing problem noting:

> British government statistics are not particularly useful as a source for estimating the number of Arab migrants ... [The] Census in general gives an underestimate of the number of Arab migrants who are of Arab nationality or Arab ethnic origin.[46]

The 1991 Census statistics shows the number of 'Other' for the population of Eccles to be 162. Considering that the ambiguous 'Other' category is unsegmented and includes all unspecified ethnic groups, this figure would include the Yemeni community, providing a very inaccurate, if not misrepresented figure. Improvements to the 2001 Census saw the creation of clearer segmentations of ethnic subgroups, which also included a number of 'mixed' ethnic origin categories. However, Arabs still remain largely 'invisible' and are only identifiable through the 'other ethnic group' category giving some credence to Halliday and al-Rasheed's claims of communities of 'invisible Arabs' in the UK. The perennial problem of identifying British Arabs through government statistics has prompted Al Rashid to conclude that, 'Arab communities in Britain remain veiled as far as policy makers are concerned'.[47] Again, this general observation would certainly be true with regards to the specific situation of the Yemenis and their community development in Eccles. A female research respondent told me of her early experiences employed as a Yemeni community worker in the 1980s:

> I was for [*sic*] the first Yemeni person that they [local authorities] got help from. So, I would represent them there at the CVS [Community Voluntary Services] and would be their spokesperson and we had our Friendship Day in 1988 I think, yeah. I did the initiation [*sic*] and they spoke on their behalf telling about their bad situation and their exclusion. That was for the first occasion to one of people [*sic*] around here and in the Salford area to know about the real situation and existence of the Yemeni community. I don't want to say they didn't ... some of them had begun to make some contacts but they weren't that strong to bring to the community to the visible stage.[48]

Al-Rasheed further asserts that this general invisibility presents a significant factor in the particular context of migrant Arab workers but, she insists that their statistical invisibility does not hide the reality that there are established migrant communities in Britain.[49]

The 2001 Census Religious Affiliation category for Eccles identifies a Muslim population of only 499. Again, this figure appears to be remarkably low particularly given that the number of identifiable ethnic subgroups: 'Indian', 'Pakistani', 'Bangladeshi', 'Other Asian' and 'Mixed Asian' total 470. Even when this figure is readjusted to allow for other religious minorities from the same ethnic subgroups to be subtracted,[50] we are left with an approximate figure of 328. By further subtracting the combined total of Muslim ethnic subgroups of 'Indian', 'Pakistani', 'Bangladeshi', 'Other Asian' and 'Mixed Asian' origin from the Religious Affiliation, 'Muslim' statistic of 499, we are left with a figure of 171. This extrapolated figure would represent the other Muslims in Eccles of non-South Asian origin, i.e., Yemenis, Libyans, Iraqis, Egyptians, Syrians, Turks, Kurds, Iranians and others. As we have seen, quantifying and segmenting Arab Muslims, and Yemenis in particular, from the Census data is fraught with difficulties and therefore establishing the official population figure for the Yemeni community is not possible based on either the 1991 or 2001 Census. A senior member of the Yemeni Eccles community, Mukbul Ahmad, who came to Eccles in 1956 and is the former Secretary of the Yemeni Welfare Society, informed me that there are approximately 100 Yemeni families living in Eccles.[51] The respondent had had limited liaisons with the local council through the Yemeni Welfare Society but he seemed convinced that the city council did not wish to help the Yemeni community:

> They don't help us; they don't listen to us. They don't give us anything. They just say yes okay, okay. I don't know why that is [they might be] racist I think. You see top one is racist, not to the ... some people is very nice. Some English people very, very good. Hazel Blears, she's MP in Eccles, she come here she's very nice, she's in Birmingham now or London. She come to here she's good she try to help before she go. Hazel Blears came to visit us here [at home] the MP was trying to help, we serious we tried but money's gone, no money. This year's money's gone wait until next year and wait until next year, now forty-four years we waiting for it![52]

If we apply Anwar's statistical research on the size of Muslim households in Britain to the respondent's estimate of a hundred families, we may be able to calculate a more precise number for the Yemeni community in Eccles. Anwar states that Muslim households are larger, five persons per household, compared with the rest of the population of (2.4 persons) per family. He also states that many Muslims live in joint and extended families.[53] Even by applying Anwar's conservative figure of five members per Muslim household and multiplying it by our estimate we are left with a figure of 500 Yemenis. By further building into this figure the 'joint and extended families' factor identified in Anwar's research, the figure of 500 could increase by up to 50%.

Whatever the exact figure for the population of the Yemeni community of Eccles is, clearly, it is far in excess of the possible 2001 Census extrapolated figure of 171. The apparent discrepancy between the 'official' population figure and the figure of around 800 based on a cross-correlation of research data and Anwar's estimates has very obvious implications with regard to the provision and service received from the local authorities. Based on the population statistics of the 2001 Census alone, it would appear that the Yemeni community is actually the largest Muslim ethnic group in Eccles, is not only indistinguishable and unidentifiable but also invisible. Subsequently, based on NABA's Report and in accordance with the 2011 Census statistics for the various 'Arab' and other relevant sub-categories, e.g. 'Other Middle Eastern', 'White and Arab' and 'White and North African or Middle Eastern', I estimate that the current population of the Yemeni community of Eccles is as follows:

Arab	1,479
Other Middle Eastern	138
White and Arab	47
White and North African or Middle Eastern	12
Total	**1,712**

Table 8.2 – Breakdown of the Relevant Arab categories for Salford taken from 'Ethnic Write-In Responses' (Information reproduced from NABA Report on 2011 UK Census – May 13)[54]

But despite the anomolies of the Yemeni population figures and their obvious 'invisibility' and social exclusion one respondent told me optimistically:

> Politics in this country gives me an assurance that I will see a change for my kids as a British ... Because how I feel now, I feel there is hatred towards Muslims, it's a hatred [*sic*]. Unless, I don't know, it might change or it might become worse. It depends on the politics and government, if Muslims still have a presence here there could be changes etc. but a number of factors could effect [*sic*] it.[55]

It is perhaps then, little wonder that Yemenis experience social exclusion and community underdevelopment and the misrepresentation of the community certainly has a wider context in that it may reflect a majority of Muslim communities throughout Britain whose continued physical and cultural segregation from the wider society has impeded and inhibited social interaction and integration.

This apparent 'ghettoization' has been identified as a major contributory factor in the race riots in the northern towns of Oldham, Burnley and Bradford in the summer of 2001.[56] The 'parallel communities' defined in the Community Cohesion report were seen as a symptomatic failure of multiculturalism and racial equality legislation in addressing community issues of social inclusion and cohesion. The report marked out the British Muslim community as being at the blunt end of exclusion, racism and discrimination. Humayun Ansari asserts that the British Muslim experience reinforces patterns of relatively high levels of socio-economic disadvantage in many communities.[57] Christopher Allen's report on the aftermath of the Bradford riots (2001), the Home Office's Community Cohesion report and the harsh sentences received by many first-time offending Muslim youths, was critical of the local authority's lack of response to the prevailing socio-economic conditions of the city's Muslim population. Allen describes the underdevelopment: unemployment, poverty, poor housing and social exclusion as, 'indices of social deprivation'.[58] This experience of exclusion would certainly appear to have been a dominant feature within the Yemeni community in Eccles until their enterprising bids for community development money through local and national government funding in the late 2000s.

8.1 – British Yemenis in Eccles, Greater Manchester, celebrating 'Eccles Day' in which they performed their tradition Yemeni tribal dances.

Increasing concerns over the perceived integration of Muslim minorities in Britain and the west, or lack thereof, have appeared to have coalesced in the discourses of social cohesion and marginalization and ideas around the currency of multiculturalism. In the process, there has been a continued blurring of the lines between what represents both the 'public' and 'private' spaces, particularly in the context of what represents 'culture' and 'politics'. The distinct framing of these discussions has been the dichotomy between liberal, secular and democratic values and conservative, religious practices specifically espoused by Islam/Muslims. The politicization of Muslim identity in Britain often means that the nuances of Muslim/Islamic cultural and ethnic identities – 'Arabness' and 'Yemeniness' – are conflated in the broader public debates and constructions of Muslim identity, albeit in a climate of deep distrust and negative stereotyping. British Yemenis have formed a community that is distinctly marked, both culturally and religiously but it is not particularly separatist or exclusive. Whilst many of their cultural traditions and religious practices have been preserved, degrees and forms of attachment are fluid and constantly negotiated both between genders and across generations. Similarly, both Yemeni traditions and Muslim practices coexist with new forms of identity and cultural manifestations that maintain 'Yemeniness' and include 'Britishness'. But these hybrid identities are often painfully forged through the intra-community dynamics of preserving tradition and identity and also against the wider social tensions of assimilation and social exclusion.

The current imposed homogeneity on divergent Muslim identities is, once again, in danger of making British Yemenis 'invisible' despite their recent efforts at transforming their invisibility into a very public presence at the national cultural level. And, whilst there has been no discernable attempt by British Yemenis generally to politicize their religious identity, it has to be noted that the wider public debates, media representations and government policies have politicized Muslim religious identity, further blurring the lines between public and private spheres and the simultaneity of religious and secular identities.[59] Largely influenced by the work of the renowned social anthropologist, Akbar Ahmad, Carol Nagel and Lynn Staeheli state that:

> The presumed lack of distinction between religion and politics in the Muslim world, therefore, signifies inherent irrationality, anti-modernism and backwardness – a conception reinforced by the constant stream of media images of suicide bombers, beheadings and *burqas* that flow from the Muslim world.[60]

It would appear that the growing collective conscious and increasing visibility of Britain's Yemeni community has unfortunately coincided with the focus of Muslim presence in the public space, along with all of the provisions that this presence demands: wearing headscarves, establishing mosques and Islamic centres, *ḥalāl* food and the provision of prayer space in the workplace and public buildings. Such demands are seen as a defying of the neutrality and secularity of national societies and as Muslims excluding themselves from the public by marking themselves out differently from wider society.[61] Hence, the comments of the former Labour Home Secretary, Jack Straw, regarding violation of social norms by Muslim women wearing the *niqāb* (face-veil) are seen to be consistent with those of the general public across liberal European societies.

Amid such discussions has been a critical evaluation of the social currency of multiculturalism, which has been deemed responsible for a reasserted 'Islamic identity' as being anti-liberal, anti-rationalist and anti-integrationist. In response, there has been a reframing of 'core national values' that appear to be increasingly secular and at the same time noticeably less inclusive, leading Nagel and Staeheli to comment:

> Overall there is a pronounced tendency in public discourse in the west ... to interpret the political claims of Muslim minorities in terms of the imposition of a fundamentalist, anti-modern Islam on a historically Christian, secularised, rational public.[62]

The evidences to challenge such gross misrepresentations and highly misleading stereotypes are simply overwhelming and recent academic research on Muslim minorities in the west have explored the diversity and complexity of Muslim identities and how they are multifariously constructed around the formation of both public and private identities. These manifold examples defy any homogenous or essentialist reading of Islam or Muslims as challenging western, secular, liberal democratic notions or as a community that is unequipped and unwilling to integrate and engage with mainstream society or to enter the public realm.[63] Nagel and Staeheli's study on young British Arabs focussed on the ambivalence expressed by their respondents towards 'Muslim' as a public and political identity. They noted that while levels of personal religiosity varied significantly among research respondents, most appeared to reject the notion of a 'British Muslim' identity because they regarded it as inherently politicized and largely unrepresentative of their own experiences of religion and politics.

The study interviewed 40 'Muslim British Arabs' of which a significant number where of Yemeni origin and the research focussed on the conflicting notions expressed by their respondents towards 'Muslim' as a public and political identity. They noted that while the levels of personal religiosity varied significantly among respondents, most appeared to reject the idea of a 'British Muslim' identity because they regarded it as inherently politicized and largely unrepresentative of their own experiences.[64] The majority of the research respondents were community activists at the local, national or international levels and some of the organizations they were affiliated with were overtly religious, others secular or non-political, while others further were political and even nationalistic: Palestinian, Iraqi, etc. As well as exploring how the personal beliefs of the respondents fitted into the wider debates about extremism, integration and citizenship, the research also studied the relationships between faith, identity and politics. The findings discussed how faith remained an intensely private and personal matter for the majority of respondents even though it appeared to shape and influence the way they viewed the world and how they engaged with it in the public realm.[65] The apparent preference for a 'British Arab' identity over that of 'British Muslim' was explained in the context of a rejection of the politicized 'Muslim' identity whilst, paradoxically, at the same time wishing to promote 'an identity and a set of political claims as Arab'.[66] The preferred hybrid 'British Arab' identity was, however, not devoid of a cultural association between Islam and 'Arabness', 'in so doing, their private identity becomes public and, to some degree, political.'[67] One respondent identified as 'Rafik', a Yemeni-Arab community leader, stated that community participation was a 'very basic principle of the Muslim faith' and that discrimination faced by the Yemeni community had reduced 'life chances' for Yemenis along with the lack of recognition and support for the community by government.[68] 'Rafik' pushed for the state to fund Islamic education in schools, despite the lack of support for the scheme by local authorities, which he sees as a matter of fairness by 'state-run schools providing cultural and religious education to different faith groups, by tutors and teachers from the same community backgrounds'.[69]

'Rafik's' scheme would provide the same opportunities for other faith communities: Jews, Sikhs, Buddhists, Hindus and Christians, but for Muslims he specifically argues that children will 'grow up as British Muslims, with no need to adopt ideologies from outside. They will be British citizens, they will be brought up with accepted and approved values and principles.'[70] What is particularly interesting is that 'Rafik' sees the future of his faith and religious identity as something that should be integrated into the state education system as a means of preserving, developing and promoting a distinctly 'British Islam' that is acculturated and indigenized, whilst at the same time impervious to 'outside' ideologies that may be either antithetical or hostile to British values. 'Rafik's' response appears to suggest a depoliticizing of Yemeni Muslim identity that is both recognized and supported by government through state education. Equally, another Yemeni community activist from Liverpool, identified as 'Ghazi', also expressed his concerns regarding the coupling of religious identity and political issues from across the wider Muslim world:

> [You] get the rise of the neo-right within the community, who are the children who have been influenced by certain elements within the community that focus on the religion. Unfortunately people ignored this in the early 1980s, and now we get a product. This is not only in the Yemeni community but the other Muslim communities worldwide – people are disillusioned with what's going on out there and are anti-western. Yes there is suffering and there are issues that need to be addressed, but sometimes, for example, the Palestinian issue or Iraq issue feeds into the Bush administration, and that feeds a culture of hate.[71]

'Rafiya' a female British-born Yemeni also expressed a clear distinction between public and private aspects of religious identity that are free from highly political motives, despite being a young woman who wears *ḥijāb*. For 'Rafiya' her wearing of *ḥijāb* is only 'a minor divergence from the "British way of life"'.[72] However, the issues of *ḥijāb* have become both a public and political statement for many non-Muslims who interpret it as a distinct expression of religious and cultural difference. 'Rafiya' acknowledges that wider society sees the distinct presence of Muslim communities across many major cities and towns in the UK as a 'threat', created by bigotry and an ignorance of Islam and Muslims.[73]

It would appear that for a number of respondents, the privacy of their own faith runs contrary to the very public and politicized view of Islam and Muslims, either as a result of the direct actions and public behaviour of a minority of British Muslims who understand their 'Muslimness' through distinctly politicized expressions and identities, or through the ignorance, misunderstandings and prejudices of non-Muslims towards Muslim practices. What is clear is that their views are in contradistinction to the 'relentless association between Islam and political extremism', whilst at the same time they acknowledge the place of religion and religious identity within the public realm.[74] This research found that the currency of the term 'British Muslim' had seriously been devalued by a majority of the British Yemenis interviewed as a direct result of the negative meanings attached to it by the media in the wake of a series of 'landmark events' previously identified by Muhammad Anwar.[75] The researchers state that, 'The British Muslim category has, for these interviewees, been irretrievably sullied by stereotypes about politically radical, extremist Islam that circulate in public discourse.'[76] 'Habeeb', another British Yemeni community activist from Sheffield, responded in quite categorical terms, 'The controversy [surrounding this term] has created a completely wrong perception about it within the social context of my life, I want to be referred to as a British citizen and that's enough for me.'[77] The ecumenicalism present within British-Arab identities highlighted by the researchers: the fact that Judaism, Christianity and Islam all feature as significant faiths within developed Arab cultures, means that the political radicalization and religious extremism now so readily associated with the term 'British Muslim', has made the term an unattractive and inappropriate descriptive for many British Arabs. 'Wajih', a Yemeni-born community activist from London, spoke of his disappointment at both the lack of mobilization and representation of Arabs in public forums and local and national councils, stating that the authorities were 'treating Arabs either as part of the Asian community or the Muslim community in general ... Arabs should be represented better by those who can speak the mind of the British Arabs.'[78]

8.2 – British Yemenis meeting with the Yemen Ambassador to the UK, H.E. Ali al-Ridhi, in 2011.

Invariably, British Yemeni identity cannot be separated from its cultural (Arab) or religious (Muslim) facets and Fred Halliday conversely claims that:

> The challenge of understanding the 'identity' of Muslims in the UK, indeed of any immigrant or indigenous community, is to gauge how far the terms of religious or cultural identity – in this case 'Muslim' – are sufficient to explaining the lives and character of the groups in question.[79]

This statement serves to illustrate how Halliday's original work, like so many pioneering minority community studies, rapidly ceases to be relevant beyond the first-generation migration and settlement experience. In the preface of his study the author recalls how during his research, conducted in the mid-1980s, he '*travelled through Britain on a Yemeni visa*' [author's italics].[80] This claim is supported by his description of the British Yemeni community as insular to the point of 'incapsulation',[81] an analysis that leads to his conclusion that their settlement represents the perpetuated 'invisible Arab' presence in the UK.[82] To some degree Nagel and Staeheli's research appears to confer with Halliday's assertion regarding 'British Muslim' identity in the British Yemeni context and they add that their respondents 'confront a paradox: what they view as a private matter – their religion and faith – has to be brought into the public sphere through cultural and educational programmes that presents a particular view of Islam.'[83] This particularly constructed view of Islam is, as we have seen, highly politicized, religiously extremist and both antithetical and antagonistic to openly tolerant and liberal multicultural European societies. The framing of 'British Muslim' identity in these narrow and negative representations present a challenge for many British Arabs who assert a distinctly private and personal facet of religious identity that is compromised by the public space, where religious identity rests upon the simultaneity of identities and beliefs that otherwise appear to be unable to occupy the same political space, reflecting the complex and contradictory nature of the relationships between religiosity and the public sphere, but seemingly devoid of the existing binaries and dichotomies of identity constructions.

I would suggest that the construction of a British Yemeni identity is an on-going process of negotiation. That is, through a process of appropriation and adaptation of certain elements of the dominant culture into the developing and acculturated forms of the minority or subjugated culture, 'Britishness' is both deterritorialized and fused into an interactive hybrid identity. A visible manifestation of this social phenomenon was observed at a Yemeni wedding I attended in Manchester where the groom wore a grey English-style morning suit complete with stiff collar, silk cravat and silver-buttoned waistcoat. His traditional English wedding apparel contrasted with his marriage celebration where he danced his Yemeni-tribal dance waving his *jambiyyah* (ceremonial dagger) and later then reclining on cushions to chew *qāt* in a huge *māqil* held honour of his wedding. The males from the bride's family chose to wear traditional Yemeni *shawāl* (headdress) and *fawṭah* (sarong) or *jalabiyyah* (long Arab gown), complete with a *jambiyyah*, which was waved around as part of the dance ritual. Here, the Yemeni traditional dress contrasted with the occasional fluent smatterings of English in a broad Liverpudlian accent. To complete the multicultural hybrid experience guests were served with neither traditional Yemeni nor English dishes, but instead, ubiquitous chicken and lamb curry dishes with *biriyānī* (rice cooked with meat) and *nān* (flat bread) supplied by the local Bengali restaurant. The whole experience appeared to serve as a living metaphor for contemporary British multiculturalism.

In its nascent stages of settlement in the UK, the British Yemeni community developed primarily through tribal connections facilitated by 'chain migration' either from the Yemen or by 'inward migration' of tribal bondsmen living in the British ports into the industrial metropolises. But, as the community expanded, tribal tensions were exacerbated in the late 1960s due to the civil war and hostilities between North and South Yemen, which brought regional and political allegiances into play within the local politics of the diaspora Yemeni communities. Yet, at the same time, tribal and regional loyalty and belonging quite often ran counter to political convictions. In the shifting Yemeni politics of independence, civil war and reunification struggles, it would appear that tribal identity often provided a stable means of self-identification in a world where geopolitical boundaries, traditional theocracies and revolutionary ideologies were in a state of constant flux. Tribal identity and affiliation amongst first-generation migrant Yemenis in Britain remains a very real and tangible facet of their self-identity.

Furthermore, tribal identity is reified through the formation of diaspora tribal 'villages' in the industrialized urban spaces of Britain, which has largely been facilitated by the process of 'chain migration' and by transnational, or what I would prefer to describe as 'translocal', networks and links with the tribal homeland. However, the notion of 'tribe' remains somewhat abstract for second-generation British-born Yemenis and tribal identity or belonging is only realized through a visit to the ancestral tribal homeland. Many of the young respondents I interviewed, particularly males, only became 'tribesmen' after a visit to their father's village in the Yemen. In contrast, female notions of tribal belonging and identity were much less pronounced even after visiting the Yemen. The female responses suggested that only an honorary sense of tribal belonging was developed, thereby lending weight to the opinion that patriarchy is the dominant factor in the construction of tribal identity and collective belonging. The experience of patriarchal domination in Yemeni tribal society is perhaps best reflected in the phrase *min jadd wāḥid* ('from one forefather') as the maxim of a collective tribal history and narrative. Translocal tribal politics forms part of the intra-community dynamics of the British Yemeni community but tribal disputes and tensions only surface occasionally and may even be virtually 'invisible' to the outsider. For example, the burden of a son's obligation to his parents is a traditional feature of tribal and village life in pre-modern societies. Betsy Hartmann and James Boyce's study of village life in Bangladesh has observed this patriarchal obligation and they note, 'in return for the love they give to their children, parents expect respect and support during their old age – a reciprocation which is basic to village society.'[84] In addition, it is because daughters leave the family home after marriage that the responsibility of care for parents ultimately falls on the son.

8.3 – Gadri Salih, community leader from the Eccles Yemeni community in his traditional Yemeni dress.

The need to conform to the collective conventions, even though one may be far beyond the cultural space and geographical place of ones ancestral homeland, is essentially self-imposed. And so, through the strongly-bonded links and tribal allegiances nurtured in both the tribal village or homeland and the 'urban village' of the diasporic tribal bondsmen, a unique dimension of tribal identity and belonging based on traditional notions of *'izzah* (honour), *'ayb* (shame), *ḥuqūq* (rights), *dam* (blood) and *'urf* (customs), has produced a new form of transnational identity. This is a phenomenon I would describe as 'translocal tribalism'. The British Yemeni community also displays aspects of its Muslim 'universalism' which extend beyond their ideas of 'Yemeniness' based on their cultural, historical, tribal and political expressions of identity. In this way, they are able to formulate notions of 'brotherhood' with other tribal bondsmen and non-Yemenis that are facilitated by both theological justifications and religious conviction. Through the process of migration it could also be argued that 'Yemeniness' has been globalized and the presence of diaspora Yemeni communities in America, Europe, Africa, South Asia and the Far East gives some credence to claims of a 'local' culture becoming global. Conversely, the understanding of local as being something small and parochial or particular to a specific space and place – defined in opposition to the 'global' – need not be merely confined to space but is perhaps more relative to size. 'Global' dimensions of 'Yemeniness' are obviously based on 'local' constructions of identity, culture, language, traditions, customs and tribe. In this context Yemeni identity would be defined through a local character yet transported and manifest in a wider global setting. This translocal form of 'Yemeniness' is a product of defining a specific identity in the wider global context of (and against) all others. Obviously, for Yemenis in the diaspora the impact and influence of the Other cannot be denied as a process to varying degrees of acculturation and integration. Equally, it may also be argued that the pervading hegemonic nature of western civilization through previous colonization, the recent phenomenon of globalization is beginning to impact and erode 'local' cultures. Alarmingly, this intrusive aspect of globalization might mean that eventually there would be no distinctiveness or local character, place or culture remaining within the globalized world. However, from the point of view of the 'local' and the 'global', they may not necessarily be terms existing in counterdistinction. In fact, in a very real way – particularly in the construction of 'Yemeniness' as a distinctive identity – the 'local' and the 'global' constitute each other.

This phenomenon is perhaps best exampled in the tribal identity as a translocal manifestation amongst the Yemeni community in Britain. To be a Yemeni, in both the traditional geo-cultural place of the Yemen and within the diaspora communities such as Britain, is a specific identity that, in contrast to the universalism of a religious (Muslim) identity, is both culturally distinctive and socially different. But, whilst Islam as a world religion can embrace the global or *ummatic* dimensions of communal identity that are also often heightened by modern global technologies, specific cultural identities would appear to be distinctly 'local', if not somewhat syncretic or even anachronistic. However, as the phenomenon of globalization appears to propagate dominant and hegemonic cultures, 'local' cultures are equally able to reach out via global connections beyond the confines of traditional space and place. As a result, minority faith communities like the British Yemeni community are able to transcend the apparent limitations of what might be considered to be their parochial tribal customs and culture, particularly when located within a new and completely different cultural and social environment. The resilience of the religious and cultural facets of British Yemeni identity raises some interesting questions relating to both the perceptions and expectations of the social integration and assimilation of minority faith communities into the wider identity constructions, notions and definitions of 'Britishness' in modern, multicultural and religiously plural Britain.

ENDNOTES

Prologue

1. For a detailed definition of the etymological origins of the word 'lascar', see Col. Yule, Henry, R.E., C.B. and, Burnell, A. C., Ph.D., C.I.E. (new edition, edited by Crooke, William, B.A.) (2000), *Hobson-Jobson; A Glossary of Colloquial Anglo-Indian Words and Phrases, and of Kindred Terms, Etymological, Historical, Geographical and Discursive*, New Delhi: Munshiram Manoharial Publishers Pvt. Ltd., pp. 507–9.
2. Seddon, Mohammad Siddique, (2005), '"Invisible Arabs" or "English Muslims"?: An inquiry into the construction of religious, cultural and national identities of the Yemeni community of Eccles', unpublished PhD thesis, Department of Religious Studies, Lancaster University.
3. Lawless, Richard, (1995), *From Ta'izz to Tyneside: An Arab community in the North-East of England during the early twentieth century*, Exeter: Exeter University Press, p. 192.
4. Ibid., p. 182–3.
5. Flynn, Tony, (1986), *The History of Eccles Cinemas and Theatres*, Manchester: Neil Richardson, p. 20.
6. Interview with Gadri Salih, 17/04/2012.
7. Ibid.
8. A term coined by Fred Halliday. See Halliday, Fred (1992) *Arabs in Exile: Yemeni Migrants in Urban Bitain*, London: I. B. Tauris, p. 135.

1. Yemen: A Brief History of *Arabia Felix*

1. Hourani, George Fadlo, (1951), *Arab Seafaring in Ancient and Early Medieval Times,* Princeton: Princeton University Press, p. 78.
2. Jenner, Michael, (1983), *Yemen Rediscovered,* London & New York: Longman, p. 29.
3. Ibid., p. 32.
4. Ibid., p. 33.
5. Ibid., p. 34.
6. Ibid., p. 35.
7. Ibid., p. 36.
8. Ibid., p. 39.
9. See al Faruqi, Ismail R., and al Faruqi, Lois Lamyah, (1986), *The Cultural Atlas of Islam*, New York: Macmillan Publishing, pp. 7–9.
10. Dresch, Paul, (2000), *A History of the Modern Yemen*, Cambridge: Cambridge University Press, pp. 3–4.
11. Latta, Rafiq, and Cooper, John P., (eds), (1994), *Yemen: Unification and Modernisation*, London: Gulf Centre for Strategic Studies, p. 8.
12. Ibid., p. 9.
13. For example, Shāfi'ī, Zaydī or Ismā'īlī.
14. Peterson, J. E., (1962), *Yemen: Search for a Modern State*, London: Cromm Helm Ltd., p. 10.
15. Ibid., p. 12.
16. Dahya, Badr Ud-Din, (1965), 'Yemenis in Britain: An Arab Migrant Community', in *Race*, vol. 3, no. 4, 1965, p. 178.
17. Ancient city of the ill-fated dam.
18. Dresch, op. cit., (2000), p. 204.
19. Ibid., p. 12.
20. 'There was for Saba', aforetime, a sign in their homeland – two gardens to the right and to the left. Eat of the sustenance (provided) by your Lord and be grateful to Him: a territory fair and happy, and a Lord oft forgiving! But they turned away (from Allah), and we sent against them the flood (released) from the dams, and we converted their two Garden (rows) into "gardens" producing bitter fruit, and tamarisks, and some few (stunted) Lote trees.' See Ali, Abdullah Yusuf, (1989), *The Holy Qur'ān: Text, Translation and Commentary*, Beirut: The Holy Qur'ān Publishing House, p. 1088, fn. 3812–14.
21. Dresch, op. cit., (2000), p. 12.
22. Literally, 'the city of Prophecy'.
23. Bashier, Zakaria, (1988), *Hijrah: Story and Significance,* Leicester: The Islamic Foundation, p. 18.
24. Haykal, Muhammad Husayn, (1976), *The Life of Muhammad*, North American Trust Publication, p. 197.

25. Bashier, op. cit., (1988), p. 18.
26. Haykal, op. cit., (1976), p. 184.
27. Balouch, N. A., (1980), *The Advent of Islam in Indonesia,* Lahore: National Institute of Historical and Cultural Research, p. 2.
28. See 'Eighteenth Century Dutch Reports on Malacca', in Bastin, John, and Winks, Robin W., (eds), (1966), *Malaysia: Selected Historical Readings*, London: Oxford University Press, pp. 101–8.
29. Ryan, N. J., (1976), A *History of Malaysia and Singapore*, Singapore: Oxford University Press, p. 22.
30. *The Encyclopedia of Islam*, refers to the term 'Hind' thus, 'Muslim geographers of the medieval period generally used the term "Hind" to denote the regions of the east of the Indus. It was also applied to practically all the countries of South East Asia.' See Bearman, P. J. et al (1960–2005) (eds), *Encyclopaedia of Islam*, 2nd edn, 12 vols, Leiden: E. J. Brill, vol. III, p. 404.
31. Bewley, Aisha, (trans.) (1997), *The Women of Madina*, London: Ta Ha Publishers, pp. 61–7.
32. Bearman et al, op. cit., vol. III, (1986), p. 454.
33. Lings, Martin, (1987), *Muhammad: His Life Based on the Earliest Sources*, London: Inner Traditions International Ltd., p. 193.
34. Qureshi, Ishtiaq Husain, (1977), *The Muslim Community in the Indo-Pakistan Subcontinent (610–1947),* Karachi: Ma'ārif Ltd., p. 45.
35. See Brown, Daniel, (1996), *Rethinking Tradition in Modern Islamic Thought*, Cambridge: Cambridge University Press, pp. 22–7.
36. Hourani, op. cit., (1991), p. 185.
37. See Daftary, Farhad, (1998), 'Sayyida Ḥurra: The Ismā'īlī Ṣulayhid Queen in the Yemen', in Hamby, Gavin R. G., (1998), *Women in the Medieval Islamic World*, New York: St. Martin's Press, p. 119.
38. Qureshi, op. cit., (1977), pp. 62–3.
39. Schimmel, Annemarie, (1980), *Islam in the Indian Subcontinent*, Leiden-Koln: E. J. Brill, p. 71.
40. Ibid.
41. Boxberger, Linda, (2002), *On the Edge of Empire,* Albany: State University Press of New York, p. 184.
42. Ibid., p. 185.
43. Ibid., p. 187.
44. *Muwallad,* literally means 'born of' but is usually used to denote someone born of a Yemeni father and a foreign mother. It is also used

for someone of Yemeni origin who is born outside Yemen.

45. Cited in Boxberger, op. cit., (2002), p. 191.

46. Ibid., p. 199.

47. Ibid., p. 203.

48. Ibid., p. 208.

49. Ingrams, Doreen, (1970), *A Time in Arabia*, London: John Murray, p. 88.

50. Jalāl al-Dīn al-Suyūṭī attributes the end of the 'rightful' succession to al-Ḥasan ibn ʿAlī ibn Abī Ṭālib (628–69) who handed the Caliphate to Muʿāwiyah ibn Abī Sufyān in 66 AH, after protracted leadership battles. See Clarke, Abdassamad, (trans.), (1995), *The History of the Khalifas Who Took The Right Way*, London: Ta Ha Publishers, pp. 197–204.

51. Al Faruqi, Ismail Ragi, and Sopher, David E., (1974), *Historical Atlas of the Religions of the World*, New York: Macmillan Publishiing Co. Inc., p. 264.

52. According to the *Encyclopedia of Islam*, the Zaydī Imāmate in Yemen was founded in 897, 'by al-Ḳāsim b. Ibrāhīm's grandson al-Hādī ilā 'l-Hād who had been invited by local tribes in the hope that he would settle feuds.' See 'The Zaydiyyah in Yemen', in Bearman et al, op. cit., vol. XI, (1986), pp. 479–81.

53. Al Faruqi and Soper, op. cit., (1974), p. 264.

54. Latta and Cooper (eds), op. cit., (1994), p. 9.

55. Dahya puts the precise date as 897CE, see, Dahya, op. cit., (1965), p. 178.

56. Stookey, Robert W., (1978), *Yemen: The Politics of the Yemen Arab Republic*, Colorado: West View Press, p. 83.

57. Peterson, op. cit., (1982), p. 14.

58. Ibid., p. 15.

59. Dresch, op. cit., (2000), p. 204.

60. Ansari, Humayun, (2004), *'The Infidel Within': Muslims in Britain Since 1800*, London: Hurst & Company, p. 37.

61. Initially called 'The Peoples Republic of South Yemen'.

62. Latta and Cooper (eds), op. cit., (1994) p. 85, fn. 17.

63. See Halliday, Fred, (1984), 'Soviet Relations with the South Yemen', in, Pridham, B. R., (ed.), *Contemporary Yemen: Politics and Historical Background*, London: Croom Helm and Centre for Arab-Gulf Studies, p. 226.

64. See El Azhary, M. S., (1984), 'Aspects of North Yemen's Relations with Saudi Arabia', in ibid., pp. 195–207.

65. Latta and Cooper (eds), op. cit., (1994), p. 37.

66. Ibid., p. 40.
67. Ibid., p. 43.
68. Ibid., p. 45.
69. Ibid., p. 46.
70. Ibid., p. 47.
71. Dresch, op. cit., (2000), p. 205.
72. Latta and Cooper, (eds), op. cit., (1994), p. 48.
73. Ibid., p. 49.
74. Which were based on the need for a longer transitional period and the boycotting of reunification by YAR Islamists because they considered the PDRY to be an atheist regime.
75. Ibid., p. 49.
76. Ibid., p. 50.
77. Ibid.
78. Dresch, op. cit., (2000), p. 185.
79. Latta and Cooper, (eds), op. cit., (1994), p. 51.
80. Dresch, op. cit., (2000), p. 185.
81. Latta and Cooper, (eds), op. cit., (1994), p. 54.
82. Van Hear, Nicholas, (1998), *New Diasporas: The mass exodus, dispersal and regrouping of migrant communities*, London: UCL Press, p. 87.
83. Dresch, op. cit., (2000), p. 187.
84. Interview with Gadri Salih, 17/01/2004.
85. Latta, Rafiq and Cooper (eds), op. cit., (1994), p. 55.
86. Ibid., p. 57.
87. Dresch, op. cit., (2000), p. 194.
88. Ibid., p. 196.
89. Ibid., p. 197.
90. Tim Mackintosh-Smith refers to the influence and role of Kuwait in the conflict who, he says were 'still smarting from Yemen's decision to call for an Arab solution to the 1990 invasion of their country'. He also footnotes a quote from the Kuwaiti newspaper, *Al-Siyāsah*, in 1993, stating, 'We have lost ten billion dollars in the Gulf War, and we are ready to lose ten billion more to ensure the partition of Yemen.' See Mackintosh-Smith, Tim, (1997), *Yemen: Travels in Dictionary Land*, London: John Murray, p. 253.
91. Dresch, op. cit., (2000), p. 198.
92. Daftary, Farhad, (1998), 'Sayyida Ḥurra: The Ismā'īlī Ṣulayhid Queen in the Yemen', in Hamby, Gavin R. G., (ed.) (1998), *Women in the Medieval Islamic World*, New York: St. Martin's Press, p. 128.
93. Dresch, op. cit., (2000), p. 201.
94. Ibid., p. 202.
95. Ibid., p. 212.
96. The terms 'Islamism' and 'Islamists' according to Eickleman and Piscatori are 'ideologically motivated Muslims ... [whose] Islamist

authority to remake the world derives from a self-confident appropriation of what they believe to be "tradition".' See Eickelman, Dale F., and Piscatori, James, (1996), *Muslim Politics*, New Jersey: Princton University Press, pp. 44–5. Francois Burgat adopts a more measured response to 'Islamism' and states, 'it may be said that academic writing on Islamism ... has produced two types of reading. The first – with most media exposure – has relied upon the radical wing (of which one the most final expressions was the assassination of Sadat) to construct an explanation of the whole phenomenon. The other ... has emphasised its cultural, national and identity-based aspects, putting the purely religious dimensions of the phenomenon into perspective and considering its extremist component as marginal and consequently denouncing its supposed antipathy to the dynamics of social modernisation and political liberalism.' See Burgat, Francois, (2003), *Face to Face with Political Islam*, London: I. B. Tauris & Co. Ltd., p. 178.

97. See Saif, Adnan, (2003), *'It's thirst for blood has not been satiated' – the ideological construction of the Yemen,* unpublished MA Dissertation, Birmingham University.

98. Eagle, A. B. D. R., (2003), 'Al-Hassan Hamid al-Din, 1908–2003: Zaidi prince in exile', *Impact International,* vol. 33, no. 10, October 2003, Shaban Ramadan, 1424, p. 44.

99. Ibid.

100 Ibid.

101. Dresch, Paul, (1993), *Tribes, Government and History in Yemen*, Oxford: Oxford University Press, p. 75.

102. Ibid., p. 76.

103. Ibid., p. 77.

104. Ibid., p. 78.

105. Ibid. p. 107.

106. Ibid., p. 79.

107. Ibid., p. 89.

108. Ibid., p. 93.

109. For a detailed account on the place of *'urf* and *sharī'ah* in the Yemen, see Donaldson, William J., (2000), *Sharecropping in the Yemen: A Study in Islamic Theory, Custom and Pragmatism,* Leiden: E. J. Brill.

110. Dresch, op. cit., (1993), pp. 81–2.

111. Ibid., p. 84.

112. Ibid., p. 97.

113. Ibid.

114. Ibid., p. 110

115. For a detailed discussion, see Seddon, Mohammad Siddique, 'Ancient Citizenry Ancient and Modern: British Yemenis and Translocal Tribalism' in Krause, Wanda (ed.), (2009), *Citizenship, Security and Democracy*, London & Istanbul: Association of Muslim Social Scientists (UK) & Foundation for Political, Economic and Social Research, pp. 89–114.

116. Dresch, op. cit., (2000), p. 207.

2. From Aden to 'Tiger Bay', 'Barbary Coast' and 'Little Arabia'

1. Chew, Samuel, (1937), *The Rose and The Crescent,* New York: Oxford University Press, p. 424, fn. 1.
2. Foster, W. (ed.), (1905), *Jourdain's Journal, 1608–1617*, Cambridge: Hakluyt Society.
3. Gavin, R., (1994), 'The Port of Aden – A Brief History', in *The Port of Aden Annual*, Ta'izz: Genpack, p. 5.
4. Ibid. 5. Ibid., p. 7. 6. Ibid. 7. Ibid.
8. See http://www.lascars.co.uk/ranks.html (accessed 25/03/2012).
9. Ansari, op. cit., (2004), p. 37. . 10. Ibid. 11. Ibid.
12. Reilly, Bernard, (1960), *Aden and the Yemen*, London: Her Majesty's Stationary Office, p. 2.
13. Halliday, op. cit., (1992), p. 141. 14. Ibid.
15. Lawless, op. cit., (1995), p. 23. 16. Ibid., p. 24.
17. Ansari, op. cit., (2004), p. 35. 18. Ibid., p. 36.
19. Ibid. 20. Ibid., p. 37. 21. Ibid. 22. Ibid., pp. 70–2.
23. Fryer, Peter, (1985), *Staying Power: The history of Black People in Britain*, London: Pluto Press, p. 262.
24. Ibid.
25. Visram, Rozina, (2002), *Asian in Britain: 400 Years of History*, London: Pluto Press, p. 27.
26. Fryer, op. cit., (1985), pp. 294–5. 27. Ibid., p. 295.
28. Visram, op. cit., (2002), p. 27. 29. Ibid., p. 54.
30. Ibid., p. 55.
31. Collins, Sydney, (1957), *Coloured Minorities in Britain*, London: Lutterworth Press, p. 193.
32. Ibid.
33. Davies, Grahame, (2011), *The Dragon and the Crescent: Nine Centuries of Welsh Contact with Islam*, Bridgend: Serenbooks, p. 107.
34. Visram, op. cit., (2002), p. 56. 35. Ibid., p. 33.
36. Salter, (1896), *The East in the West*, London: Partridge, pp. 70–2.
37. Ibid., p. 150. 38. Ibid., p. 143.
39. Visram, op. cit., (2002), p. 58.

40. Salter, op. cit., (1896), p. 152.
41. Ibid., p. 154.
42. Ibid., p. 152–3.
43. Ibid., p. 154.
44. Ibid., p. 37.
45. Ibid., p. 24.
46. Ibid., p. 39.
47. Ibid., p. 18.
48. Ibid., p. 70.
49. Ibid., p. 74.
50. Ibid., p. 24.
51. Ibid., p. 43.
52. Ibid., p. 127.
53. Ibid., p. 118.
54. Ibid., p. 37.
55. Ibid., p. 25.
56. Ibid., p. 44.
57. Ibid., p. 53.
58. Ibid., p. 71.
59. Ibid., p. 76.
60. Ibid., p .81.
61. Ibid., p. 83.
62. Ibid., pp. 91–2.
63. Ibid., p. 92.
64. Ibid., p. 101.
65. Ibid., p. 104.
66. Ibid., pp. 107–8.
67. Ibid., p. 116.
68. Ibid., p. 165.
69. Ibid., p. 125.
70. Ibid., p. 127.
71. Ibid., p. 134.
72. Ibid., pp. 135–7.
73. *South Shield Gazette*, March 1939, cited in Collins, op. cit., (1957), p. 188, fn. 1.
74. Davies, op. cit., (2011), p. 114.
75. Ibid., pp. 113–14.
76. Salter, op. cit., (1896), p. 138.
77. Ibid., pp. 139–40.
78. Ibid., p. 144.
79. Ibid., p. 158.
80. *The Crescent: A Weekly Record of Islam in England*, Liverpool: The Crescent Printing Company, vol. II, no. 27, 22 July 1893, pp. 212–13.
81. Ibid., p. 213.
82. Ibid.
83. *The Crescent: A Weekly Record of Islam in England*, Liverpool: The Crescent Printing Company, vol. II, no. 28, 29 July 1893, p. 224.
84. Deane, Phyllis, (1969), *The First Industrial Revolution*, Cambridge: Cambridge University Press, p. 85.
85. Redford, A., (1934), *Manchester Merchants and Foreign Trade*, vol. 1, Manchester, p. 199.
86. Salter, Joseph, (1873), *The Asiatic in England: Sketches of Sixteen Years' Work Among Orientals*, London: Seeley, Jackson and Halliday, p. 224.
87. However, his name seems remarkably similar to a 'Jan Abdool' referred to in Salter's later monograph. Abdool was visited by the London Christian Mission whilst in prison in the capital for opium dealing. If Salter's account is to be believed opium smoking was an epidemic amongst the lascars of Britain in the nineteenth century. See Salter, Joseph, op. cit., (1896), p. 24.
88. Salter, op. cit., (1873), p. 224.

89. Quoted in, Leese, Peter, Piatek, Beata, and Curyllo-Klag, Izabela, (2002), '"Monkey Abraham" and other "Orientals" in Manchester and Salford, 1873', in *The British Migrant Experience, 1700–2000: An Anthology*, Basingstoke: Palgrave Macmillan, pp. 252–3.
90. Rosenthal, Eric, (reprinted 1982), *From Drury Lane to Mecca*, Cape Town: Howard Timmins Publishers, pp. 22–4.
91. Anon., (1994), *Barbary Coast Revisited*, Salford; Bridging the Years, Salford Quays Heritage Centre, p. 6.

3. First World War: From Sacrifice to Sufferance

1. Ally, Mashuq, (1981), *History of Muslims in Britain 1850–1980*, Unpublished MA Dissertation, Faculty of Arts, University of Birmingham, p. 5.
2. Abram, Jake, (1996), *Tugs, Boats and Me: Manchester Ship Canal and Bridgewater Canal Memories*, Manchester: Neil Richardson Publications, p. 47.
3. Ibid., p. 49.
4. Ally, op. cit., (1981) p. 7.
5. Ibid., p. 8.
6. Little, K. L., (1947), *Negroes in Britain: A Study of Racial Relations in English Society*, London: Kegan Paul, Trench, Truber & Co. Ltd., pp. 34–5.
7. Ibid., p. 35, fn. 1.
8. Ibid., p. 36.
9. Ibid.
10. Ibid.
11. Ibid., p. 37.
12. Fryer, op. cit., (1984), p. 295.
13. Williams, John Jones, (1983), *Llanongwr o Ros-Lan*, Pen-y-groes, p. 91, cited in Davies, op. cit., (2011), p. 116.
14. Ibid., p. 295.
15. Visram, op. cit., (2002), p. 56.
16. Ibid.
17. Ibid., p. 57.
18. Ibid.
19. Ibid., p. 58.
20. Ibid.
21. Ansari, op. cit., (2004), p. 39.
22. Visram, op. cit., (2002) p. 55.
23. Davies, op. cit., (2011), p. 108.
24. Ansari, op. cit., (2004), p. 40.
25. Visram, op. cit., (2002), p. 170.
26. Fryer, op. cit., (1984), p. 296.
27. Ibid., p. 304.
28. Ansari, op. cit., (2004), p. 41.
29. Cited in Lawless,op. cit., (1995), p. 75.
30. Visram, op. cit., (2002), p. 197.
31. Ibid.
32. Cited in Carr, Barry, (1992), 'Black Geordies' in Colls, Robert, and Lancaster, Bill, (eds) (1992), *Geordies: Roots of Regionalism*, Edinburgh: Edinburgh University Press, p. 135.

33. Cited in, Fryer, op. cit., (1984), p. 303. 34. Ibid., p. 299.

35. Ibid. 36. Little, op. cit., (1948), p. 59.

37. Halliday, op. cit., (1992), p. 24. 38. Cited in Ibid., p. 27.

39. Cited in Ibid. 40. Ansari, op. cit., (2004), p. 74.

41. Cited in Halliday, op. cit., (1992), p. 18.

42. A former 'Barbary Coast' resident, cited in Anon., (1992), *Bridging the Years: A history of Trafford Park and Salford Docks as remembered by those who lived and worked in the area*, Salford: Salford Quays Heritage Centre, p. 14.

43. Lawless, op. cit., (1995), p. 48. 44. Ibid., p. 53.

45. Davies, op. cit., (2011), p. 108. 46. Dahya, op. cit., (1965), p. 184.

47. Ibid. 48. Lawless, op. cit., (1995), p. 49. 49. Ibid.

50. Interview with Aziz Bugati, 14/11/2003.

51. Interview with respondent, 22/11/2003.

52. Interview with respondent, 16/01/2004.

53. Collin, op. cit., (1957), p. 21.

54. Interview with respondent, 04/10/2003.

55. Collins, op. cit., (1957), p. 194. 56. Ibid., p. 211.

57. Ansari, op. cit., (2004), p. 135. 58. Halliday, op. cit., (1992), p. xii.

59. For a detailed explanation and discussion of this term, see Chapter 5.

60. Interview with Tariq Mahyoub, 13/11/2003.

61. Interview with respondent, 04/10/2003.

62. Interview with respondent, 14/11/2003.

63. *Eccles and Pendleton Journal*, 30/11/1972, p. 6.

64. Lawless, op. cit., (1995), p. 50. 65. Ibid., pp. 50–1.

66. Ibid., p. 52–3. 67. Ibid., p. 53.

68. Ibid., p. 54. 69. Ibid., p. 72.

70. Cited in Ibid., pp. 72–3. 71. Fryer, op. cit., (1984), p. 356.

72. Ibid. 73. Ansari, op. cit., (2004), p. 92.

74. Cited in, Fryer, op. cit., (1984), p. 357.

4. Interwar Period: Shaykh Abdullah Ali al-Hakimi and the ʿAlawī *Ṭarīqah*

1. This racial discrimination did not change in the UK until the implementation of the Race Relations Act 1976.
2. Salter, Joseph, (1873), *The Asiatics and England*, London: Selly Jackson, and Salter, Joseph, (1896), *The East in the West*, London: Partridge.
3. Seddon, Mohammad Siddique, (2004), 'Muslim Communities in Britain: A Historiography', in Seddon, Mohammad Siddique, et al, (2004), *British Muslims Between Assimilation and Segregation*, p. 9, n. 22.
4. A *zāwiyah* (pl. *zawāyā*) is, according to *The Encyclopaedia of Islam*, 'lit. a "corner, nook [of a building]", originally the cell of a Christian monk and then in the Islamic context, a small mosque or oratory room ... the term came to designate a building designed to house and feed travellers and members of local sufi brotherhood.', in Bearman et al, op. cit., vol. XI, p. 44.
5. Lings, Martin, (1971), *A Sufi Saint of the Twentieth Century,* Berkeley: University of California Press, p. 116, fn. 3.
6. Lawless, Dick, (1993), 'British-Yemeni Society: Sheikh Abdullah Ali al-Hakimi', at http://www.al-bab.com/bys/articles/lawless93.htm (accessed 29/03/2010).
7. Lings, Martin, (1961), *A Moslem Saint of the Twentieth Century*, London: George Allen & Unwin Ltd., p. 63, fn. 3.
8. Cited in ibid., p. 9.
9. The book was eventually posthumously published in 1941.
10. Lings, op. cit., (1961), pp. 64–6.
11. Ibid., p. 68.
12. Ibid., p. 74, fn. 1.
13. Ibid., p. 116, fn .3.
14. Serjeant, R. B., (1944), 'Yemeni Arabs in Britain', in *The Geographical Magazine*, vol. 17, no. 4, 1944, pp. 143–7.
15. This conservative figure would appear to be inconsistent with contemporaneous accounts which suggest the South Shields Yemeni population to have been around 2–3000.
16. Ibid., p. 147
17. Ibid., p. 143
18. Ibid.
19. Serjeant, op. cit., (1944), p. 143.
20. 'Shaykh' – literally, 'old man' but, understood to mean learned elder as in, tribal leader or religious scholar.
21. Ibid.
22. Ibid.
23. Ibid.
24. Ibid.

25. For a detailed study of his life, see Chapter 6. 26. Ibid.

27. Ibid. 28. Ibid. 29. Ibid. 30. Ibid.

31. Ibid. 32. Ibid. 33. Ibid. 34. Ibid.

35. Ibid. 36. Ibid. 37. Ibid.

38. *Dhikr,* according to *The Encyclopaedia of Islam*, literally means, 'reminding oneself'. In the Islamic context and particularly within the Sufi traditions, the act of *dhikr* is based on the Qur'ānic verse, 'And remember your Lord when you forget, and say you: "Perchance my Lord will guide me to something nearer to right direction than this."' (18: 24). See Daryabadi, Abdul Majid, (2001), *The Glorious Qur'ān: Text, Translation and Commentary*, Leicester: The Islamic Foundation, p. 531. *Dhikr*, then, is 'possibly the most frequent form of prayer, its *mukābal* ('opposite correlative') is *fikr* [q.v.] (discursive) reflection, meditation.', see Bearman et al, op. cit., vol. II, pp. 223–6.

39. Serjeant, op. cit., (1944), p. 147. 40. Collins, op. cit., (1957), p. 186.

41. Ibid., p. 143. 42. Halliday, op. cit., (1992), p. 10.

43. See Fryer, op. cit., (1984), pp. 298–316; and Seddon, Mohammad Siddique, (2003), '400 Years of Muslim Deportation from Britain', in *Q-News*, no. 350, October 2003/Shaban 1424, pp. 18–21.

44. Al-Masaybi, Muhammad, (1991), 'Obituary: Shaikh Muhammad Qassim al-'Alawi (1909–99)', at http://www.al-bab.com/bys/obits/alawi.htm (accessed 25/03/2012).

45. Ibid. 46. Ibid. 47. Ibid.

48. Halliday, op. cit., (1992), pp. 29–30. 49. Ibid., p. 30.

50. Collins, op. cit., (1957), p. 180.

51. Cited in Halliday, op. cit., (1992), p. 31.

52. Serjeant, op. cit., (1994), p. 144. 53. Halliday, op. cit., (1992), p. 33.

54. Ibid. 55. Ibid. 56. Ibid. 57. Ibid.

58. Cited in Collins, op. cit., (1957), pp. 226–7.

59. Anon., (1993), *Prayer Timetable 1993 to 2000*, Eccles: Eccles/Salford Mosque & Islamic Centre, p. 3.

60. Clark, Jim, (1982), 'A visit to the Eccles Mosque', *The Eccles and Patricroft Journal*, 12/01/1982.

61. *Prayer Timetable*, op. cit., (1993), p. 3.

62. Ali, A. Y., (1989), *The Holy Qur'ān: Text, Translation and Commentary*, Maryland: Amana Corporation, p. 49.

63. Ibid., p. 1628.

64. Ibid., p. 49, fn. 117.

65. The Wahhābīs or Wahhābiyyah, are defined by *The Encyclopaedia of Religion*, as 'An Islamic renewal group established by Muḥammad ibn 'Abd al-Wahhāb (d. AH 1206/1792 CE), the Wahhābiyyah continues to the present in the Arabian Peninsula. The term Wahhābī was originally used by opponents of the movement, who charged that it was a new form of Islam, but the name eventually gained wide acceptance ... The Wahhābiyyah often refer to "the mission of the oneness of God (*da'wat al-tawḥīd*)" and call themselves "those who affirm the oneness of God", or Muwaḥḥidun'. For a detailed explanation, see Voll, John O., 'Wahhābiyyah', in Eliade, Mircea, et al, (eds) (1987), *The Encyclopaedia of Religion*, New York: Macmillan, vol. 15, pp. 313–16.

66. The Salafīs or Salafiyyah, are a reformist movement inspired by the modernist scholars like Muhammad 'Abduh and Rashīd Riḍā from Egypt. *The Encyclopedia of Islam* describes the Salafiyyah as '[a] neo-orthodox brand of Islamic reformism originating in the late 19th century and centred on Egypt, aiming to regenerate Islam by a return to the tradition represented by the "pious forefathers" (*al-salaf al-ṣāliḥ*, hence its name) of the primitive name.' See, Bearman et al, op. cit., vol. VIII, pp. 900–9.

67. Quoted in Halliday, op. cit., (1992), p. 31.

68. Lawless, op. cit., (1995), p. 220.

69. Halliday, op. cit., (1992), p. 30.

70. Ibid., p. 31.

71. Lawless, (1993), 'Sheikh Abdullah Ali al-Hakimi', http://www.al-bab.com/bys/articles/lawless93.htm (accessed 12/02/2012).

72. Halliday, op. cit., (1992), p. 31.

73. Lawless, op. cit., (1993), http://www.al-bab.com/bys/articles/lawless93.htm (accessed 12/02/2012).

74. Ibid.

75. Ibid.

76. Collins, op. cit., (1957), p. 224.

77. Lawless, op. cit., (1993), http://www.al-bab.com/bys/articles/lawless93.htm (accessed 12/02/2012).

78. For a detailed discussion on this subject see Seddon, Mohammad Siddique, (2009), 'Global Citizenry Ancient and Modern: British Yemenis and Tranlocal Tribalism', in Krause, W., (ed.) (2009), *Citizenship, Security and Democracy: Muslim Engagement with the West*, pp. 89–114.

79. See Ibn 'Abd al-Wahhāb, Muhammad, (trans. Al Faruqi, Ismail R.) (1991), *Kitāb al-Tawḥīd*, Riyadh: International Islamic Publishing House, pp. xv-xvii.

5. Post-World War Two Migration, The *Muwalladūn* and Shaykh Hassan Ismail

1. Halliday, op cit., (1992), p. 58.
2. Ibid.
3. Ibid., p. 59.
4. Anwar, Muhammad, (1979), *The Myth of Return*, London: Heinnimann Educational Books Ltd., p. 14.
5. For a detailed study on the phenomenon of migration 'fanning' movement, see Werbner, Pnina, (1994), 'Avoiding the Ghetto: Pakistani migrant and settlement shifts in Manchester', in Drake, Michael, (ed.) (1994), *Time, Family and Community: Perspectives on Family and Community History*, Oxford and Cambridge, Mass.,: The Open University and Blackwell.
6. Halliday, op. cit., (1992), p. 60.
7. See Seddon, Mohammad Siddique, (2004), 'Muslim Communities in Britain: A Historiography' in Seddon et al, (2004), *British Muslims between Assimilation and Segregation*, Markfield: The Islamic Foundation, pp. 1–42.
8. Interview with respondent, 15/11/2003.
9. Seddon in Seddon et al, op. cit., (2004), p. 121.
10. Ibid., p. 129.
11. Ibid., p. 130.
12. Little, op. cit., (1947), p. 34.
13. Ibid., p. 35.
14. Ibid.
15. Ibid., pp. 38–9.
16. Ibid., p. 46.
17. Cited in ibid., p. 82, fn. 1.
18. Ibid., p. 84.
19. Ibid.
20. Massey, Philip, (1940), *Industrial South Wales: a detailed survey*, London: Gollancz, pp. 85, 122.
21. Ibid., p. 86.
22. Ibid., p. 89.
23. Ibid.
24. See Seddon, Mohammad Siddique, 'Locating the Perpetuation of "Otherness": Negating British Islam', in Seddon et al, op. cit., (2004), p. 127.
25. Interview with respondent, 09/01/2004.
26. Chalmeta, Pedro, 'Muwallad', in Bearman et al, (eds), (1960 2005) *The Encyclopedia of Islam*, Leiden: E. J. Brill, vol. VII, p. 807.
27. Interview with Adnan Saif, 23/03/2004.
28. Freitag, Ulrike, (2003), *Indian Ocean Migrants and State Formation in Hadhramaut,* Leiden: Brill, p. 6.

29. Interview with respondent, 15/11/2003.
30. Freitag, op. cit., (2003), p. 6.
31. Interview with respondent, 22/11/2003.
32. Ibid.
33. Ibid.
34. Ahsan, M. Manazir, (1996), 'Arrival, Expulsion and Return: Muslim Experience in Europe', in *Al-Mizan*, vol. 2, no. 1, 1996, p. 25.
35. Dozy, Reinhart, (1913), *Spanish Islam: A History of the Muslims of Spain,* London: Chatto & Windus, p. 240.
36. Ahsan, op. cit., (1996), p. 26.
37. Arnold, Thomas, W., (1892), *The Preaching of Islam: A History of the Propagation of Muslim Faith*, (reprinted 1979), Lahore: Sh. Muhammad Ashraf, p. 142.
38. Ahsan, op. cit., (1996), pp. 26–7.
39. Ali, Sayed Amir, (1987) [1899], *A Short History of the Saracens*, New Delhi: Nusrat Ali Nasri for Kitab Bhavan, p. 482, fn. 3.
40. Ibid., p. 141.
41. Boxberger, Linda, (2002), *On the Edge of Empire: Hadramawt, Emigration and the Indian Ocean*, Albany: State Univeristy of New York Press, p. 52.
42. Ibid., p. 53.
43. Freitag, op. cit., (2003), p. 267.
44. See the homepage of the Yemeni Community Association of Sandwell, http://www.yca-sandwell.org.uk/ (accessed 01/09/2004).
45. Boxberger, op. cit., (2002), pp. 41–2.
46. Ibid.
47. Interview with respondent, 09/01/2004.
48. See Abdul-Wali et al, (2001), *They Die Strangers*, Austin: Center for Middle Eastern Studies.
49. Morton, Rachel, (2000), *One Island Many Faiths,* London: Thames Hudson, p. 40.
50. Interview with respondent, 17/10/2003.
51. Interview with respondent, 26/09/2003.
52. Interview with respondent, 16/01/2004.
53. Little, op. cit., (1947), p. 111.
54. Collins, op. cit., (1957), p. 191.
55. Ibid., p. 192.
56. Ibid., p. 203.
57. Little, op. cit., (1947), p. 94.

58. Ibid. 59. Ibid. 60. Ibid., p. 111.

61. Ibid. 62. Ibid.

63. Collins, op. cit., (1957), pp. 14–15. 64. Ibid., p. 151.

65. Ibid., p. 152. 66. Ibid. 67. Ibid., p. 153. 68. Ibid.

69. See Umar, Zubayda, (1985), 'Yemen to South Shields', *Al-Afkar*, May 1985, pp. 62–3.

70. Collins, op. cit., (1957), p. 154.

71. *South Shields Gazette*, 8 November 1937, cited in ibid., p. 154.

72. *South Shields Gazette*, 25 January 1935, cited in ibid., p. 157.

73. *South Shields Gazette*, 23 March 1935, cited in ibid.

74. *South Shields Gazette*, 14 April 1935, cited in ibid.

75. Ibid., p. 155. 76. Ibid., p. 156. 77. Ibid., p. 161.

78. Ibid., p. 197. 79. Ibid., p. 161.

80. See Seddon, Mohammad Siddique, (2003), '400 years of Muslim deportations from Britain' in *Q-News*, October 2003, pp. 18–21.

81. Collins, op. cit., (1957), p. 162. 82. Ibid., p. 162.

83. Ibid., p. 167. 84. Ibid., p. 166. 85. Ibid., p. 160.

86. Ibid., p. 171. 87. Ibid., p. 173. 88. Ibid.

89. Ibid., p. 174. 90. Ibid. 91. Ibid., p. 179.

92. Ibid., p. 176. 93. Ibid. 94. Ibid., p. 176, fn. 1.

95. See Chapter 4 for a full discussion on the origins of the 'Alawī *ṭarīqah*.

96. Collins, op. cit., (1957), p. 177. 97. Ibid., p. 179.

98. Ibid., p. 180. 99. Ibid., pp. 180–1. 100. Ibid., p. 182.

101. Ibid., p. 184, fn. 1. 102. Ibid., p. 222. 103. Ibid., p. 223.

104. Interview with Shaykh Said Hassan Ismail conducted by author in 1993.

105. *Daily Herald*, January 10, 1956.

6. Shaykh Said Hassan Ismail and 'Second Wave Migration'

1. Aithie, Patricia, (2011), 'Sheikh Said Hassan Ismail (1930–2011)', at http://www.al-bab.com/bys/obits/ismail.htm (accessed 11/02/2012).

2. Anon., (2011), 'Sheikh Said Ismail', *Meeting Point*, April, (2011), p. 15.
3. Anon., (2005), 'Sheikh Said', *Agenda*, Winter (2005–6), p .5.
4. Aithie, op. cit., (2011), http://www.al-bab.com/bys/obits/ismail.htm (accessed 11/02/2012).
5. Ibid. 6. Ibid. 7. Ibid. 8. Ibid.
9. *Agenda*, op. cit., (2005–6), p. 5.
10. *Meeting Point*, op. cit., (2011), p. 15.
11. *Agenda*, op. cit., (2005–6), p. 5.
12. Ibid. 13. Ibid. 14. Ibid.
15. Morton, Rachael, (2000), *One Island Many Faiths*, London: Hudson, p. 40.
16. *Meeting Point*, op. cit., (2011), p. 15.
17. For a detailed discussion on this subject, see Seddon, Mohammad Siddique, (2009), 'Global Citizenry Ancient and Modern: British Yemenis and Translocal Tribalism' in Krause, Wanda, (ed.) (2009), *Citizenship, Security and Democracy: Muslim Engagement with the West*, London and Istanbul: AMSS(UK) and SETA, pp. 89–112.
18. See Seddon, Mohammad Siddique, (2010), 'Constructing Identities of "Difference" and "Resistance": The Politics of Being Muslim and British', *Social Semiotics Journal*, November 2010, pp. 557–71.
19. Searle, Kevin, (2009), *From Farms to Foundries: An Arab Community in Industrial Britain*, Bern: Peter Lang AG, p. 163.
20. Ibid. 21. Dahya, op. cit., (1965), p. 177.
22. Mashuq Ally, (1982), *History of Muslims in Britain 1850–1980*, unpublished MA dissertation, University of Birmingham, p. 84.
23. Khan, Muhammad Akram, (1979), *Islam and the Muslims in Liverpool*, unpublished MA Dissertation, University of Liverpool, p. 42.
24. Ansari, op. cit., (2004), p. 343.
25. Halliday, op. cit., (1992), p. 10.
26. Dahya, op. cit., (1965), pp. 177–8. 27. Ibid., p. 178.
28. Boxberger, op. cit., (2002), pp. 24–5.
29. Ibid. p. 19. 30. Ibid. p. 25. 31. Ibid. p. 27. 32. Ibid. p. 27.
33. Dahya, op. cit., (1965), p. 179.
34. See Anwar, Muhammad, (1979), *The Myth of Return,* London: Heinemann.

35. Dayha, op. cit., (1965), p. 182.

36. El-Solh, Camilla Fawzi, (1992), 'Arab Communities in Britain: Cleavages and Commonalities' in *Islam and Christian–Muslim Relations*, vol. 3, no. 2, December 1992, pp. 236–58, citation at p. 240.

37. Dahya, op. cit., (1965), p. 182. 38. Ibid., p. 180.

39. El-Solh, op. cit., (1992), p. 241. 40. Ibid.

41. Ibid., p. 181. 42. Ibid. 43. Ibid., p. 182.

44. Ibid., p. 183. 45. Ibid. 46. Ibid., p. 184.

47. Ibid. 48. Ibid., p. 190. 49. Ibid., p. 186.

50. Halliday, op. cit., (1992), p. 68. 51. Ibid.

52. Ibid., p. 70. 53. Ibid., p. 71. 54. Ibid.

55. Ibid., p. 72. 56. Ibid. 57. Ibid.

58. Ibid., p. 73. 59. Ibid.

60. Dresch, op. cit., (1993), p. 17. 61. Halliday, op. cit., (1992), p. 8.

62. Ibid. p. 11. 63. Ibid. p. 13. 64. Ibid. p. 12.

65. Ibid. p. 7. 66. Ibid. p. 11.

67. A fact confirmed by respondent who proudly showed me photographs of his abundant *qāt* crop growing on his plot of land in his tribal village. Interview with respondent, 11/10/2003.

68. Abdul-Wali, Mohammad, op. cit., (2001).

69. Halliday, op. cit.,(1992), p. 12.

70. Dresch, op. cit., (1993), p. 302.

71. Halliday, op. cit., (1992), p. 15.

72. Cited in Halliday, op. cit., (1992), p. 15. 73. Ibid., p. 4.

74. Ibid., p. 73. 75. Ibid., p. 75.

76. El-Solh, op. cit., (1992), p. 240.

77. Halliday, op. cit., (1992), p. 76. 78. Ibid., p. 77.

79. Ibid. 80. Ibid., p. 81. 81. Ibid., p. 91.

82. Ibid., p. 105. 83. Searle, op. cit., (2009), p. 157. 84. Ibid.

85. Most suffered with acute tinnitus, a permanent ringing in the ears.

86. Searle, op. cit., (2009), p. 156. 87. Ibid., pp. 153–61.

88. Ibid., p. 161. 89. See Carr, op. cit., (1992), p. 137.

90. Ibid., p. 80.

91. See Kevin Searle's published PhD thesis on Yemeni migrants in Sheffield, Searle, Kevin, (2009), *From Farms to Foundries: An Arab Community in Industrial Britain*, Bern: Peter Lang AG.
92. Halliday, op. cit., (1992), p. 81.
93. Climes, Michael, (2006), 'The Prince's Place in History', *Eastside Boxing*, 4 January 2006, http://www.eastsideboxing.com/news.php?p=6498&more=1, (accessed 14/03/2012).
94. Ibid. 95. Ibid. 96. Ibid. 97. Ibid.
98. Interview with respondent, 14/11/2003.
99. Interview with respondent, 26/09/2003.
100. Interview with respondent, 15/11/2003.
101. Interview with respondent, 17/10/2003.
102. See Werbner, Pnina, (2002), *Imagined Diasporas among Manchester Muslims*, Oxford and Santa Fe: James Currey and School of American Research Press, pp. 199–232.
103. Interview with respondent, 17/10/2003. 104. Ibid.
105. Interview with respondent, 26/09/2003.
106. Kucukcan, T., (2004), 'The making of Turkish-Muslim diaspora in Britain: Religious collective identity in a multicultural public sphere' in *Journal of Muslim Minority Affairs,* 24, no. 2, pp. 243–58.
107. See Ramadan, T., (2002), 'Europeanization of Islam or Islamization of Europe?, in Hunter, S., (ed.) (2002), *Islam, Europe's second religion: The new social, cultural and political landscape,* Westport, CT: Praeger, p. 208; Winter, T. J., (2003), 'Muslim loyalty and belonging: Some reflections on the psychosocial background' in Seddon, M. S., et al, (eds) (2003), *British Muslims: Loyalty and Belonging,* Markfield: The Citizen Organising Foundation and The Islamic Foundation, pp. 8–9.
108. Nasser, N., (2005) 'Expressions of Muslim identity in architecture and urbanism in Birmingham, UK', in *Islam and Christian–Muslim Relations*, vol. 16, no. 1, pp. 61–78.
109. Malik, N., (2004), 'Friends, Romans, Countrymen?' in Seddon, M. S., et al, (2004), *British Muslims Between Assimilation and Segregation: Historical, Legal and Social Realities*, Markfield: The Islamic Foundation, p. 147.
110. Ibid., p. 147. 111. Carr, op. cit., (1992), p. 145.
112. Ibid., p. 148.

7. Becoming Visible: the Emergence of British Yemenis

1. For a detailed discussion, see Chapter 3 of this study.
2. Searle, op cit., (2009), p. 129.
3. Aswad, Barbara C., (1974), 'The Southeast Dearborn Arab Community Struggles for Survival against Urban "Renewal"', in Aswad, Barbara C., (ed.) (1974), *Arab Speaking Communities in American Cities*, New York: Centre for Migration Studies, pp. 53–83.
4. Searle, op. cit., (2009), p. 131.
5. Ibid., p. 138.
6. Ansari, op. cit., (2004), p. 254.
7. Ibid.
8. See ibid., pp. 258–66.
9. Umar, Zubayda, (1985), 'From Yemen to South Shields', *Afkar,* May 1985, pp. 62–3.
10. For a detailed discussion, see Chapter 3 of this publication.
11. Umar, op. cit., (1985), p. 62.
12. Ibid.
13. Ibid.
14. Ibid., p. 63
15. See Chapters 4 and 5 of this publication.
16. Umar, op. cit., (1985), p. 63.
17. Searle, op. cit., (2009), p. 187.
18. Ibid.
19. Ibid.
20. Ibid.
21. Ibid.
22. Ibid.
23. Dalrymple, William, (1989), 'The Arabs of Tyneside', *The Independent Magazine*, 7 October 1989.
24. Ibid.
25. Ibid.
26. Ibid.
27. Ibid.
28. Ibid.
29. Ibid.
30. Ibid.
31. Ibid.
32. Ibid.
33. Ibid.
34. Ibid.
35. Actually pronounced in the Yemeni dialect of Arabic as '*gāt*'.
36. Ibid.
37. See Serjeant, op. cit., (1944), p. 147.
38. Ibid.
39. Ibid.
40. Ibid.
41. Scott, Hugh, (1942), *In The High Yemen*, London: John Murray, p. 95.
42. Reilly, op. cit., (1960), p .4.
43. Ingrams, Harold, (1942), *Arabia and the Isles*, London: John Murray, pp. 109–10.
44. Whitaker, Brian, (2001), 'Where the qat is out of the bag', *The Guardian*, 28/05/2001.

45. Vidal, John, (2004), 'Getting high on the road to Addis', *The Guardian*, 05/05/2004.

46. Dresch, op. cit., (1993), p. 20.

47. Ibid., p. 245.

48. Halliday, op. cit., (1992), p. 124.

49. Whitaker, *The Guardian*, op. cit., 28/05/2001.

50. El-Solh, op. cit., (1992), p. 242.

51. Halliday, op. cit., (1992), p. 122.

52. Ibid., p. 51.

53. Turnell, Cat, 'This is the drug khat: banned in the USA, bought legally in Leicester', *The Leicester Mercury*, 14/08/ 2004, p. 4.

54. Cited in Halliday, op. cit., (1992), p. 126.

55. See Whitaker, *The Guardian*, op. cit. 28/05/2001, and Turnell, *The Leicester Mercury*, op. cit., 14/8/2004, p. 4.

56. Whitaker,*The Guardian*, op. cit. 28/05/2001.

57. See Turnell, Cat, 'Crazy dreams and my mouth looks like its mowed the lawn!', *The Leicester Mercury*, 14/08/2004, p. 4. and Vidal, John, 'Getting high on the road to Addis', *The Guardian*, 05/05/2004.

58. Whitaker,*The Guardian*, op. cit. 28/05/2001.

59. Rushby, Kevin, (1999), *Eating the Flowers of Paradise: A journey through the drug fields of Ethiopia and Yemen,* New York: New York St. Martin's Press . For another account, see Mortimer, Peter, (2005), *Cool For Qat, A Yemen Journey: Two Countries, Two Times,* Edinburgh and London: Mainstream Publishing.

60. Rushby, op. cit., (1999), p. 57.

61. Ibid., p. 67.

62. Ibid., p. 234.

63. I have previously argued that the European sexual obsession and fetish with the orient repeats the same imperial motifs of conquest and domination. See Seddon, Mohammad Siddique, (2004), 'Unveiling Imperial Conquest', *Emel,* March/April, 2004, pp. 16–17.

64. Rushby, op. cit., (1999), p. 56.

65. Ibid., p. 58.

66. My own experience of *qāt* as a traveller through Tanzania, Kenya and Uganda and then later, in the 'chewing sessions' with Yemenis in Britiain and Yemen, are far less lurid, sensational or exotic than any of the accounts cited above.

67. Interview with respondent, 15/11/2003.

68. For a detailed description of the *mafraj*, see, Kirkman, James, (ed.) (1976), *The City of Ṣan'ā'*, London: London Museum of Mankind, Department of Ethnography of the British Museum and World Festival

of Islam, p. 16.

69. Interview with respondent, 17/10/2003.
70. Interview with respondent, 26/09/2003.
71. Interview with respondent, 15/11/2003.
72. See Fryer, op. cit., (1984), pp. 298–316.
73. Interview with Adnan Saif, former Executive Director, The Muath Welfare Trust, The Bordesley Centre, Birmingham, undertaken 24/03/2004.
74. Ibid.
75. Ibid.
76. Anon., (2003), *The Bordesley Centre for Further & Higher Education, Prospectus 2003–2004*, p. 2.
77. Anon., (2000), *Muath Welfare Trust, Annual Report 2000*, p. 11.
78. Interview with Adnan Saif, 24/03/2004.
79. Ansari, op. cit., 2004, p. 170.
80. See http://www.yemeni-community-manchester.org.uk/about/history (accessed 20/03/2012).
81. Interview with Adnan Saif, op. cit., 24/03/2004.
82. Ibid.
83. Ibid.
84. For more on this subject, see Seddon in Krause (ed.), op.cit., (2009), pp. 89–114.
85. Ibid.
86. Ibid.
87. Carr, Barry, (1992), 'Black Gordies', in Colls, Robert, and Lancaster, Bill, (eds) (1992), *Geordies: Roots in Regionalism*, Edinburgh: Edinburgh University Press, pp. 131–49.
88. Ibid., p. 132.
89. Assimilation is a complex sociological process by which, usually, one culture is absorbed into a 'host society'. For a detailed study, see Gordon, Milton, M., (1964), *Assimilation in American Life*, New York: Oxford University Press, 1964.
90. Integration, the means by which a society's various elements hold together or bond with each other. Essentially, in the context of ethnic minorities, integration refers to the process by which different races fuse together through social, economic and political interaction. See Abercrombie, Nicholas, Hill, Stephen, and Turner, Bryan S., (1985), *The Penguin Dictionary of Sociology*, London: Penguin Books, 1985, p. 112.

91. Acculturation is, according to John Lewis, 'the process by which culture is transmitted through contact of groups with different cultures, usually one having a more highly developed civilisation'. For a more detailed explanation, see Lewis , John, (1982), *Anthropology Made Simple*, London: William Heinmann Ltd, p. 141.
92. Umar, op. cit., 1985, p .63.
93. See Halliday, op. cit., (1992).
94. Ibid., p. iv.
95. For example, during the 1976 revolution Yemeni worker organisations in Britain often collected donations to fund projects in the Yemen.
96. Ibid., p. 97.
97. In addition to reporting the expansion of the Yemeni population in Liverpool, he also states that when North and South Yemen were unified after a brief war in 1992, a significant number of Yemenis actually returned home.
98. Halliday, op. cit., (1992), p. 140.
99. Halliday's term.
100. See Seddon, Mohammad Siddique, (2004), 'Muslim Communities in Britain: A Historiography' in Seddon et al, op. cit., (2004), pp. 13–17.
101. Ibid., p. 129.
102. Seddon, Mohammad Siddique, (2011), 'Engaging with young Muslims: Some paradigms from the Qur'an and *Sunnah*', in Ahmad, Fauzia and Seddon, Mohammad Siddique, (eds) (2011), *Muslim Youth: Challenges, Opportunities and Expectations*, London: Continuum, pp. 267–8.
103. Halliday, op. cit., (1992), p. 130.
104. Anwar, op. cit., (1979).
105. See Halliday, Fred, (2010), *Britain's First Muslims: Potrait of an Arab Community*, London: I. B. Tauris.

Epilogue

1. Al-Rasheed, Madawi, (1991), 'Invisible and Divided Communities: Arabs in Britain', in Riad al-Rayyes (1991), *Arabs in Britain: Concerns and Prospects*, London: Riad Al-Rayyes Books, pp. 1–14.
2. Ibid., p. 2.
3. Ibid., p. 3.
4. Ibid., p. 5.
5. Ibid.
6. The *Economist*, 17 September 1988.
7. Al-Rasheed, op. cit., (1991), p. 9.
8. Ibid.

9. Ibid., p. 11.
10. Ibid., p. 12.
11. Ibid.
12. El-Solh, Camilla, Fawzi, (1992), 'Arab Communities in Britain: Cleavages and Commonalities', in *Islam and Christian–Muslim Relations*, vol. 3, no. 2, December 1992, pp. 236–88, citation at p. 236.
13. Ibid., p. 255.
14. Ibid., p. 243.
15. Ibid., p. 237.
16. Ibid., pp. 237–8
17. Ibid., p. 238.
18. Ibid., p. 239.
19. See *London Country of Birth Profiles – The Arab League: An Analysis of Census Data*, London Greater Authority, June 2005, available at http://wwww.naba.org.uk/the-library/reports/LGA-ArabLeague-Study-2005.pdf. (accessed 14/07/2013).
20. See Yafaie, Y., (2009), *British Arabs: Identity, Politics and Community*, Results of an Exploratory Survey by the Atlantic Forum, Spring 2009, available at http://www.naba.org.uk/the-library/reports/BritshArabsYafaiF.pdf (accessed 14/07/2013).
21. Arabs and Arab League Population in the UK: Report on the 2011 Census, May 2012, The National Association of British Arabs, p. 3, available at http://naba.og.uk/the-library/reports/NABA-Census-2001-FinalReport-May%202013.pdf) (accessed 14/07/2013).
22. Ibid., p. 6.
23. Ibid., p. 4.
24. Ibid., p. 5.
25. Ibid.
26. Cited in ibid.
27. Ibid., p. 7.
28. Ibid.
29. Ibid., p. 8.
30. Ibid.
31. Ibid.
32. Ibid., p. 243.
33. For a detailed study, see Seddon, Mohammad Siddique, (2007), 'Muslim and Jewish Communities in Nineteenth Century Manchester' in Ansari, Humayun and Cesarani, David, (eds) (2007), *Muslim–Jewish Dialogue in a 21st Century World*, Egham: Centre for Minority Studies, Royal Holloway University of London.
34. See, Seddon, Mohammad Siddique (2005), '"Invisible Arabs" or "English Muslims"?: An inquiry into the construction of religious, cultural and national identities of the Yemeni community of Eccles, unpublished PhD. Thesis, Lancaster University.
35. Interview with respondent, 24/03/2004.
36. Halliday, op.cit., (1992), p. 135.
37. Dahya, Badr Ud-Din, *South Asian Urban Immigration*, 1967, p. 332, cited in Halliday, op. cit., p. 316.
38. See Fryer, op. cit., (1984), pp. 298–326, and Seddon in *Q-News*, op. cit., (2003), pp. 18–21.
39. Malik, Iftikhar, (2003), *Islam and Modernity*, London: Pluto Press, p. 93.

40. Anwar, Muhammad, 'British Muslims: Socio-Economic Position', in Seddon et al (eds), op. cit., (2003), p. 58.
41. Ibid. pp. 57–8.
42. Ibid. p. 95.
43. Malik, op.cit., (2003), p. 85.
44. See http://www.ons.gov.uk/ons/dcp171776_310454.pdf, p. 4.
45. Email correspondence with Roselyn Baker, Ethnic Minority Monitoring Unit, Salford City Council, 29/11/2002.
46. Al-Rasheed, op. cit., (1991), p. 3.
47. Ibid., p. 12.
48. Interview with respondent, 13/12/2003.
49. Al-Rasheed, op. cit., (1991), p. 12.
50. According to a cross-tabulation of Ethnic and Religious Affiliation categories for England and Wales undertaken by Yahya Birt, who states that 12.5% of the Indian origin population of Britain are Muslim and that 92% and 92.5% of both Bengali and Pakistani origin populations, respectively, are Muslim with a further 37.5% of British Other Asian being Muslim. However, he acknowledges the problem of locating precise and specific population figures based on the Census data stating, 'Of course statistics do not tell the human story in all its complex glory, but they do help us to debunk a few myths and tell us where we might start looking to understand the complex reality', see Birt, Yahya, 'Lies! Damn Lies! Statistics and Conversions', in, *Q-News*, no. 350, October 2003, Shaban 1424, p. 20.
51. Interview with respondent on 22/11/03.
52. Interview with respondent, 22/11/2003.
53. Anwar and Bakhsh, *British Muslims and State Policies*, Warwick: Centre for Research in Ethnic Relations, University of Warwick, (2003), p. 10.
54. NABA, May 2013, op.cit., (2013), p. 15.
55. Interview with respondent, 09/01/2004.
56. A detailed analysis of the causes of the riots, along with a series of recommendations aimed at tackling and preventing their reoccurrence, has been outlined in the Community Cohesion report produced by the Home Office. See *Community Cohesion – Report of the Independent Review Team*, Chaired by Ted Cantle, Home Office, December 2001.
57. Ansari, op. cit., (2004), p. 391.
58. Allen, Christopher, (2003), *Fair Justice: The Bradford Disturbances, the Sentencing and the Impact*, London: Forum Against Racism and Islamophobia, p. 17.

59. Nagel, Carol, and Staeheli, Lynn, (2009), 'British Arab Perspectives on Religion, Politics and "The Public"', in Hopkins, Peter, and Gale, Richard, (eds) (2009), *Muslims in Britain: Race, Place and Identities*, Edinburgh: Edinburgh University Press, pp. 95–112, citation at p. 96.

60. Ibid., p. 98.
61. Ibid.
62. Ibid., p. 99.
63. Ibid., p. 100.
64. Ibid.
65. Ibid., p. 101.
66. Ibid.
67. Ibid.
68. Ibid., p. 102.
69. Ibid.
70. Ibid.
71. Ibid., pp. 102–3.
72. Ibid.
73. Ibid., p. 105.
74. Ibid.
75. Anwar in Seddon et al (eds) op. cit., (2003), pp. 60–1.
76. Nagel and Staeheli, op. cit., (2009), p. 105.
77. Ibid.
78. Ibid., p. 107.
79. Halliday, op. cit., (2010), p. ix.
80. Ibid., p. x.
81. Ibid., pp. 141–2.
82. Ibid., pp. 131–40.
83. Nagel and Staeheli, op. cit., (2009), p. 108.
84. Hartmann, Betsy, and Boyce, James, (1983), *A Quiet Violence: View from a Bangladesh Village*, London: Zed Books, p. 112.

GLOSSARY

aba – father.

adab – ettiquitte, manners, or politeness.

akhlāq – morality and ethics. In the singular form the word means character, manners and etiquette.

aṣl – origin or, geneaology.

'aṣabiyyah – tribal belonging and allegiance.

'ayb – shame or disrespect.

asīd – a dough-like Yemeni dish.

ayah (Persian/Urdu) – oriental nanny or child minder.

Bāb al-Mandab – the geographical strait running from the southern tip of Yemen along the Red Sea to Saudi Arabia.

baḥrī (pl., *baḥriyyah*) – of the sea, a term used for a sailor.

barakah (pl., *barakāt*) – blessings, both spiritual and Divine.

bay'ah – an oath of allegiance usually associated with Sufism or tribal belonging.

bid'ah – innovation, usually associated with erroneous religious practices.

bilād – country or, region.

bint al-saḥān – a Yemeni sweet dish made of filo pastry and honey.

biriyānī (Persian/Urdu) – a rice dish made with meat from south Asia.

dā'ī – an individual Muslim devoted to religious proselytizing.

dam – blood, or genealogical relatives.

dars – lesson, usually associated with traditional Islamic learning.

da'wah – invitation, usually understood as religious proselytizing.

dhikr – rememberance or recollection of the Divine.

Eid ['Īd] al-Aḍḥā – 'the celebration of the sacrifice', the festivity associated with completion of *ḥajj*.

Eid ['Īd] al-Fiṭr – 'the celebration of the opening', the festivity associated with the completion of the fast of Ramadan.

faqīr (pl., *fuqarā'*) – beggar, or destitute, a name given to adherents of Sufism as indigents utterly dependent on God.

fiqh – body of jurisprudential rulings derived from *sharī'ah* by legal scholars exercising their understanding of the law.

fidyah – compensation for breaking tribal or religious laws.

fawṭah – a sorong-like lower garment worn by Yemeni men.

ghaṣṣan – chew, a term used for communal *qāt* chewing sessions.

hadīth (pl., *aḥādīth*) – saying or narrative usually associated with the Prophet Muhammad.

ḥaḍīr – settled, townspeople.

ḥajj – Islamic religious pilgrimage to the holy precinct in Makkah.

ḥalāl – permitted, allowed according to *sharī'ah*.

ḥarām – prohibited, not permitted according to *sharī'ah*.

al-ḥaqq al-qahwah – 'the right of coffee', a euphemism for a bribe.

ḥijāb – female head covering in accordance with *sharī'ah*.

ḥilbah – fenugreek, a Yemeni sauce to accompany meat dishes.

Hind – India, or contemporary south Asia.

ḥaqq (pl., *ḥuqūq*) – a legal right, ordained by religious or customary law.

ifṭār (pl., *fuṭūr*) – meal taken to break the fasting of Ramadan.

ijāzah – permission or, licence from the Sufi shaykh to guide others.

ijmā' – consensus, the majority opinion of religious legal scholars on religious matters.

imām – the leader of prayer, usually in the *masjid*.

'izzah – honour, dignity, or self-respect.

jalabiyyah – a long garment worn by Arab men.

jama'dār – commander or, one in military service.

jihād – struggle, i.e. the spiritual and physical struggle to establish or defend Islam.

jinn – creatures of the unseen who, like humans, are endowed with free will.

jumu'ah – Friday congregational prayer in Islam.

kayf – a state of cerebral contentment.

kāfir (pl., *kuffūr*) – disbeliever, one who rejects belief in the Divine.

khalīf – leader or 'vicegerent' of the *ummah* after Muhammad's death.

lahjah – colloquial, or dialect Arabic.

madhhab – religious legal school according to Islam.

madrasah – school, where Qur'ānic lessons are taught.

mafraj – large room to receive guest in Yemeni homes.

majlis al-dhikr – 'remembrance gatherings' associated with the practice of Sufism.

makrūh – reprehensible, a legal religious category of disliked actions.

maqām (pl., *maqāmāt*) – station, a spiritual level within Sufism.

māqil – oratory, a place where Yemeni men gather to chew *qāt*.

maqṣūrah – a reception room usually annexed to the *masjid*.

masjid – place of prostration, understood as 'the mosque'.

mawlid – birthday festivity of the Prophet Muhammad or a Sufi saint.

miḥshī – a Yemeni dish of meat and vegetables.

min jadd wāḥid – 'from one forefather', the maxim of tribal belonging.

al-minṭaqah al-wusṭā – the geographical 'middle region' of Yemen.

muqaddam (pl., *muqaddamūn*) – representative or deputy; in the context of Sufism, of a Sufi shaykh.

murīd – one in need, usually meaning a Sufi initiate.

murshid – one who is guided, usually used to refer to a Sufi shaykh

musākin – (pl., *musākinūn*) sedentary tribesmen.

muṭ'ah – temporary marriage, permitted by Shii Muslims but prohibited by Sunnis.

muwallad (pl., *muwalladūn*) – literally meaning 'born of', but usually used to refer to 'mixed race' progeny of a Yemeni father and non-Yemeni mother.

muwassiṭ (pl., *muwassṭūn*) – middleman or agent.

nān (Persian/Urdu) – a flat bread made with flour and yeast.

niqāb – a cloth used by some Muslim women to cover the face.

qabīlah (pl., *qabā'il*) – Arab tribe.

qāt (*'gāt'*) – a plant leaf chewed by Yemenis and East Africans.

qirā'at al-Qur'ān – recitation of the Qur'ān.

qurā – villages or rural hamlets; in Yemeni dialect, the plural form can be used for the singular.

Ramadan (*Ramaḍān*) – the lunar month of fasting according to Islam.

ribā – interest, or usury prohibited according to *sharī'ah*.

ṣalāh (pl., *ṣalawāt*) – formal ritual Islamic prayer.

salṭah – a Yemeni meat dish served hot in a clay pot.

sayyid, al-sādah, sādūn – all names for the descendants of the Prophet Muhammad's bloodline family.

sharaf – nobility or dignity.

sharī'ah – Divine law according to the teachings of the Qur'ān.

shawāl – a cloth usually worn as a headdress by Yemeni men.

shaykh (pl., *mushā'ikh*) – lit., 'old man', usually understood to be a religious teacher or tribal leader.

shayṭān – rejected or,accursed, understood to be Satan, the Devil.

Shia (*Shī'ah*) – derived from *shī'at 'Alī* ('the party of 'Alī'). They are the minority sect in Islam who contest that 'Alī should have been the first *khalīfah* after Muhammad's death and follow 12 bloodline (*sayyid*) *imāms* after 'Alī.

shirk – polytheism, or associationism, the antithesis of *tawḥīd*, absolute monotheism, Islam's primary creed.

silsilah – chain, understood in Sufism as a spiritual link of Sufi shaykhs.

subḥah – rosary or remembrance beads.

ṭarīqah (pl., *ṭurūq*) – spiritual 'pathway' associated with Sufism.

taṣawwuf – spirituality or Sufism.

tawẓīf – legal or official document.

tawḥīd – the concept of absolute monotheism, the primary creed of Islam.

'ūd – a guitar-like, stringed instrument played throughout the Middle East.

'ulamā' (sing., *'ālim*) – meaning 'one with knowledge' but, referring to Islamic religious scholars.

ummah – the universal 'family' or brethren of Islam.

'urf – custom or tradition.

'urf al-qabīlah – the 'custom or tradition of the tribe'.

wādī – valley.

wajh – face or the tribal concept of 'keeping face' or honour.

waqf (pl., *awqāf*) – endowment, usually as a religious charity.

waṭan – nation or country.

zāwiyah (pl., *zawāyā*) – lit., 'corner', but understood to be a place of spiritual retreat or contemplation and prayer within Sufism.

PICTURE CREDITS

Frontispiece Courtesy of *Yemeni Roots Salford Lives: A Community in Eccles* – Jenny Vickers and Jackie Ould-Okojie, Ahmad Iqbal Ullah Educational Trust.

0.1. Gadri Salih's family photographic collection.

0.2. Gadri Salih's family photographic collection.

0.3. Gadr Salih's family photographic collection.

1.1. By permission of Crown Copyright.

2.2. Peter Fryer's collection, www.peter-fryer.com.

2.3. Author's collection.

2.4. Peter Fryer's collection, www.peter-fryer.com.

2.5. Peter Fryer's collection, www.peter-fryer.com.

2.6. Peter Fryer's collection, www.peter-fryer.com.

3.1. Gadri Saleh's family photographic collection.

3.2. Courtesy of *Shields Gazette*, www.shieldsgazette.co.uk.

3.3. Peter Fryer's collection, www.peter-fryer.com.

3.4. Peter Fryer's collection, www.peter-fryer.com.

4.1. Gadri Salih's family photographic collection.

4.2. Origin unknown, but attributed to *Evening Chronicle*, Newcastle-upon-Tyne, in Lawless, op.cit. (1995), p. 182.

4.3. Photograph presented to author by al-Hakimi's grandsons.

4.4. By permission of Crown Copyright.

5.1. Gadri Saleh's family photographic collection.

5.2. Author's collection.

5.3. Courtesy of *South Wales Echo*, Cardiff.

5.4. Gadri Salih's family photographic collection.

6.1. Rabiea Sharker's family photographic collection.

6.3. Gadri Salih's family photographic collection.

6.4. By permission of Crown Copyright.

6.5. Peter Fryer's collection, www.peter-fryer.com.

7.1. Author's collection.

7.2. Author's collection.

7.3. Peter Fryer's collection, www.peter-fryer.com.

8.1. Courtesy of the Yemeni Community Association, Eccles.

8.2. Courtesy of the Yemeni Community Association, Eccles.

8.3. Gadri Salih's family photographic collection.

BIBLIOGRAPHY

Primary Sources

Ally, M. M., (1982), 'History of Muslims in Britain 1850–1980', unpublished MA thesis, University of Birmingham.

Anon., (1992), *Bridging the Years: A history of Trafford Park and Salford Docks as remembered by those who lived and worked in the area*, Salford: Salford Quays Heritage Centre.

———, (1993), *Prayer Timetable 1993 to 2000*, Eccles: Eccles/Salford Mosque & Islamic Centre.

———, (1994), *Barbary Coast Revisited*, Salford; Bridging the Years, Salford Quays heritage Centre.

———, (2000), *Muath Welfare Trust, Annual Report 2000.*

———, (2003), *The Bordesley Centre for Further & Higher Education, Prospectus 2003–4.*

———, (2005), 'Sheikh Said', *Agenda*, Winter (2005–6), p. 5.

———, (2011), 'Sheikh Said Ismail', *Meeting Point*, April, (2011), p. 15.

Birt, Yahya, 'Lies! Damn Lies! Statistics and Conversions', *Q-News*, no. 350, October 2003, Shaban 1424, p. 20.

Clark, Jim, (1982), 'A visit to the Eccles Mosque', *The Eccles and Patricroft Journal*, 12/01/1982.

Community Cohesion – Report of the Independent Review Team, chaired by Ted Cantle, Home Office, December 2001.

Daily Herald, 10 January 1956.

Dahya, Badr Ud-Din, (1967), *South Asian Urban Immigration*, unpublished Ph.D. thesis, University of London.

Dalrymple, William, (1989), 'The Arabs of Tyneside', *The Independent Magazine*, 7 October.

Eagle, A. B. D. R., 'Al-Hassan Hamid al-Din, 1908–2003: Zaidi prince in exile', *Impact International*, vol. 33, no. 10, October 2003, Shaban-Ramadan, 1424, p. 44.

Eccles and Pendleton Journal, 30/11/72.

Khan, M. A., (1979), 'Islam and the Muslims of Liverpool', unpublished MA thesis, University of Liverpool.

Redford, A., (1934), *Manchester Merchants and Foreign Trade*, vol. 1, Manchester.

Saif, Adnan, (2003), *'Its thirst for blood has not been satiated' – the ideological construction of the Yemen,* unpublished MA Dissertation, Birmingham University.

Seddon, Mohammad Siddique, (2003), '400 Years of Muslim Deportation from Britain', *Q-News*, No.350. October 2003/Shaban 1424, pp. 18–21.

———, (2004), 'Unveiling Imperial Conquest', *Emel*, March/April, 2004, pp. 16–17.

———, (2005), '"Invisible Arabs" or "English Muslims"?: An inquiry into the construction of religious, cultural and national identities of the Yemeni community of Eccles, unpublished PhD. Thesis, Lancaster University.

Serjeant, R. B., (1944), 'Yemeni Arabs in Britain', *The Geographical Magazine*, vol. 17, no. 4, 1944, pp. 143–7.

South Shields Gazette, 14 April 1935.

———, 25 January 1935.

———, 23 March 1935.

———, 8 November 1937.

The Crescent: A Weekly Record of Islam in England, Liverpool: The Crescent Printing Company, vol. II, no. 27, 22 July 1893, pp. 212–13.

———, Liverpool: The Crescent Printing Company, vol. II, no. 28, 29 July 1893, p. 224.

The Economist, 17 September 1988.

Turnell, Cat, (2004), 'Crazy dreams and my mouth looks like its mowed the lawn!', *Leicester Mercury*, 14/08/2004.

———, (2004), 'This is the drug khat: banned in the USA, bought legally in Leicester', *Leicester Mercury*, 14/08/2004.

Umar, Zubayda (1985), 'From Yemen to South Shields', *Afkar*, May 1985, pp. 62–3.

Vidal, John, (2004), 'Getting high on the road to Addis', *The Guardian*, 05/05/2004.

Whitaker, Brian, (2001), 'Where the qat is out of the bag', *The Guardian*, 28/05/2001.

Secondary Sources

Abdul-Wali, Mohammad, (2001), Bagader, Abubaker, and Akers, Deborah (trans.), *They Die Strangers: A novella of stories from Yemen,* Austin: Center for Middle eastern Studies.

Abercrombie, Nicholas, Hill, Stephen, and Turner, Bryan S., (1985), *The Penguin Dictionary of Sociology*, London: Penguin Books.

Abram, Jake, (1996), *Tugs, Boats and Me: Manchester Ship Canal and Bridgewater Canal Memories*, Manchester: Neil Richardson Publications.

Ahsan, M. Manazir, (1996), 'Arrival, Expulsion and Return: Muslim Experience in Europe', *Al-Mizan*, vol. 2, no. 1, 1996.

Aithie, Patricia, (2011), 'Sheikh Sa'id Hassan Ismail (1930–2011)', http://www.al-bab.com/bys/obits/ismail.htm.

Al Faruqi, Ismail R., and al Faruqi, Lois Lamyah, (1986), *The Cultural Atlas of Islam*, New York: Macmillan Publishing.

Al Faruqi, Ismail R., and Sopher, David E., (1974), *Historical Atlas of the Religions of the World*, New York: Macmillan Publishiing Co. Inc.,

Ali, A. Y., (1989), *The Holy Qur'ān: Text, Translation and Commentary*, Maryland: Amana Corporation.

———, (1989), *The Holy Qur'ān: Text, Translation and Commentary*, Beirut: The Holy Qur'ān Publishing House.

Ali, Sayed Amir, (1987) [1899], *A Short History of the Saracens*, New Delhi: Nusrat Ali Nasri for Kitab Bhavan.

Allen, Christopher, (2003), *Fair Justice: The Bradford Disturbances, the Sentencing and the Impact*, London: Forum Against Racism and Islamophobia.

Al-Masaybi, Muhammad, (1991), 'Obituray: Shaikh Muhammad Qassim al-'Alawi (1909–99)', http://www.al-bab.com/bys/obits/alawi.htm.

Al-Rasheed, Madawi, (1991), 'Invisible and Divided Communities: Arabs in Britain, in Riad al-Rayyes (ed.) (1991), *Arabs in Britain: Concerns and Prospects*, London: Riad Al-Rayyes Books, pp. 1–14.

Ansari, H., (2004), *'The Infidel Within': Muslims in Britain since 1800*, London: Hurst & Company.

Anwar, Muhammad, (1979), *The Myth of Return,* London: Heinemann.

———, (2003), 'British Muslims: Socio-Economic Position' in Seddon, Mohammad Siddique et al, (eds) (2003), *British Muslims: Loyalty and Belonging*, Leicester: The Islamic Foundation and The Citizen Organising Foundation, pp. 57–67.

Anwar, Muhammad and Bakhsh, Qadir, (2003), *British Muslims and State Policies*, Warwick: Centre for Research in Ethnic Relations, University of Warwick.

Arnold, Thomas, W., (1892), *The Preaching of Islam: A History of the Propagation of Muslim Faith*, (reprinted 1979), Lahore: Sh. Muhammad Ashraf.

Aswad, Barbara C., (1974), 'The Southeast Dearborn Arab Community Struggles for Survival against Urban "Renewal"' in Aswad, Barbara C., (ed.) (1974), *Arab Speaking Communities in American Cities*, New York: Centre for Migration Studies, pp. 53–83.

Balouch, N. A., (1980), *The Advent of Islam in Indonesia*, Lahore: National Institute of Historical and Cultural Research.

Bashier, Zakaria, (1983), *The Makkan Crucible*, Leicester: The Islamic Foundation.

———, (1988), *Hijrah: Story and Significance,* Leicester: The Islamic Foundation.

Bastin, John, and Winks, Robin W., (eds), (1966), *Malaysia: Selected Historical Readings*, London: Oxford University Press.

Bearman, P. J. et al (1960–2005) (eds), *Encyclopædia of Islam*, 2nd edn, 12 vols with indexes and etc., Leiden: E. J. Brill.

Bewley, Aisha, (trans.) (1997), *The Women of Madina*, London: Ta Ha Publishers

Boxberger, Linda, (2002), *On the Edge of Empire: Hadramawt, Emigration and the Indian Ocean*, Albany: State University of New York Press.

Brown, Daniel, (1996), *Rethinking Tradition in Modern Islamic Thought*,

Cambridge: Cambridge University Press.

Burgat, Francois, (2003), *Face to Face with Political Islam*, London: I. B. Tauris & Co. Ltd.

Carr, Barry, (1992), 'Black Gordies', in Colls, Robert, and Lancaster, Bill, (eds) (1992), *Geordies: Roots in Regionalism*, Edinburgh: Edinburgh University Press, pp. 131–49.

Chalmeta, Pedro, 'Muwallad' in, Bearman et al, (eds), (1960–2005) *The Encyclopedia of Islam*, Leiden: E. J. Brill, vol. VII, p. 807.

Chew, Samuel, (1937), *The Rose and The Crescent,* New York: Oxford University Press.

Clarke, Abdassamad, (trans.), (1995), *The History of the Khalifas Who Took The Right Way,* London: Ta Ha Publishers.

Climes, Michael, (2006), 'The Prince's Place in History', *Eastside Boxing,* 4 January 2006, http://www.eastsideboxing.com/news.php?p=6498&more=1.

Col. Yule, Henry, R.E., C.B. and, Burnell, A. C., Ph.D., C.I.E. (new edition, edited by Crooke, William, B.A.) (2000), *Hobson-Jobson; A Glossary of Colloquial Anglo-Indian Words and Phrases, and of Kindred Terms, Etymological, Historical, Geographical and Discursive*, New Delhi: Munshiram Manoharial Publishers Pvt. Ltd.

Collins, Sydney, (1957), *Coloured Minorities in Britain*, London: Lutterworth Press.

Daftary, Farhad, (1998), 'Sayyida Hurra: The Isma'ili Sulayhid Queen in the Yemen', in Hamby, Gavin, R. G., (ed.) (1998), *Women in the Medieval Islamic World*, New York: St. Martin's Press.

Dahya, Badr Ud-Din, (1965), 'Yemenis in Britain: An Arab Migrant Community', in *Race*, vol. 3, no. 4, 1965.

Daryabadi, A. M., (2001), *The Glorious Qur'an: Text, Translation and Commentary*, Markfield: The Islamic Foundation.

Davies, Grahame, (2011), *The Dragon and the Crescent: Nine Centuries of Welsh Contact with Islam*, Bridgend: Serenbooks.

Deane, Phyllis, (1969), *The First Industrial Revolution*, Cambridge: Cambridge University Press.

Donaldson, William J., (2000), *Sharecropping in the Yemen: A Study in Islamic Theory, Custom and Pragmatism,* Leiden: E. J. Brill.

Dozy, Reinhart, (1972), *Spanish Islam: a History of the Muslims of Spain,*

London: Frank Cass.

Dresch, Paul, (1993), *Tribes, Government and History in Yemen*, Oxford: Oxford University Press.

———, (2000), *A History of the Modern Yemen*, Cambridge: Cambridge University Press.

Eickelman, Dale F., and Piscatori, James, (1996), *Muslim Politics*, New Jersey: Princton University Press.

El Azhary, M. S., (1984) 'Aspects of North Yemen's Relations with Saudi Arabia', in Pridham, B. R., (ed.), *Contemporary Yemen: Politics and Historical Background*, London: Croom Helm and Centre for Arab-Gulf Studies.

Eliade, M., et al, (eds) (1987), *The Encyclopaedia of Religion*, vol. 15, New York: Macmillan Publishers.

El-Sohl, Camilla, Fawzi, (1992), 'Arab Communities in Britain: Cleavages and Commonalities', in *Islam and Christian–Muslim Relations*, vol. 3, no 2, December 1992, pp. 236–88.

Flynn, Tony, (1986), *The History of Eccles Cinemas and Theatres*, Manchester: Neil Richardson.

Foster, W. (ed.), (1905), *Jourdain's Journal, 1608–1617*, Cambridge: Hakluyt Society.

Freitag, Ulrike, (2003), *Indian Ocean Migrants and State Formation in Hadhramaut*, Leiden: Brill.

Fryer, Peter, (1985), *Staying Power: The History of Black People in Britain*, London: Pluto Press.

Gavin, R., (1994), 'The Port of Aden – A Brief History', in *The Port of Aden Annual*, Ta'izz: Genpack.

Gordon, Milton, M., (1964), *Assimilation in American Life*, New York: Oxford University Press.

Halliday, Fred, (1984), 'Soviet Relations with the South Yemen', in Pridham, B. R., (ed.), *Contemporary Yemen: Politics and Historical Background*, London: Croom Helm and Centre for Arab-Gulf Studies.

———, (1992), *Arabs in Exile: Yemeni Migrants in Urban Britain*, London: I. B. Tauris.

———, (2010), *Britain's First Muslims: Potrait of an Arab Community*, London: I. B. Tauris.

Hamby, Gavin R. G., (ed.) (1998), *Women in the Medieval Islamic World*, New

York: St. Martin's Press.

Hartmann, Betsy, and Boyce, James, (1983), *A Quiet Violence: View from a Bangladesh Village,* London: Zed Books.

Haykal, Muhammad Husayn, (1976), *The Life of Muhammad,* North American Trust Publication.

Hourani, George Fadlo, (1951), *Arab Seafaring in Ancient and Early Medieval Times,* Princeton: Princeton University Press.

Ibn Abd Al Wahhab, Muhammad, (trans. Al Faruqi, Ismail, R.,) (1991), *Kitāb al-Tawḥīd,* Riyadh: International Islamic Publishing House.

Ingrams, Doreen, (1970), *A Time in Arabia,* London: John Murray

Ingrams, Harold, (1942), *Arabia and the Isles,* London: John Murray.

Jenner, Michael, (1983), *Yemen Rediscovered,* London & New York: Longman.

Kirkman, James, (ed.) (1976), *The City of San'a',* London: London Museum of Mankind, Department of Ethnography of the British Museum and World Festival of Islam.

Krause, W., (ed.) (2009), *Citizenship, Security and Democracy: Muslim Engagement with the West,* London and Istanbul: The Association of Muslim Social Scientists, UK (AMSS (UK)) & The Foundation for Political, Economic and Social Research (SETA, Turkey).

Kucukcan, T., (2004), 'The making of Turkish-Muslim diaspora in Britain: Religious collective identity in a multicultural public sphere', *Journal of Muslim Minority Affairs,* vol. 24, no. 2, pp. 243–58.

Latta, Rafiq, and Cooper, John P., (ed.), (1994), *Yemen: Unification and Modernisation,* London: Gulf Centre for Strategic Studies.

Lawless, Dick, (1993), 'British-Yemeni Society: Sheikh Abdullah Ali al-Hakimi', http://www.al-bab.com/bys/articles/lawless93.htm.

Lawless, Richard, (1995), *From Ta'izz to Tyneside: An Arab community in the North-East of England during the early twentieth century,* Exeter: Exeter University Press.

Leese, Peter, Piatek, Beata, and Curyllo-Klag, Izabela, (2002), *The British Migrant Experience, 1700–2000: An Anthology,* Basingstoke: Palgrave Macmillan.

Lewis, John, (1982), *Anthropology Made Simple,* London: William Heinmann Ltd.

Lings, Martin, (1961), *A Moslem Saint of the Twentieth Century,* London: George Allen & Unwin Ltd.

———, (1971) *A Sufi Saint of the Twentieth Century*, Berkeley: University of California Press.

———, (1987), *Muhammad: His Life Based on the Earliest Sources*, London: Inner Traditions International Ltd.

Little, K. L., (1947), *Negroes in Britain: A Study of Racial Relations in English Society*, London: Kegan Paul, Trench, Truber & Co. Ltd.

Mackintosh-Smith, Tim, (1997), *Yemen: Travels in Dictionary Land*, London: John Murray (Publishers) Ltd.

Malik, Iftikhar, (2003), *Islam and Modernity*, London: Pluto Press.

Malik, N., (2004), 'Friends, Romans, Countrymen?', in Seddon, M. S., Hussain, D., and Malik, M., (2004), *British Muslims Between Assimilation and Segregation: Historical, Legal and Social Realities*, Markfield: The Islamic Foundation.

Massey, Philip, (1940), *Industrial South Wales: A detailed survey*, London: Gollancz.

Mortimer, Peter, (2005), *Cool For Qat, A Yemen Journey: Two Countries, Two Times*, Edinburgh and London: Mainstream Publishing.

Morton, Rachel, (2000), *One Island Many Faiths*, London: Thames Hudson.

Nagel, Carol, and Staeheli, Lynn, (2009), 'British Arab Perspectives on Religion, Politics and "The Public"', in Hopkins, Peter, and Gale, Richard, (eds) (2009), *Muslims in Britain: Race, Place and Identities*, Edinburgh: Edinburgh University Press, pp. 95–112.

Nasser, N., (2005) 'Expressions of Muslim identity in architecture and urbanism in Birmingham, UK', *Islam and Christian-Muslim Relations*, vol. 16, no. 1, pp. 61–78.

Peterson, J. E., (1962), *Yemen: Search for a Modern State*, London: Cromm Helm Ltd.

Pridham, B. R., (ed.), *Contemporary Yemen: Politics and Historical Background*, London: Croom Helm and Centre for Arab-Gulf Studies.

Qureshi, Ishtiaq Husain, (1977), *The Muslim Community in the Indo-Pakistan Subcontinent (610–1947)*, Karachi: Ma'arif Ltd.

Ramadan, T., (2002), 'Europeanization of Islam or Islamization of Europe?' In Hunter, S., (ed.) (2002), *Islam, Europe's second religion: The new social, cultural and political landscape*, Westport, CT: Praeger.

Reilly, Bernard, (1960), *Aden and the Yemen*, London: Her Majesty's Stationary Office.

Rosenthal, Eric, (reprinted 1982), *From Drury Lane to Mecca*, Cape Town: Howard Timmins Publishers.

Rushby, Kevin, (1999), *Eating the Flowers of Paradise: A journey through the drug fields of Ethiopia and Yemen,* New York: New York St. Martin's Press.

Ryan, N. J., (1976), A *History of Malaysia and Singapore*, Singapore: Oxford University Press.

Salter, Joseph, (1873), *The Asiatic in England: Sketches of Sixteen Years' Work Among Orientals*, London: Seeley, Jackson and Halliday.

———, (1896), *The East in the West*, London: Partridge.

Schimmel, Annemarie, (1980), *Islam in the Indian Subcontinent*, Leiden-Koln: E. J. Brill

Scott, Hugh, (1942), *In The High Yemen*, London: John Murray.

Searle, Kevin, (2009), *From Farms to Foundries: An Arab Community in Industrial Britain*, Bern: Peter Lang AG.

Seddon, Mohammad Siddique, (2004), 'Locating the Perpetuation of "Otherness": Negating British Islam', in Seddon et al, (2004), *British Muslims Between Assimilation and Segregation: Historical, Legal and Social Realities*, Markfield: The Islamic Foundation, pp. 119–44.

———, (2004), 'Muslim Communities in Britain: A Historiography' in Seddon, Mohammad Siddique et al, (2004), *British Muslims Between Assimilation and Segregation: Historical, Legal and Social Realities*, Markfield: The Islamic Foundation, pp. 1–42.

———, (2007), 'Muslim and Jewish Communities in Nineteenth Century Manchester', in Ansari, Humayun and Cesarani, David, (eds.) (2007), *Muslim-Jewish Dialogue in a 21st Century World*, Egham: Centre for Minority Studies, Royal Holloway University of London, pp. 63–84.

———, (2009), 'Global Citizenry Ancient and Modern: British Yemenis and Translocal Tribalism', in Krause, Wanda (ed.) (2009), *Citizenship, Security and Democracy: Muslim Engagement with the West*, London & Istanbul: AMSS UK & SETA, pp. 89–114.

———, (2010), 'Constructing Identities of 'Difference' and 'Resistance': The Politics of Being Muslim and British', *Social Semiotics Journal*, November 2010, pp. 557–71.

———, (2012), 'Engaging with young Muslims: Some paradigms from the Qur'an and *Sunnah*', in Ahmad, Fauzia and Seddon, Mohammad Siddique, (eds) (2011), *Muslim Youth: Challenges, Opportunities and Expectations*, London: Continuum, pp. 248–69.

Stookey, Robert W., (1978), *Yemen: The Politics of the Yemen Arab Republic*, Colorado: West View Press.

Van Hear, Nocholas, (1998), *New Diasporas: The mass exodus, dispersal and regrouping of migrant communities*, London: UCL Press.

Visram, Rozina, (2002), *Asians in Britain: 400 Years of History*, London: Pluto Press.

Voll, John O., (1987),'Wahhabiyah', in Eliade, Mircea, et al, (eds) (1987), *The Encyclopaedia of Religion*, New York: Macmillan, vol. 15, pp. 313–16.

Werbner, Pnina, (1994), 'Avoiding the Ghetto: Pakistani migrant and settlement shifts in Manchester', in Drake, Michael, (ed.) (1994), *Time, Family and Community: Perspectives on Family and Community History*, Oxford and Cambridge, Mass.: The Open University and Blackwell.

———, (2002), *Imagined Diasporas among Manchester Muslims*, Oxford and Santa Fe: James Currey and School of American Research Press.

Winter, T. J., (2003), 'Muslim loyalty and belonging: Some reflections on the psychosocial background.' in Seddon, M. S., Hussain, D., and Malik, M., (eds) (2003), *British Muslims: Loyalty and Belonging*, Markfield: The Citizen Organising Foundation and The Islamic Foundation, pp. 3–22.

Websites

http://www.eastsideboxing.com/news.php?p=6498&more=1

http://www.ons.gov.uk/ons/dcp171776_310454.pdf

http://www.lascars.co.uk/ranks.html

http://wwww.naba.org.uk/the-library/reports/LGA-ArabLeague-Study-2005.pdf

http://www.naba.org.uk/the-library/reports/BritshArabsYafaiF.pdf

http://naba.og.uk/the-library/reports/NABA-Census-2001-FinalReport-May%202013.pdf

http://www.yemeni-community-manchester.org.uk/about/history

http://www.yca-sandwell.org.uk/

INDEX